OCT 17

D0848665

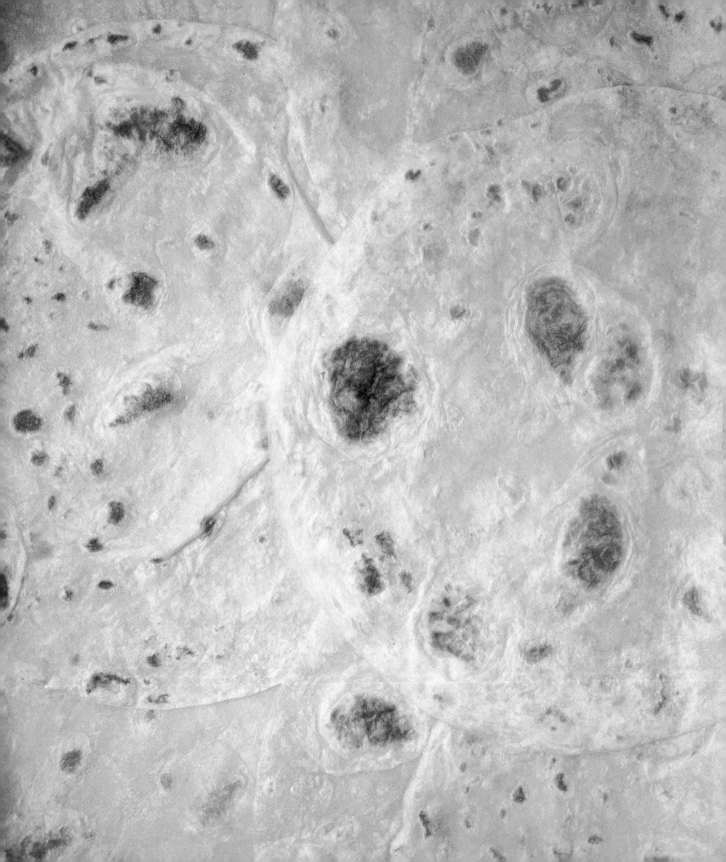

Published by Prospect Park Books
2359 Lincoln Avenue
Altadena, California 91001
www.prospectparkbooks.com

Distributed by Consortium Books Sales & Distribution
www.cbsd.com

Library of Congress Cataloging in Publication Data is on file with the Library of Congress
The following is for reference only:

Esparza, Bill
L.A. Mexicano: Recipes, People & Places / by Bill Esparza — 1st ed.
   p. cm.
ISBN: 978-1-945551-00-0
1. Cooking, Mexican. 2. Cooking, California. 3. Cooking, Los Angeles, CA. I. Title.

Edited by Colleen Dunn Bates
Editorial team: Jenn Garbee, Pat Jalbert-Levine, Dorie Bailey, Elizabeth Ovieda, Anna Russell, Daphne Liu, and Emily Peters

Photography by Staci Valentine
Designed by Amy Inouye, Future Studio

First edition, first printing

Printed in China by Imago on sustainably produced, FSC-certified paper

L.A. MEXICANO
RECIPES, PEOPLE & PLACES

BY BILL ESPARZA

INTRODUCTION BY **GUSTAVO ARELLANO** ★ PHOTOGRAPHS BY **STACI VALENTINE**

PROSPECT
PARK
BOOKS

CONTENTS

The Magellan of Menudo *Gustavo Arellano* 6

L.A. Mexicano:
Winning Our Hearts Through Our Stomachs 8

Mexico's Culinary Regions 16

Nuestra Cocina *Our Kitchen* 19

Pocho Cuisine 29

Regional Mexican Cuisine 51

Alta California Cuisine 113

Bebidas *Drinks* 153

Ambulantes *Trucks & Takeout* 165

Centro de Abastos *Marketplaces* 185

Neighborhood Resources 195

Diccionario 231

Reconocimiento *Acknowledgments* 235

Index 236

THE MAGELLAN OF MENUDO

Gustavo Arellano

The most precious memory I have of Bill Esparza is him lecturing me for a good half an hour about why I'm wrong about my favorite meal of all time.

It was over cell phone, while I was trying to get somewhere with my wife, with me simultaneously wanting the conversation to end as fast as possible and yet being mesmerized by the knowledge Bill was dropping on me, like Yahweh telling Job to shut up and listen. The topic at hand was birria de res, a beef stew from the Mexican state of Zacatecas that still isn't readily available in the United States. Growing up, I only ate it at family parties, and ached for it all other times: stringy beef stewed in a spicy sauce made from chiles sourced only in Mexico, usually served alongside beans, rice, and corn tortillas but sometimes found in burritos. Spicy, savory, sweet: perfect. Birria de res is heritage, it's culture, it's delicious—and Bill was telling me it wasn't true birria.

"But, Bill," I kept telling him. "My mom calls it birria. My dad calls it birria. My grandparents called it birria. Everyone from my hometown calls it birria. And now you're telling us we've been wrong all these years—and our birria de res is not actually birria?"

"Yes," Bill would respond, before launching into another detailed explanation of why he was right.

Coming from anyone else, Bill's arguments would sound like the juvenile, arrogant blabbering of crazy Yelp kids or pretentious Instagrammers. But instead, I let him talk. He is America's finest chronicler of Mexican food right now, the Livingstone of lengua, the Magellan of menudo, the Captain Cook of carnitas. He tracks down the most obscure Mexican regional dishes, whether in a tiny Mexican village or an alley in the middle of the San Fernando Valley, and lets the world know about it, bringing big, necessary business to mom-and-pop shops. And he does all of this with no formal journalism training and while playing sax across the world.

Screw Dos Equis: Bill is the Most Interesting Man in the World. So not only did I decide to shut up and take my birria de res lecture, I decided to write down everything that he was saying.

When I wrote my 2012 book, *Taco USA: How Mexican Food Conquered America*, I let audiences know that it was merely the first draft of what I hoped would be a blossoming of studies on the history of Mexican food in the United States. My book tells all the big stories—how Doritos were invented, the biographies of little-known pioneers, why more tequila is sold in the United States than in Mexico. It was important to document such history, much of which had never been chronicled before, but my bigger intention was to motivate people to find the local pioneers and tell their tales. Even if they didn't warrant a mention in a national release, their life's work was worthy of being captured and celebrated.

Despite Los Angeles being the second-largest Mexican city in the world, the story of Mexican food in this metropolis has been criminally untold. Seriously: You can count on two hands all of the books ever published specifically on Mexican food in Los Angeles—really, one hand and a thumb. A new generation of scholars is starting to rectify this, but I know those books will mostly be academic gobbledygook that no one will read outside of a PDF or university library.

That's why I was so thrilled when Bill told me about this book, and why I'm honored to write the foreword. Bill is not some fancy *paisa* anthropologist; he's real. The pages here not only tell stories and recipes, but capture a moment in time before it disappears: an era in which the pioneers of a "new" style of Mexican food from the last couple of decades are still cooking while newcomers are already creating the next evolution of Mexican food. Far too much history has left us already, and *L.A. Mexicano* is arriving on the scene at the perfect time.

Bill is the only person who could've written this book. No one has logged more miles in L.A. and Mexico to forge the relationships that have encouraged people to talk, and this book is a testament to that. If you need further proof, just visit the annual Tacolandia Festival in Olvera Street, the greatest food event in Southern California, if not the nation: 125-plus taqueros from Los Angeles to Monterrey to London (!) slinging the best stuff around.

As a professional food critic, I've long witnessed the reluctance of immigrant restaurateurs to participate in anything mainstream—yet Bill gets them to overcome their doubts. I've been with Bill in South Central L.A. tire shops, at Ensenada sea-urchin carts, in high-end Tijuana eateries, and the reaction by these men and women is always the same: *Beel!* It's chefs and cooks greeting their John the Apostle, the prophet who shares their gospel with the rest of the world.

Here, then, gentle reader, is your Bible. History, food, humor—*L.A. Mexicano* will be the best read this year, and it joins *City of Quartz* and *Southern California Country: An Island on the Land* as a Los Angeles literary classic.

Buen provecho! And Bill: When do you want to go grab some birria de res?

L.A. MEXICANO: WINNING OUR HEARTS THROUGH OUR STOMACHS

"BECOMING" MEXICAN AMERICAN

For me, the journey toward *L.A. Mexicano* began standing atop the Pyramid of the Sun looking down upon the Valley of Mexico at Teotihuacan in the summer of 2002. My father had just passed away, and I'd asked my grandmother to connect me with our family in Aguascalientes, Mexico. I feared that with only my grandmother remaining, I'd lose my roots. I hadn't visited Mexico since I was ten years old, which turned out to be the last trip I'd take with my grandparents to their hometown.

My father, Ignacio Esparza Jr., was born in Aguascalientes, Mexico, but came to the United States before his first birthday. My grandfather, Ignacio Sr., was from Aguascalientes, but his dad, my great-grandfather Blas Esparza, had a ranch in California that had been in his family for several generations. After bringing his family to the US and a failed effort at being a rancher, my grandfather found work as a truck driver for Tri Valley Growers, hauling tomatoes from the Central Valley down to Bakersfield. He tricked my grandmother into coming to the US, as she'd always say, leaving behind a privileged life in Aguascalientes for life in Stockton and backbreaking work in a tomato canning plant. I had cousins who worked as pickers, and my father became a millwright, servicing the heavy machinery that canned tomatoes. Despite their humble beginnings, my grandfather's generation bought homes and good cars and pursued the American dream.

As a child in the 1950s, however, my father experienced the ugliness of racism. Spanish-speaking children like him were placed in schools for the severely handicapped because they didn't speak English. He told me about visiting Texas as a kid and seeing signs on businesses that read "No Dogs or Mexicans Allowed," a humiliation sharpened by angry slurs and hateful stares as he walked down the street with his parents.

To survive, he did what others of his generation did to blend in. He learned to speak English with a clean accent, and I'd only hear him speak Spanish a couple more times in my life. He was fiercely proud of our Aztec heritage and would point out every actor and musician who was Mexican, but he was ashamed to speak Spanish in public and even around me. Instead of Nacho, the nickname for Ignacio, he became Nash, and his Chicano friends were Pete, Bob, Rick, Ernie, Joe, and Manuel—and Manuel was just plain old "man-yoll." They were Chicanos who listened to Jimi Hendrix, wore tie-dyed T-shirts, and ate steak a la chicana with Miller Genuine Draft. But while my dad identified as a cholo in high school and later embraced the Chicano biker culture of the '70s, he restricted the culture for me. One of the first lessons I learned was that I wasn't allowed to learn Spanish—he once caught my grandparents addressing me in Spanish and snapped, "Don't speak Spanish to him, ever!" I obeyed and wasn't given an explanation other than, "This is America, and you don't need to speak Spanish" (little did he know). But it cut deeper than that—I knew that I was to blend in.

"And we gotta prove to the Mexicans how Mexican we are, and we gotta prove to the Americans how American we are, we gotta be more Mexican than the Mexicans and more American than the Americans, both at the same time. It's exhausting. Damn. Nobody knows how tough it is to be a Mexican American." So goes a rant by Edward James Olmos in the 1997 movie *Selena*. Truer words have never been spoken.

My grandparents with family

By the sixth grade, I was Mexican only at my grandmother's house and in the safety of my extended family, where I'd hear the sound of hot oil amplified by crackling, gurgling eggs bathed in salsa ranchera, and where the aroma of refried beans and of handmade flour tortillas being toasted on a comal would jolt me out of bed at 6 a.m. on weekends. At my grandmother's house, we went to the panaderia for sweets, watched Spanish-language television—for an adolescent boy, no words were needed to watch *Sabado Gigante*—and for the holidays, and ate (always) tamales, beans, tortillas, and rice with the turkey.

My first trip to Mexico was to Aguascalientes with my grandparents. My grandfather drove a brand-new Chrysler New Yorker Brougham for three days straight from Stockton, stopping in Indio and El Paso. He was a truck driver who knew the ropes, so we flew through Mexico, bribing soldiers at checkpoints and eating street food along the way. It's more vivid than any other of my childhood memories—I had the most amazing roadside carnitas, eating an entire lunch bag full of the confit-style pork after my grandparents made themselves some tacos. I remember every face and every aroma that floated out of my aunt's kitchen, but for those two weeks I wasn't able to communicate with any of my relatives. No hablo español.

At my aunt's house, a courtyard separated all the rooms. There was a chicken pen, and we had to boil the milk in the morning. My cousins were nicer than all of us Americanized Mexicans, and I had a kid's crush on several of the pretty girls in my family who would just smile and giggle at me because we couldn't talk.

We were there for the posadas, where kids threw firecrackers and hit piñatas; I'll never forget seeing a kid get whacked instead of the piñata because he stood too close. Mostly, though, I couldn't get over the food. In my grandmother's house in Stockton and here in Aguascalientes, I was Mexican, but at school in California I was not.

The Mexican American kids in my Stockton neighborhood were fully assimilated; at school, we were accepted by the multicultural kids, and with names like Bill, Jared, and Krystal, and the Americanized pronunciation of our last names, our Mexicanness wasn't a threat. We even laughed along with the beaner jokes made at our own expense, sometimes said by the parents of our non-Latino friends. But around middle school age, we faced unexpected pressure from new Mexican-immigrant kids whose parents had come to work in the

fields. They gave me a lot of shit, asking why I didn't speak Spanish and why I was hanging out with the white kids, the same ones who'd make those beaner jokes. I felt the weight of my dad's shame; I wanted to learn Spanish, but that was forbidden.

An escape from this cultural purgatory came from music. I took up the saxophone and hid in the band room throughout high school and college with fellow music geeks, earning a bachelor of music degree and beginning a career as a musician. In the days when saxophone could still be heard on the radio, I occasionally performed with Bryan Adams, the Brian Setzer Orchestra, Slash, Bobby Caldwell, Colin Hay, Diane Schuur, Khaled, Santana, and others. My first road gig was with Chris Cain, when I was twenty-

On the road with an appetite

two, and we played the blues circuit, traveling the country in a van doing one-night stands. On the road, I encountered two kinds of musicians: the ones who were all about vice and the ones who read and became experts on various useless pursuits. I ended up learning about food, becoming an accidental expert on the regional cuisines of Latin America—which turned out not to be useless after all. It was a hobby that most musicians found peculiar, so I often explored alone, but it helped me get closer to my dad, as we'd often talk about Mexican food and even cooked some of our family recipes together when I was home from the road.

In those touring years, I traveled throughout Mexico with the Mexican pop star Marisela, and that's when the passion for food that I'd inherited from my grandmother and father became an obsession that I pursued with an insatiable fury—from the time soundcheck was over until lobby call, I was out eating. I sacrificed many a good night's sleep so I could explore Mexico's markets, fondas, and taquerias, sometimes having to get my own cab to the airport because the van had left.

In 2002, while rehearsing for a tour through Colombia, Honduras, and El Salvador, my mother called to say that my father had died; he'd been in bad health for years, so it was something we'd been anticipating. I had to leave for the tour in a few weeks, but I felt an urgency like I'd never felt before to see my family—his family—in Aguascalientes. It was the only thing that could assuage my grief.

Reclaiming my roots in Mexico

I went for my father, but I finally found myself, the pocho he'd spent his entire life protecting. I was now free to fully embrace my culture, and I needed to make up for lost time. I still didn't speak Spanish, so once again, I couldn't talk to many of my relatives, but with a dictionary and a phrase book, I painfully constructed sentences for the first time. They called in my English-speaking cousins who'd studied abroad for backup. I'm sure I annoyed them, asking so many damn questions about language and the food—but I had to know it all, because it was now okay to be Mexican, and food was becoming a way for me to share my heritage with others.

L.A.'S MEXICAN FOOD COMES INTO ITS OWN

By 2007, now living in Los Angeles, I was seeking out the regional dishes I'd enjoyed in my Latin American travels: Salvadoran pupusas at Pentecostal churches, Brazilian acarajé from a house in Palms, and regional Mexican lamb barbacoa from backyard pits. I started a blog called Street Gourmet LA, earning a reputation for finding hidden gems, and then I was recruited by the *Los Angeles Times* to write features. Since then I've written for *Los Angeles Magazine* and a few others. I'm a regular "fixer" (research consultant) and onscreen personality for TV food shows. I've consulted for restaurants, and I curate a food festival called Tacolandia for *LA Weekly*. I was fortunate to have come along at a time just before the national demand for Mexican food, especially tacos, exploded in the US, yet there were only a very few from our community talking knowledgeably about our food.

I've always found it curious that a cuisine so beloved and deeply woven into the American fabric could be the least understood by its fans and even by the Mexican American community, which is too often eager to attack cultural appropriators yet won't pay for quality ingredients or support our Alta California chefs. It's a revelation when a white American chef talks about mole, but all the Oaxacan restaurants in L.A. are just holes in the wall. This hasn't been the case with other cuisines, which garner deference on behalf of immigrant chefs: the sushi master, the Burgundian chef, the émigré from Chengdu.

The story of Mexican food is an asymmetrical narrative told by outsiders, its origins discredited by self-appointed food anthropologists and prone to the fetishizing of delicious but less relevant snacks and treats like elotes, paletas, and chips and salsa (an Orange County food critic once claimed that he judged a Mexican restaurant by its chips and salsa). This is much less of an issue with Asian cuisines in America, where chefs like Roy Choi, Sang Yun, David Chang, and Kris Yenbamroong are rock stars who legitimately represent Asian American food. Where are the Roy Chois and David Changs of the Mexican community? It turns out they've always been right here in Los Angeles, and now their time has come.

When Colleen Bates of Prospect Park Books approached me to write *L.A. Mexicano*, we talked about our mutual amazement that this book hadn't been written already—Los Angeles has been the center of Mexican cuisine in America since before we were a nation. From the pioneers of Mexican American cuisine, to the keepers of old-country tradition, to the young, revolutionary Chicano chefs (an inspired group on the precipice of one of the most important food movements in American history), a collective voice has emerged. These virtuosos are in a fight to take back their cuisine, because as Mexican cooking has become dominant in America's culinary landscape, brown faces have been missing from the discussion. Mexican Americans are not on food television (with the exception of the talented Tijuana native Marcela Valladolid), are barely mentioned in major magazines, and are absent at major food festivals.

And if that isn't enough, gringos tell our chefs they can't charge top dollar for lowly Mexican food, while third-generation Mexican Americans who haven't even been to Mexico bitch about pozole made with a miso broth. L.A.'s chefs, cooks, and restaurateurs have been dealing with extremes from both sides of the aisle for generations.

But although you don't see them on TV, Mexicans in Los Angeles have led this cuisine from the founding of the legendary Cielito Lindo and other Olvera Street vendors in the 1930s. In order to make a living, Aurora Guerrero and her peers had to cater to a white America that only wanted to see Mexican food served by women in adelita dresses and men in sombreros. Hard-shell tacos, combo plates, and taquitos spread all over the United States from Los Angeles. People loved the food but hated the Mexican. The lynching of

Mexicans from the mid-nineteenth century to the twentieth century, the Zoot Suit Riots, and all manner of discrimination have long set the Mexican American community apart. Restrictive covenants physically segregated them to live in Chicano sanctuaries in Boyle Heights, Lincoln Heights, and East L.A., where a regional style of pocho cuisine developed in the 1950s and '60s. East L.A. has terroir; burritos just don't taste the same outside the barrio, for the same reasons that New York's pizza doesn't travel well. I remember one afternoon loitering around the La Estrella Truck for a story when I noticed something peculiar—every Anglo customer ordered tacos, and every Mexican ordered burritos. At the time I thought, *What the hell, I don't get it?* Later I figured it out. For Mexicans living in L.A.'s barrios, a burrito for dinner is legit—we pochos mostly eat tacos at 3 a.m., launching a preemptive strike against a hangover. Eating tacos after hittin' the club, a bar, or after a movie is our way of life.

The origin of the Mexican American burrito, whether it's made in the Mission, San Diego, or Texas, must have been inspired by East L.A. and Boyle Heights. El Tepeyac (1955) led the way for a Mexican American–style menu that was pure eastside. The eastside even has its own regional variety of corn tortillas, which are inexplicably thick, almost like a Salvadoran-style tortilla. At Al & Bea's, Lupe's No. 2, Los Cinco Puntos, Ciro's, and, later, La Azteca Tortilleria (which has existed as a tortilleria since 1945 but first introduced its award-winning burritos in 2010), burritos, taquitos, combination plates, and steak picado are axioms of a Chicano manifesto.

TO ALTA CALIFORNIA AND BEYOND

Yes, there's such a thing as authentic cuisine. It's a living, breathing thing that's eternally evolving—a snapshot in time of dishes, traditions, cooks, and ingredients that have survived through natural selection, with innovation adding layers of complexity. What's popular today that sticks around becomes authentic tomorrow, but authenticity has to come from a place. We have such a place right here in Alta California, where there's a culinary reconquista afoot in the barrios and kitchens of Aztlán.

The story of today's Alta California cuisine begins with Ricardo Diaz and Thomas Ortega in 2008, when they opened (respectively) Cook's Tortas and Ortega 120. In 2009 came Eagle Rock's Cacao Mexicatessen. These pioneers suffered often-crippling frustration from closed-minded raza and our crabs-in-a-bucket mentality, and it wasn't any easier finding support from Anglos who valued Mexican food only as a cheap novelty. To non-Latinos, these restaurants weren't serious kitchens—that is, until 2012, when the first classically trained pocho chef, Wes Avila, opened Guerrilla Tacos.

Soon thereafter, Avila was joined by Carlos Salgado, Eduardo Ruiz, Josef Centeno, and Ray Garcia to become the first generation of chefs to elevate the Chicano American kitchen. Their tacos, tamales, and guisados mingled with California's bounty of ingredients and L.A.'s multicultural aesthetic. As the second-largest Mexican city on the planet, L.A. is home to a new movement led by chefs who earned their stripes in the hallowed temples of California cuisine, but who also understand the roots, regions, and artistry of Mexican cooking.

Chef José Andrés illustrated this movement during a talk at the SLS Beverly Hills in 2011, where he spoke with Ferran Adrià and Juan Mari Arzak. He narrated a video that broke down his version of his mom's cheese and almond plate. "No one does a better plate of cheese and almonds than my mom," he said. "But I can't just serve it the way she does it—I'm a chef and I have to create something new."

Alta California cuisine is relevant because it is legitimate, an original cuisine from L.A.'s zona chicana: East L.A., Pico Rivera, Pacoima, Huntington Park, Whittier, y mas (and more).

For the first time in the history of the US, Mexico's greatest chefs are inviting pochos to cook modern Chicano gastronomy at events in Mexico. As I sit here writing on this alarmingly hot fall day in Hollywood, chef Wes Avila is in Mexico City cooking with Latin America's 50 Best chef Diego Hernandez (Corazón de Tierra), and in a week I'll be attending a series of anniversary dinners at Taco Maria with famed chefs Javier Plascencia (Misión 19), Hernandez, and Enrique Olvera (Pujol). These same chefs from Mexico are beginning to appear at festivals here in the US; they're receiving national press, winning awards, and appearing on food television. Yet when I attended L.A.'s biggest food festival in the summer of 2016, only three of the one hundred chefs were Latino. We still have a long way to go, but there's a strong sense of community and collaboration within this group—both here in California and with their counterparts in Mexico, who serve as mentors, peers, and collaborators.

L.A. MEXICANO

L.A. Mexicano is but a few slices off the trompo (vertical spit), just enough to fill you up with deliciousness— the forty fascinating individuals profiled here all play a part in one of the richest culinary journeys in American history. Some are pioneers, some represent the future, and others work a comal with generations of muscle memory and secrets in their hands. They represent the waves of Mexican immigrants who've come to Los Angeles for a better life and have triumphed to earn their piece of the American dream through hard work, taking risks as entrepreneurs in order to feed their families.

In collecting and editing recipes for this book, I learned a valuable lesson about what it means to cook other people's food, a topic that's been raised by people like brassy restaurateur, author, and *Fresh Off the Boat* host Eddie Huang. I was careful to ask for recipes with the utmost respect, thinking that many would not want to jeopardize their businesses. When a family member dies in America, the estate is divided: houses, cars, mutual funds. In Mexican culture, the big question is who gets the recipes. But I was surprised at who didn't want to give away a recipe and who offered one up without hesitation. For certain recipes, I wouldn't even dare to ask. There's no way, for instance, that I'd ask for Maria Ramos's goat barbacoa recipe, which has been in her family for at least three generations. It's not because you or I might exploit it—they know we can't do it like them anyway—but because these are more than recipes. "It's our patrimony," said David Padilla, Maria's husband/partner at Gish Bac. Those recipes represent memories working alongside parents and grandparents, absorbing the thousands of lessons involved in toasting just a single item in a mole.

Is it okay to cook other people's food? Absolutely, but it's not okay to claim ownership or assume to represent the cuisine. My esteemed colleague Gustavo Arellano and I are huge supporters of everyone who cooks Mexican cuisine, but it's time to give Mexican cooks and chefs the same appreciation given their Korean, Japanese, and Italian counterparts. It is my wish that this book helps to direct attention to the people who are the true leaders of this cuisine in America—something that most Angelenos have known for years.

Los Angeles has three principal styles of Mexican cuisine: Mexican American (what I call pocho cooking), regional, and Alta California. The recipes in these pages represent all of these interconnected traditions, and in the back of the book you'll find a guide to some of the restaurants, markets, bars, and stores whose flavors speak volumes in chiles, masa, and stews.

In some ways this book may be premature, because Alta California is just taking off and Mexican cuisine in the City of Angels is growing and changing so rapidly, but a history, memoir, and cookbook of my city's Mexican gastronomy is long overdue. It's an exciting time to be eating Mexican food in America, especially in Los Angeles, and I hope to inspire your appetite through the recipes, people, and places of *L.A. Mexicano*. Buen provecho!

MEXICO'S CULINARY REGIONS

In the 1970s in L.A., regional specialists like La Flor de Yucatán and Carnitas El Momo began to target homesick Mexicans looking for an authentic dining experience, and in 1985, haute Mexican cuisine first appeared in Boyle Heights. This was ignored by the national food press, which was distracted by the PR machine behind a white American chef from Oklahoma who appropriated regional recipes and was given the title of best Mexican chef in the US by people who knew nothing about the cuisine.

In 1985, before Rick Bayless and even Sonoran-born Zarela Martinez, Mexican fine dining arrived in L.A. at La Serenata de Garibaldi, and then a few years later at Roberto Berrelleza's La Moderna. The Mexican-restaurant culture matured to include serious Oaxacan restaurants and refined fondas serving elevated traditional plates and Mexican haute standards, like La Casita Mexicana, Chichén Itzá, and the chile-and-spice trail of eateries fashioned by Oaxacan chef Rocio Camacho, our own Goddess of Moles. While Mexican chefs and traditional cooks erected monuments to Mexican gastronomy in plain view of what Huang called the "oppressive whiteness of the food world," Bayless flat-out seized the title of standard-bearer, which food writers and bloggers hoisted high above the Mexican chefs serving ancestral traditions that the food media dismissed as nothing but ethnic restaurants—holes in the wall.

This all happened under the assumption that Mexican fine dining and modern Mexican cooking could only exist as long the plates were rectangular, the proteins were from fancy farms, and the dining room was elegant enough for customers who wouldn't be caught dead at a "Mexican" restaurant. Well, we had those places here, too, but only pioneering writers like Barbara Hansen of the *Los Angeles Times* and, later, Jonathan Gold covered these places.

Tlapazola Grill introduced Oaxacan mole to L.A. diners in 1992. Two years later, Oaxacalifornia (the name for the large number of Oaxacans in California) cuisine experienced a food boom when Soledad Lopez, the first person to commercially import Oaxacan products for L.A.'s Oaxacan community, opened Guelaguetza on 8th Street in Koreatown, where Sabores Oaxaqueños is now located. El Texate in Santa Monica opened that same year, and soon Oaxacan restaurants were springing up all over Koreatown, West L.A., and Mid-City. Their success led to a greater explosion of southern Mexican cuisine, with restaurants serving food not just from Oaxaca but also from Puebla, Michoacán, and the Yucatán.

By the 2000s, an avalanche of Mexican ingredients was crossing the border from Tijuana by car and in overstuffed suitcases that stressed the delivery belts of LAX's baggage carousels. This gave rise to an escalation of regional and hyper-regional Mexican restaurants. Experienced artisans and taqueros continue to arrive in L.A. at a faster rate every year, and dishes hidden in plain sight for decades within L.A.'s barrios are now being discovered, satisfying L.A.'s ever-growing appetite for Mexican cuisine.

Today, half of Mexico's states are represented on L.A.'s culinary map. Sinaloa, Jalisco, Nayarit, and Oaxaca, as well as the antojitos of Mexico City and the state of Mexico, form the base of the city's Mexican restaurants, stands, trucks, markets, and underground establishments. Los Angeles doesn't do Mexican cuisine better than Mexico, but you won't find as many regions represented anywhere else on the planet. Our Oaxacan restaurant scene ranks second in the world after Oaxaca itself, and when you have new spots opening up regularly that serve Coliman antojitos, corundas from Michoacán, and chivichangas from Sonora, a whole other universe opens up, invariably redefining what is L.A. Mexicano from one year to the next.

Following is a roster of Mexico's culinary regions and towns with some key dishes they're known for.

Aguascalientes: red enchiladas, red pozole, tacos de lechón, bolillos de crema, gorditas, mole de espinazo de puerco, lamb birria, cueritos encurtidos, esmeriles, condonches, lomo en salsa de chile bola, piratas

Baja California: seafood tacos, roasted lamb, tuna ceviche, sea urchin tostadas, marciano a la diabla, geoduck ceviche, pork loin tortas, adobada, beef birria, lobster Puerto Nuevo style, chorizo de abulón, wine, olive oil, craft beer

Baja California Sur: sweet bean empanadas, chocolate clams, grilled clams, damiana liqueur, manta ray machaca, grilled lobster, callo garra de león, seafood tacos, chilorio de abulón

Campeche: pan de cazón, dogfish panuchos, chile X'catic filled with dogfish, pompano en escabeche

Chiapas: sopa de pan, chalupas, tamal jacuané, tamal de chipilín, chanfaina, cochito hornedo, kistan en mole

Chihuahua: burritos, chile relleno, cheese, sotol, caldillo de carne seca, beef barbacoa, quesadillas, carne asada, discada

Coahuila: gorditas de harina, burritos, lonches, sotol, elotes, cabrito al pastor, carne asada, nachos, discada

Colima: pepena, tuba, bate, enchiladas dulces, pozole seco, sopitos, fish ceviche, cuachala, tatemado, chilayo, taco de pez vela, albondigas de chacal, tacos tuxpeños, iguana con salsa de cacahuate

Districto Federal (D.F.): tortas cubanas, tacos de guisado, tacos de canasta, tacos de fritanga, tacos al pastor, migas, quesadillas, pambazos, huaraches, guajolotas, comida corrida, torta de chilaquil, caldo de gallina, pancita, snails in mole

Durango: mezcal, caldillo durangüense, gorditas, tacos laguneros, torta india, pipián rojo, gallinas borrachas

Estado de Mexico: barbacoa, green chorizo, obispo, queso de puerco, carnitas, wild mushroom soup, sopa de medulla, escamoles, tlacoyos, mixiotes de conejo, pulque, huitlacoche, cecina

Guanajuato: guacamayas, cebadina, enchiladas mineras, pico de gallo de xoconostle, cajeta de Celaya, gorditas de queso y migajas, carnitas

Guerrero: pozole (green and white), pescado a la talla, nacatamales, mole teloloapan, chilate, mezcal, huaxmole, mole de iguana, caldo de cuatete, fiambre

Hidalgo: lamb barbacoa, escamoles, zacahuil, pastes, bocoles, gusanos, gualumbos, pulque, molotes, rabbit mole, ximbó

Jalisco: goat birria, tortas ahogadas, lonches, tejuino, menudo, carne en su jugo, tequila, raicilla, pozole, jericalla, tacos al vapor, rompope, charales en la ribera, patitas de puerco en escabeche, enchiladas tapatías, pozole blanco

Michoacán: carnitas, mole, morisqueta, chavindecas, enchiladas placeras, mezcal, corundas, pozole batido, atoles, pescado blanco de Patzcuaro, sopa Tarasca, aporreadillo

Morelos: cecina Yecapixtla, jumiles, clemole, mole verde, tacos acorazados, tlacoyos de frijol, tortitas de flor de colorín, tamales de bagre, quesadillas, conejo en chileajo

Nayarit: pescado zarandeado, lisa ahumada, shrimp albondigas, tlaxtihuilli, oyster sopes, pollo al estilo Ixtlán del Río, pipián, shrimp tamales, camarones a la diabla, paté de camarón, aguachile

Nuevo León: cabrito al pastor, cabrito en salsa, tacos de trompo, frijoles con veneno, cortadillo, machitos, asado rojo, machacado con huevo, tortas compuestas, agujas a las brasas (carne asada)

Oaxaca: mole negro, pipián, moles, tlayudas, chapulines, empanadas de amarillo, mezcal, estofado, tacos de cazuela, chileajo, tamales de chepil, caldo de piedra, garnachas, tejate, chocolate, alambres, molotes

Puebla: mole poblano, pipián, cemita poblana, tacos placeros, al pastor, mole de caderas, chalupas, chiles en nogada, pelonas, tacos arabes, memelas, camotes, tortitas de Santa Clara, chileatole, huauzontles, mixiotes, mole de olla

Querétaro: zacahuil, lamb barbacoa, enchiladas queretanas, mole de Amealco, tostadas de arriero, chivito tapeado, mole de xoconostle, pollo almendrado, nopales en penca

Quintana Roo: frijol con puerco, chirmol, panuchos, salbutes, queso relleno, pipían verde, cochinita pibil, tikinxic, papadzules, relleno negro, empanadas de cazón, ceviche de caracol, mucbilpollo

San Luis Potosi: zacahuil, enchiladas potosinas, bocoles, coldo Xochitl, rabo de mestizo, tamales huastecos, carnitas, tacos rojos, gorditas, tamales de palmito, guiso borracho, fiambre potosino, asado de boda

Sinaloa: chilorio, machaca, pescado zarandeado, mochomos, vampiros, ceviche de sierra, chorreadas, aguachile, callo de lobina, tamales estilo Sinaloa, tamales barbones, tacos dorados de camarón, callo de hacha, cauques, enchiladas del suelo

Sonora: carne asada, carne con chile colorado, bacanora, burritos percherrones, burritas de machaca, caldo de queso, dogos, sobaqueras, gallina pinta, frijoles mandeados, coyotas, chivichangas, sopa de teparí, carne seca, pozole de trigo, menudo blanco

Tabasco: pejelagarto asado, tamales de pejelagarto, albondigas de chaya, chicharrón con platano, mondongo con garbanzos, torta de iguana, tortilla de coco, pato en chirmol, tamales de caminito, pochitoque en verde

Tamaulipas: jaibas rellenas, tortas de la barda, masita tamaulipeca, cortadillo de res, tamal de chilpán, guayín, mole de papas con camarón, asado de puerco, machaca con tortillas de harina, salpicón de jaiba

Veracruz: mole de xico, mole de Naolinco, zacahuil, chilpachole, picadas, tamal de flor de izote con cerdo, huatape, pazkal de gallina, sopa de chochoyotes, pulpos en su tinta, iguana en moxte

Yucatán: cochinita pibil, huevos motuleños, poc chuc, vaporcitos, sopa de lima, panuchos, lechón asado, panuchos, brazo de reina, kibis, mucbilpollo, frijol con puerco, papadzules, mondongo a la andaluza, relleno blanco, lomitos de Valladolid, pavo en relleno negro

Zacatecas: asado de boda, prickly pears, mezcal, gorditas, birria, tamales de la Bufa, pacholes, tostadas de Jeréz, enchiladas zacatecanas, mole zacatecano, picadillo de asadura, burritos norteños (Burritos La Palma)

NUESTRA COCINA
OUR KITCHEN

Kitchen Equipment 20

Techniques 20

Ingredients 22

Beans & Rice 24

Salsas & Guacamole 27

KITCHEN EQUIPMENT

Cazuela de barro: Look for lead-free clay casserole dishes for cooking stews, soups, and moles

Cheese grater: For grating cheese in pocho gastronomy

Chinois: For straining salsas

Citrus squeezer: For making lime juice for tacos, soups, seafood dishes, and more

Comal: A traditional flat, circular grill made of clay, used for warming tortillas, tacos, and other foods; today it includes a variety of flat-top grills made of metal or clay in a variety of shapes. Mexican markets sell circular comals that fit stovetop burners.

Joint knife: A construction tool useful in flipping tacos on a comal, tortillas too, and can be used to scrape off the comal

Mandoline: Vegetable slicer

Masher: For mashing beans for refried beans

Molcajete: Mortar and pestle made of vesicular basalt. Use a blender if you don't have a molcajete.

Olla: A clay pot for making beans, soups, and stews; can substitute with a stockpot

Pressure cooker: A favorite device used by Mexican home cooks to expedite cooking beans, stews, and more

Spoons: Be sure to have plenty of wooden and enamel spoons handy

Strainers: For straining salsas, lime juice, and other foods

Tongs: You need lots of tongs for moving ingredients in the many multi-step dishes in Mexican cuisine

Tortilla press: For pressing corn tortillas, if you want to take the time to learn—but unless you're going to really put in the time, and I mean years, leave it to the pros at your local tortilleria.

Tortilla warmer: For keeping your tortillas warm; wrapping them in a dishtowel also works just fine

Vaporera: A steam pot used for making tamales

TECHNIQUES

Cleaning chile peppers: For fresh chiles. Wear gloves. Use a paring knife to make a T-cut toward the top of the pepper and leave a little space toward the bottom to keep the peppers intact if you are stuffing them. Carefully cut away the seeds and membrane and discard. For dried chiles, you can use kitchen scissors to remove the stem and cut the pepper lengthwise to easily remove the seeds and stringy membrane. The seeds can also be saved for adding heat to salsas or other dishes.

When to clean chiles (and when not to): Stems and seeds carry more of the heat than the flesh of a chile. Typically you should remove stems and seeds of dry and fresh chiles when making soups, stews, moles, and stuffed peppers, because the purpose in those dishes is to get the complex flavors without so much heat. In making salsas, where you will be using chiles as a condiment, stems and seeds are essential to add heat. For dried chiles, soaking them in lukewarm water or boiling them is necessary to soften them enough for cooking. Use a variety of cooking techniques in making salsas for different flavors and textures. Take a pepper like chile de árbol and make the same salsa with different chile-preparation methods—boiling, frying, toasting, blackening, even raw—and you'll get five very different salsas.

Roasting fresh chiles: Wash and pat dry the chiles, then apply cooking oil to the flesh with a paper towel and place one directly on an open flame. Turn frequently to evenly blacken the chile, being careful not to burn it, and avoid cooking the stem, as you'll need it to handle the chile. Place the charred peppers in a plastic bag, seal it, and let the flesh steam in the bag for about 5 minutes. Remove the chiles and carefully peel the charred skin by rubbing with your fingers (wear gloves) or by grabbing a wadded-up paper towel with a pair of tongs and gently scraping off the flesh with the coarse paper towel.

Toasting: Cooking chiles, herbs, vegetables, and fruits to release aromatics for making stews, salsas, soups, and moles.

Molcajete: Ingredients should be ground in a circular motion until you reach the desired consistency. Be sure your molcajete has been cured before you use it, if not, wash the molcajete with soap and water then grind a handful of beans into a fine powder, repeating three more times, and then do four more passes with raw rice (same amount), then brush out the residue after discarding all the ground ingredients. Rinse with water. Clean with a lime wedge and leave upside down to dry.

Rolling a burrito: To roll a burrito restaurant style, place your flour tortilla on a flat top grill, layer the ingredients then shift them to one side of the tortilla and fold in the sides that are perpendicular to your filling, then pull the top over to cover the ingredients. Roll the burrito away from your body and then serve or wrap in foil. For the best results, continue cooking the rolled burrito on the flat top to lightly toast the outside.

Tortillas: Set the comal to low heat and place a tortilla (corn or flour) on the comal and cook until the tortilla starts to fluff (about 15 seconds), then turn it by hand, with a spatula, or with a joint knife and cook for another 30 seconds, then turn one more time and cook for 15 more seconds. Remove from the heat and place it in a dish towel or tortilla warmer.

INGREDIENTS

The following are staples or common ingredients in L.A. Mexican cooking. You can find all of them at Latino-focused markets, and many at general supermarkets. Some, of course, are available online.

Bayo beans: A bean varietal

Birotes salados: A hard bread roll from Jalisco

Blanditas: Oaxacan-style corn tortillas

California chiles: Dried Anaheim chiles essential to Sonoran cuisine; in Sonora, they're called chiles colorado

Chicharrón: Deep-fried pork rind (sometimes with a small amount of meat attached) for making stews, eating as a snack, or for adding texture to a dish

Chile de árbol: A spicy pepper used in fresh and dried form

Chilhuacle negro chiles: Oaxacan chile peppers used in moles

Chipotle chiles: Smoked, dried jalapeños

Chipotle peppers in adobo (canned): Smoked, dried jalapeños canned in adobo marinade

Chocolate, Mexican: Gritty chocolate tablets for making hot chocolate or to be used in some moles

Costeño chiles: Spicy dried chiles essential to Guerreran cuisine, also used in other regions

Crema mexicana: Mexican sour cream

Epazote: Pungent Mexican herb

Fideos: Mexican pasta dish

Guajillo chiles: Dried chiles essential to Mexican stews, soups, salsas, moles, and many other dishes

Güeros chiles: Blond chiles

Jalapeño chiles: Medium to hot fresh chiles

Jalapeño chiles, pickled: Used as a table condiment

Habanero chiles: Hot peppers from the Yucatán peninsula, used all over Mexico to add heat to dishes

Masa: Corn dough made from ground nixtamalized corn

Milanesas: Breaded meat

Mulato chiles: Dark dried chiles used in sauces and moles

Nixtamal: Prehispanic technique of cooking corn in an alkaline solution that's then hulled and ground into masa for making tortillas, tamales, and a variety of other antojitos

Nopal: Cactus paddle

Oregano, Mexican: A strong-tasting oregano grown in Mexico

Pasilla chiles: Dried chile peppers used in sauces, and the Oaxacan varietal is used in moles

Peruano beans: Mayacoba or canary varietal of bean used in Mexican cooking

Piloncillo: Brown sugar cones

Queso chihuahua: Fresh cheese made by Mennonites in Chihuahua

Queso cotija: A salty, dry cheese for crumbling on sauces and moles from Cotija de la Paz, Michoacán

Queso fresco: Fresh cow's milk cheese

Queso Oaxaca: String cheese, aka quesillo

Sal de Colima: Sea salt from Colima

Sal de San Felipe: Sea salt from San Felipe, Baja California

Saladitas crackers: Saltine crackers

Salsa Huichol: Popular brand of bottled salsa for Mexican seafood

Telera roll: Bread roll for tortas

Tomatillos: Green tomatoes

Tortillas: Thin flatbreads made from nixtamalized corn, corn flour, or wheat flour

Tortillas recien hecha: Tortillas made at a tortilleria, usually pressed and cut by machine

Tostadas (packaged): Fried or baked corn tortillas used as a base for a variety of regional Mexican toppings

BEANS & RICE

BASIC BEANS

Frijoles de la olla, or pot beans, can be used to make a northern bean stew or refried beans, or they can become a meal by adding crumbled queso fresco, diced onions, oregano or cilantro, sliced avocado, chiles, salsa, and/or whatever you fancy. Note that while many bean recipes include onion and garlic, this is a basic preparation that you then can use to make refried beans. In northern Mexico, whole beans are cooked for making frijoles charros, refritos, and other dishes.

The beans favored by my family in Aguascalientes are the yellow peruano beans found at most any supermarket in California. They are technically mayacoba beans but are labeled as peruanos (sometimes canaries) in the Mexican American markets as well as the Mexican section in supermarkets. Despite the name, they are not actually Peruvian. I recommend the Rancho Gordo beans.

Makes 6 cups

2 cups (1 pound) beans (peruano, canario, bayo, or pinto)
4¼ cups water
½ teaspoon sea salt

Sift through the beans to remove any small rocks or other materials and rinse the beans in a colander. There's no need to soak them.

Place beans and water in a pot (a Mexican-style olla if you have one) and set the burner to a medium flame. Once the beans start to boil, lower the heat, cover the pot, and cook until tender, about 2 hours. Check them regularly to make sure they don't run out of water and burn. Keep some hot water on reserve in case you need it—if using an olla, you can place an earthenware bowl filled with water on top of the olla as a lid. This will keep your reserve water at the same temperature as your cooking liquid, so there's no disruption to the cooking process if you add more water.

To check for doneness, remove a bean and press it with a spoon on a hard surface. If it mashes easily, your beans are ready. When they are done, remove them from the heat, add salt, and taste. Add more salt if desired.

BLACK BEANS

Makes 6 cups

2 cups (1 pound) black beans
4¼ cups water
½ medium onion, peeled

1 to 2 cloves garlic, peeled
½ bunch fresh epazote, tied
1½ teaspoons sea salt

Place beans in a pot (a Mexican-style olla if you have one) with water, onion, and garlic and set over medium heat. Once the beans start to boil, add the epazote, lower the heat, cover the pot, and cook until tender, about 2 hours. Check them regularly to make sure they don't run out of water and burn. Keep some hot water on reserve in case you need it—if using an olla, you can place an earthenware bowl filled with water on top of the olla as a lid. This will keep your reserve water at the same temperature as your cooking liquid, so there's no disruption to the cooking process if you add more water.

To check for doneness, remove a bean and press it with a spoon on a hard surface. If it mashes easily, your beans are ready. When they are done, remove them from the heat, discard the onion, garlic, and epazote, add salt, and taste. Add more salt if desired.

REFRIED BEANS

2 tablespoons lard
½ onion, finely diced

3½ cups cooked beans
     (black, peruano, bayo, or pinto)
Sea salt to taste

Set a pan over medium-high heat and add the lard and onion. Lift the pan off the burner and swirl the onion in the lard to avoid burning the onion. Swirl until it is translucent. Return the pan to the heat and add the beans with some of their liquid, mashing them with a potato masher in the pan until you make a smooth purée, or use an immersion blender for a smoother texture. Add more of the bean liquid or hot water for a creamier consistency, or you can cook out the liquid for a more dense texture. Stir constantly to avoid burning. When you're happy with the consistency, taste and add salt as you prefer.

MEXICAN RICE

Makes about 8 cups

1 large tomato or one 8-ounce can tomato sauce
2 teaspoons vegetable oil
½ onion, diced
2 cloves garlic, minced

2 cups basmati rice
2½ teaspoons sea salt, or to taste
2 cups chicken stock

Place tomato in a blender and purée with a little water until it's smooth. If tomatoes aren't in season, use canned tomato sauce, or blend homemade canned tomatoes if you have any in your pantry.

Heat a heavy-bottomed pot over medium-high heat, then add oil, onions, and garlic. Cook, stirring constantly to avoid burning, until translucent. Add rice and cook until it becomes opaque, stirring constantly so it doesn't burn. Add tomato purée and continue to sauté and stir until the tomato has colored the rice red, about 2 to 3 minutes, then add salt.

Add chicken stock and bring to a boil. Reduce the heat to low, cover (with a translucent lid if possible to stop the cooking if the liquid has cooked off), and simmer for 15 to 20 minutes. Remove from the heat. Do not remove the lid to check the rice for at least another 5 minutes. Once the rice is done, remove the lid, stir, add salt to taste, and serve hot.

WHITE RICE

This lightly seasoned white rice is the perfect fit with such richly flavorful main dishes as mole and pipián.

Makes about 8 cups

2 teaspoons vegetable oil
½ onion, finely diced
2 cloves garlic, minced

2 cups rice
4 cups water
2½ teaspoons sea salt, or to taste

Heat a heavy-bottomed pot over medium-high heat, then add oil, onions, and garlic. Cook, stirring constantly to avoid burning, until translucent. Add rice and cook until it becomes opaque, stirring constantly so it doesn't burn.

Add water and bring to a boil. Reduce the heat to low, cover (with a translucent lid if possible), and simmer for 15 to 20 minutes. Remove from the heat. Do not remove the lid to check the rice for at least 5 minutes. Once the rice is done, remove the lid, stir, add salt to taste, and serve hot.

SALSAS & GUACAMOLE

SALSA VERDE

For a milder salsa, remove the seeds from the chiles after cooking and/or use one chile instead of two.

2 tomatillos, cleaned
2 serrano chiles
½ onion, cut into chunks

Juice of 1 lime
1 sprig cilantro, chopped
Sea salt to taste

Fill a medium saucepan three-quarters full with salted water and bring to a boil. Add tomatillos and chiles, reduce heat to medium-low, and simmer for 20 minutes. Remove tomatillos and chiles and discard water. Remove stems from the chiles and place the tomatillos, chiles, onion, lime juice, and cilantro in a blender or food processor and purée to a smooth and even consistency. Taste and add salt as needed.

CHILE DE ÁRBOL SALSA

You can adjust the ratio of tomato to chile de árbol for a hotter or milder salsa as you see fit.

½ cup vegetable oil
12 chiles de árbol, stems removed

2 roma tomatoes, charred and peeled
Sea salt to taste

Heat oil in a skillet over medium-high heat. Add chiles and fry until they change color, about 3 minutes. Place chiles and tomatoes in a blender or food processor and blend until the mixture is smooth, adding a little water if it seems too thick. Taste and add salt as needed.

GUACAMOLE

2 Haas avocados, pitted and peeled
¼ cup finely diced onion

2 tablespoons chopped cilantro
Sea salt to taste

Place avocado, onion, cilantro, and salt in a serving bowl and stir with a fork until combined.

POCHO CUISINE

"Pocho" (or "pocha") was originally a pejorative term used by Mexicans to describe Mexican Americans, but today its use is openly embraced by Mexican Americans, who often speak "broken Spanish" and embrace their Mexican heritage. Pocho cooking is the original L.A. Mexicano, the food that many second- and third-generation Mexican Americans grew up eating, and the dishes that everyone in L.A. considered truly Mexican until we started knowing better in the 1990s: the enchiladas and tostadas that L.A.-born college kids craved when away at college, the trays of taquitos served at Cinco de Mayo parties, the huevos rancheros inhaled by surfers after an early morning session. Are these dishes authentic? Absolutely—they are authentically L.A., created in L.A. by Mexican-born cooks with the ingredients they had available to them from the 1920s through the 1970s.

PEOPLE

Oscar Gonzalez 30

Susanna MacManus 33

Christy Vega Fowler 38

Elena Rojas 43

John Anthony 49

RECIPES

Steak Picado Ciro's 32

Taquitos with Avocado Sauce . . 36

Molcajete 41

Enchilada Sauce 42

Hollenbeck Burrito 45

Chile Rojo 46

Chile Relleno Burrito,
    La Azteca Style 47

Eastside Pico de Gallo 48

OSCAR GONZALEZ

1972 was the summer of Chicano love, when songs from Malo's legendary album *Suavecito* dripped out of the rear speakers of vintage Impalas on Brooklyn Avenue (now César Chavez) like nectar from the gods, and every smooth cholo in Boyle Heights imagined holding his ruca like the Mexica warrior from the album's cover art by Mexican painter Jesus Helguera. That same year, in an era that woke la raza to join the civil rights movement and saw Mexican American pride soaring through the barrio, the Gonzalez family opened the pocho restaurant Ciro's.

The Gonzalez family arrived in L.A. from Ciudad Juárez, Chihuahua, in 1966. Oscar's grandmother opened a few bakeries, where his dad, a baker, worked alongside his mother. His grandmother then bought a burger joint on Evergreen in 1972, but business was slow. "In 1973, my parents took over after my grandmother left—my dad would have us stand outside in a line to make it look like we were busy," remembers Oscar. They needed help, which came from an unlikely source: Manny Rojas, the affable owner of the beloved El Tepeyac Café just down the street, who started sending his customers down to try Ciro's. "We had different food, so I guess he didn't think it was a big deal, but that's the way Manny was," adds Oscar.

In 1968, two years after the Gonzalez family landed in Boyle Heights, thousands of Mexican American high school students participated in the L.A. Blowouts, one of the nation's largest organized protests ever against a school district—in this case, L.A. Unified, which was providing subpar educations and facilities to students in Boyle Heights and East L.A. Throughout the struggles for civil rights, the challenges of gang violence, and the current backlash against gentrification in Boyle Heights, Ciro's has remained neutral territory, where lumbering plates of pocho cuisine bind the community together in a tapestry of melted cheese. For Mexican American actors and rock stars, it's the closest thing to the famed Café de la Rotonde in Paris, but with badass avocado salsa and flautas. The guys from Los Lobos come in from time to time, and Danny Trejo ate there more than once while filming *Blood In, Blood Out,* but you won't find their pictures up on the wall.

"My dad always catered to the customers," says Oscar, who owns Ciro's today. "We'd help the old ladies, even dropping them off at their houses—I was Uber before there was Uber." His dad thought that if they put any pictures on the wall, they should be of the regulars, not the occasional celebrity visitor.

The food was regional cuisine from Ciudad Juárez, and the name Ciro's came from a family street stand of the same name. But cooking regional cuisine under the bias and scrutiny of the health department proved a challenge, as did the nature of dining in the pocho community. In Mexico, for example, elongated flautas (flutes) were cooked over open flames in large metal pans filled with oil—a big no-no for the health depart-ment—but commercial fryers were financially out of reach. "So we decided to just cut them in half and cook them in a frying pan," says Oscar. The dish lays three pairs of taquitos filled with chicken or beef end to end to form faux flautas—into the gap goes the tomato sauce and a covering of guacamole and sour cream. In Mexico, flautas were considered a snack to tide you over while on the go, but in Boyle Heights, Mexican im-migrants worked long, hard hours and came in hungry. "We added the rice and beans because our customers were blue-collar workers—we wanted them to eat like they were in our home," says Oscar. "My dad always said that rice and beans shouldn't be in burritos because our customers aren't animals." Rice and delicious refried beans on the side, always, with a warm, wilted shredded-lettuce salad dressed with vinegar.

Pocho cuisine in Boyle Heights and East L.A. shares some aspects of El Torito's Americanized Mexican bill of fare, but the menus have a closer tie to traditional Mexican dishes. Ciro's versions of mole, machaca, chile relleno, tongue red salsa, and chicharrones in green salsa have roots in Ciudad Juárez. The beans, rice, giant burritos, and combo plates are Chicano fuel for the long journey toward the American dream, but Oscar's desires weren't wrapped in tortillas. He left L.A. to study advertising and graphic design at Seattle University, and still wonders what his life could've been if he'd pursued his dreams. But he stepped up to help out at Ciro's after his sister got married and began to raise a family. Any second-guesses about his career choices are interrupted by his great customer-service reflexes, when he greets every customer warmly with, "*Bienvenidos, por donde gustes,*" meaning "Welcome, sit where you like."

As is true with so many family businesses, Oscar inherited cooks, waitresses, and bussers (some related and some not) who have been around for a long time. "Here, we promote dishwashers to preps and then to cooks—we do everything within," he says. His sister, Adriana "Lenny" Tenorio, cooks on the weekends and has all the recipes down, recipes that marinate in the senses of generations of pochos who've both left the barrio and remained. From customers to vendors, all of Oscar's business is done with a handshake—if you ask anyone from the 'hood, "Ese vato Oscar is a true camarada" (comrade), as a former marine from Boyle Heights once wrote.

Everyone—cops, politicians, celebrities, DWP and Edison workers, even gang members (they don't beef here)—keeps coming back for the food. "Little by little I've accepted my fate," says Oscar, beaming. "I love interacting with the people, and the happiness and memories that people have when they eat our food, that's what keeps me going." As I dig in to a plate of steak picado, a passing group looks me in the eye and says "provecho" (bon appétit). *Suavecito's* celestial layers of falsetto fill the dining room with nostalgia. It's just another Sunday in Chicano paradise.

STEAK PICADO CIRO'S

Oscar Gonzalez, Ciro's

You can find steak picado in any legit Mexican American restaurant. It's a pocho version of a northern Mexican dish that's part of the Mexican American trinity of Chicano guisados: steak picado, chile verde, and chile colorado. Ciro's makes this dish with a fiery punch of chiles—I calmed it down somewhat for this recipe, but feel free to add more if you can handle it.

Serves 4

Vegetable oil
1½ pounds ribeye steak
2 cups chopped onions (about 2 medium onions), chopped into 1-inch pieces
2 jalapeño chiles, sliced

3 güeros chiles, sliced
1½ teaspoons cumin
1 tablespoon sea salt, plus more if needed
1 tablespoon garlic powder
Freshly ground black pepper to taste

Preheat a grill or a skillet with a grate to medium-high heat, add a tablespoon or so of vegetable oil and cook steaks until browned, 3 to 4 minutes per side. Remove to a cutting board, reserving the juices, and cut meat into medium chunks. Set aside.

Heat a saucepan over medium heat, add about 2 tablespoons oil, and sauté onions until they are translucent. Add both chiles and cook for another 10 minutes, stirring constantly. Add cumin, salt, garlic powder, and reserved beef juices, cooking for another 2 to 3 minutes. Add chopped steak and simmer for another 10 minutes. Taste and add pepper and more salt if needed.

Serve with refried beans, Mexican rice, pico de gallo, a salad of shredded lettuce, a large tomato slice, and warm flour tortillas. Guacamole is always a good addition, too. To enjoy the steak Mexican style, tear off a piece of flour tortilla and scoop up a bit of meat, rice, salsa, and beans, just enough for a hearty bite.

SUSANNA MacMANUS

Los Angeles is a taco city—America's first city of Mexican cuisine—and it all started on Olvera Street, where patient zero got a first taste of the taco. Later it spread to every corner of L.A.'s urban sprawl, eventually afflicting the entire country with taco fever.

When Los Pobladores (the original forty-four families who settled Los Angeles) arrived in 1781, it is certain that those brave souls, two-thirds of them Mexicans recruited in Sonora and Sinaloa (including mestizos, Afro-Mexicans, and indigenous people), enjoyed a hearty serving of Mexican cuisine as their first meal—probably fideos, beans, lentils, and vegetables to cure their hunger after a nine-mile trek that ended on what today is Placita Olvera.

By the 1880s, settlers from the southern states had arrived to bolster the town's growing English-speaking population, and they preferred the surrounding land and left Placita Olvera for neglect. As Mexican immigration increased in the 1920s (and with the support of *Los Angeles Times* publisher Harry Chandler), Christine Sterling—fondly referred to as the Mother of Olvera Street—stepped in to restore California's past through the corny outfits, trinkets, and Mexican food that had once been forbidden anywhere off Olvera Street.

Aurora Guerrero arrived in Los Angeles from Huanusco, Zacatecas, at the age of twenty-two with her eight-year-old daughter, Ana Natalia Guerrero, in tow. She supported them by cleaning houses and churches. Years later, Ana Natalia had found work on Olvera Street, and she heard that one of the vendors wanted to go back to Mexico—so with the approval of Christine Sterling, Aurora Guerrero took his spot in 1934, called it Cielito Lindo, and started selling tacos.

"My grandmother came up with the avocado salsa, enchiladas rojas, and taquitos—I think they might have originally been barbacoa de borrego (lamb), but that didn't sell," says Susanna MacManus, Aurora's granddaughter and the face of Cielito Lindo and Las Anitas, also on Olvera Street. Originally Aurora served a variety of foods, but she switched to just beef to attract the white American tourists looking for Mexican food—just not anything "too Mexican."

It wasn't long before Susanna's grandmother's beef taquitos with avocado salsa became a hit with tourists and celebrities alike. "At first, she cooked the beef over charcoal, and then they built the stall around the grill," says Susanna. "Orson Welles, who was introduced to us by Rita Hayworth, once ate forty-three taquitos in one sitting!" By the time Susanna was born in 1943, Cielito Lindo was a veteran stall that had paved the way for the taquito, tamal, chile relleno, and enchilada hawkers on Olvera Street.

In 1944, to satisfy the city's growing taco fever, Aurora opened a commissary on Broadway called Las Anitas and brought in family from Zacatecas to help cook the fillings and roll taquitos. Outside of Olvera Street, Mexican restaurants identified themselves as Spanish to avoid the stigma of serving dirty Mexican food, unless waitresses wore peasant blouses like Margarita Cansino (Rita Hayworth's real name) did in *The Loves of Carmen* and portrayed romantic caricatures from Alta California's past.

Struggles came to Broadway and Olvera Street in the 1960s as L.A. began emptying out into the suburbs. "More than once, my mom had to go to the track and gamble on long shots to raise the money for our rent—the sheriff was there ready to shut us down," says Susanna. She'd help out in high school and college, and noticed that La Casita, a nightclub across the street, was packed; she asked her mom to let her keep Cielito Lindo open late one night, and she made more in those extra few hours than they had sold all day.

Susanna went on to earn a BA and a MA in medieval Spanish, and stopped just short of a PhD in order to help maintain her grandmother's recipes and handle the marketing while her sister, Dianna Robertson, managed the books.

"We've had our ups and downs with all the changes the city has gone through since the '30s—we opened some other Las Anitas but they closed," says Susanna. "But now a new generation of writers, bloggers, and Instagrammers are spreading the word." All Aurora Guerrero wanted was to be able to buy each family member a house, a goal she achieved long ago when she purchased seven houses in a row in Lincoln Heights. She accomplished so much more, though, including the founding of a signature L.A. dish, not to mention a dining experience that has touched so many lives.

When I met up with Susanna for lunch at Las Anitas, seated next to us was a young pocho couple on a date—they were sharing taquitos and combination plates of enchiladas soaked in a blood-red sauce that stained the flanking perimeters of rice and beans, with the whole ensemble covered in *Blair Witch* twig-men figures of melted yellow and white cheese. It's a wickedly delicious plate of hearty, old-school Mexican American flavors, the aromas commemorating familial occasions and courtships, as a new generation of Mexican Americans have become eager to taste what their tio would certify as real Mexican food.

In the last decade, Olvera Street's manager Chris Espinoza has done a great job of bringing the Mexican American community together for cultural events, concerts, and festivals. Cielito Lindo's business is booming, and its famous runny, tangy avocado sauce—poured over a pair of taquitos whose sole purpose is to act as a pair of crisp, well-seasoned utensils for that liquefied Chicano gold—has been drawing devotees to L.A.'s first street for more than eighty years. Yes, you can still get great Mexican American food at Placita Olvera, where Cielito Lindo and Las Anitas have remained to witness a new version of Alta California—one that they can finally call their own.

TAQUITOS WITH AVOCADO SAUCE

Susanna MacManus, Cielito Lindo

This Olvera Street landmark makes its corn tortillas the old-school way via nixtamalization, the pre-Hispanic method of transforming corn into masa, but fresh tortillas from a tortilleria will work just fine for home cooks. Look for a Mexican brand of tortilla that is thick, like from Los Cinco Puntos or Carnitas Uruapan Market and Bakery on the eastside.

The crockpot results in very tender machaca (beef), but if you don't have one, you can use a large saucepan—follow the same procedure, but cook the stew over low heat, covered, for 1½ to 2 hours.

Makes 12 taquitos

1 pound boneless chuck roast or other inexpensive cut of beef
½ tablespoon black peppercorns
Sea salt to taste
1 clove garlic, chopped
1 bay leaf
1 dozen fresh corn tortillas
Toothpicks
Peanut oil or lard
Avocado Sauce (recipe follows)

Place beef in a crockpot and add water to cover. Add peppercorns, salt to taste, garlic, and bay leaf. Bring to a boil, reduce heat to low, and cook on low for 8 to 10 hours.

Remove beef from crockpot and set aside to cool. (Discard garlic, peppercorns, and bay leaf, but you can reserve the stock for another use.) When it's cool enough to handle, shred the beef and set aside.

Heat tortillas on a comal or griddle until pliable and place in a towel to keep them soft. Set a tortilla on a work surface and add about 1 ounce of machaca near one end. Curl the tortilla over the beef with your fingers and roll it up. Insert a toothpick lengthwise across the fold so it doesn't unravel. Repeat with each tortilla.

Place a cast-iron skillet over high heat. Add enough oil or lard to submerge the taquitos halfway. Using tongs, carefully place the taquitos into the hot oil, 2 or 3 at a time, and cook until golden brown, about 1 minute per side. Do not turn over more than once on each side, unless you have to do so to achieve the crispness you desire. Set taquitos on a paper-towel-lined dish to drain the oil. Remove toothpicks and salt to taste.

To serve, arrange taquitos on a platter and pour over enough avocado sauce to cover. Grab a taquito and don't stop until all the avocado sauce is gone!

AVOCADO SAUCE

Makes 2 quarts

13 medium tomatillos
7 güeros chiles, stems removed
4 cloves garlic
2 medium ripe avocados
2 cups roughly chopped cilantro
1 tablespoon sea salt, more to taste

Peel husks off the tomatillos and rinse under cold water. Pour 6 cups water into a large stockpot and turn heat to high. Add tomatillos, chiles, and garlic and bring to a boil. Lower to a medium heat and cook for 5 minutes. Use a slotted spoon to remove tomatillos, chiles, and garlic, reserving most of the water, and place strained ingredients into a food processor or blender. Add avocado, cilantro, and salt. Add 1 cup of the reserved water and blend on low speed. Add another cup of water and continue to blend, progressing to higher speed. Blend, adding more water as needed, until sauce has the consistency of a light gravy. It should be smooth, without any chunks.

You can use the sauce immediately, or cover and refrigerate until needed. It will keep in the refrigerator for about a week.

CHRISTY VEGA FOWLER

Casa Vega in Sherman Oaks represents a style of Mexican American dining that will never die: painfully tart margaritas, hot combo plates where undressed lettuce supports the high temperature of the canopy of greasy yellow cheese, and a dimly lit den of leatherette booths, where what happens in the dark never comes to light. It's a paparazzi-and-social-media-free zone, in which even the most eagle-eyed photographer can't tell a bowl of chips from a Hermès clutch. "That's why celebrities have been coming here for years," says owner Christy Vega Fowler. "Like Jane Fonda, Gig Young, Dyan Cannon, and Al Pacino—today, it's Selena Gomez, Miley Cyrus, and the Kardashians, who've been regulars for a long time and have even filmed here." At Casa Vega, anonymity comes with chips and salsa and a whole lot of history.

The food is different than what you'll find in East L.A. or in San Fernando—it's more about seafood enchiladas, taco salads, and fajitas. But it finds common ground with its cousins in burritos (with beans and rice on the side), combo plates, and such traditional dishes as chile colorado, steak picado, and mole. Casa Vega's history represents a continuum of Mexican flavors, from Prohibition-era Tijuana, to the founding of Olvera Street's romanticized Mexican marketplace for Anglos, to today's lobster quesadillas and Mexican pizzas.

Christy's father, Rafael "Ray" Vega, was born in National City and grew up in Tijuana and, later, Los Angeles. He was a natural restaurateur—his parents had worked at Tijuana's Caesar's Restaurant, the birthplace of the salad found on nearly every menu on the planet, and in 1938, they opened Café Caliente on Olvera Street. (It's now El Paseo Inn, which still serves some dishes from the old Café Caliente.) "My dad wanted to find a new location, but was worried people wouldn't eat Mexican food off Olvera Street—until he had an offer from an old lady who owned a restaurant and knew my family," says Christy. With an incentive of two months free rent, he opened Casa Vega in 1956 in that old lady's Sherman Oaks space (now a Barbecues Galore). Two years later, Ray Vega had become one of L.A.'s pioneering Mexican restaurateurs, and he moved to a larger space, where Casa Vega remains today.

Christy grew up in Las Vegas, where the mob's decline had opened up opportunities in the hospitality business. While the restaurant kept running, her father sold bar supplies and handled food service for Vegas resorts; he became an honorary consul general to Mexico and a member of the state's Commission of Economic Development. Christy went off to St. Mary's College and moved to L.A. in 1999, business degree in hand, to handle accounting and back-office tasks at Casa Vega. Eventually, Ray sold his Vegas holdings and came back to run his popular San Fernando Valley den of margaritas, combo plates, and kisses in the dark.

Christy eventually found her way into the kitchen, helping prepare tamales and learning the recipes from Chef Conoso, who'd been at Casa Vega for fifty years. "All of our employees have been around for decades," she says. "Braulio was our chef for twenty-seven years, working with Conoso, and even our waiters have been around forever." Though she too had been around for a long time, it took a while for this bubbly, Irish-Mexican girl to earn the respect of her father and the employees. "It was ten years before my father finally said, 'Okay, you got this,'" she says, laughing. But the customers were another story—to them, she got it.

"I can hardly change anything here," she adds. "If I move a plant or a painting, someone complains that they proposed to their wife in that booth. And there's no way we could ever change the food." She is a caretaker of a cuisine and an era in which the only Mexican food you ate had melted cheese on it, but today she's using better proteins, has added vegetarian items, and has updated the bar prep with fresh ingredients. "That was another challenge—it's more work to make cocktails from scratch using fresh ingredients, and the bartenders had always used mixes," she says.

The employees who watched her grow up no longer pat Christy on the head when she tells them what to do, and she's branched out as a television personality doing cooking demos on the *Today Show*, *This Morning*, and *Rachael Ray*. Last summer, both an ailing Ray Vega (who looked like a million bucks that night) and Christy Vega Fowler celebrated Casa Vega's sixtieth anniversary with guest chef and Christy's cousin, Tijuana-based Javier Plascencia, and his parents. On that occasion, history and mythos became one; the Plascencias, who'd resurrected the legendary Caesar's Restaurant from the grave, came together with the Vegas to renew a Mexican dynasty that began in Tijuana eighty years earlier.

Casa Vega—it's where the combined flavors of prohibition-era Tijuana, Olvera Street, and Mexican food's journey into suburbia converge onto a plate, a culinary history preserved in a tapestry of persimmon red and annatto-tinted orange-yellow.

MOLCAJETE

Christy Vega Fowler, Casa Vega

A dish named for the large Mexican mortar and pestle in which it is served, a molcajete is a hallmark of a Mexican American family restaurant. This version is one of the most popular dishes at Casa Vega, and it's perfect for entertaining at home, particularly when served with Casa Vega margaritas (*see page 158*).

Serves 4

½ cup extra-virgin olive oil, plus more
6 cloves garlic, minced
1 teaspoon Mexican oregano
1 teaspoon cumin
1 teaspoon paprika
1 teaspoon sea salt, plus more
1 teaspoon freshly ground black pepper, plus more
1 pound flank steak
12 ounces boneless chicken breast, pounded to an even thickness

Juice of 2 lemons
12 tiger shrimp, peeled and deveined
8 whole green onions
4 Anaheim chiles
2 cups Enchilada Sauce (*recipe follows*)
1 cup queso fresco
1 cup guacamole (*see recipe page 27*)
1 cup sour cream
18 corn and/or flour tortillas

Preheat the oven to 400°.

In a medium bowl, whisk together ½ cup olive oil, garlic, oregano, cumin, paprika, salt, and pepper. Pour half the marinade into another bowl. Add steak to one bowl and chicken breast to the other. Cover each and set aside in the refrigerator for 1 hour.

Heat grill to medium-high. Remove meat from marinade and shake off liquid. Grill steak for 3 to 4 minutes per side for medium rare. At the same time, grill chicken breast until internal temperature reaches 165°, also about 3 to 4 minutes per side. Remove both from heat, cover with foil, and leave to rest for 5 minutes.

Put a large molcajete in the oven to heat.

While steak and chicken are resting, toss shrimp in a bowl with about 1 tablespoon olive oil, lemon juice, and salt and pepper to taste. Grill shrimp until they turn pink, 2 to 3 minutes per side. Set aside.

Rub green onions and Anaheim chiles in olive oil to coat and grill until both are slightly charred. Place chiles in a plastic bag (a leftover produce bag works well), seal the bag, and set aside until the skin loosens, about 3 to 5 minutes. If the pepper is too hot to handle, ball up a paper towel, grab the chile with a pair of tongs, and gently rub off the charred skin with the paper towel. If it's cool enough to handle, the skin should come off by rubbing it gently with your fingers. This is easier under running water, but you'll lose some of the flavor and char by doing this.

In a small bowl, whisk together the Enchilada Sauce, ½ cup water, and a hearty pinch each of Mexican oregano and black pepper. This is the "special sauce."

Slice steak and chicken into thick, even strips, cutting against the grain. Remove hot molcajete from the oven with oven mitts, and pour the special sauce into it. Add steak, chicken, shrimp, green onions, and Anaheim chiles, arranging the pieces uniformly and stacking ingredients as you see fit. Serve with crumbled queso fresco, guacamole, sour cream, and corn and/or flour tortillas.

ENCHILADA SAUCE

Makes 2 cups

¼ cup canola oil
¼ cup flour
2 tablespoons chile paste
1 cup cold water, divided
½ cup chicken stock
1 tablespoon chicken base
1 teaspoon cumin
1 teaspoon garlic powder

Heat oil in a medium saucepan over medium-high heat. Add flour and cook, stirring, for 1 minute. Add chile paste and stir to combine. Stir in ½ cup cold water and chicken stock, bring to a boil, and reduce heat to simmer.

In a small mixing bowl, stir together chicken base, cumin, garlic powder, and remaining ½ cup water. Pour mixture into saucepan, stir to combine, and simmer for 10 minutes.

ELENA ROJAS

The day that Ramon Manuel Rojas, known as Manny, quit drinking, he opened a bottle of Jose Cuervo and started pouring shots for his family at El Tepeyac Café in Boyle Heights. And when I say family, I mean his customers. "His doctor told him he couldn't drink anymore, so he decided to let everyone else drink instead," says his daughter, Elena Rojas, who now runs the famed shrine to gut-bursting burritos and smoldering plates of pocho excess.

Manny was famous for pouring generous shots of Cuervo, working the room, and crafting his prodigious burrito—called the Hollenbeck—which is filled with beans, rice, guacamole, and stew and then blanketed with the same stew. The burrito was named for the fine public servants at the LAPD's Hollenbeck division, who have been regular customers for decades. "Let's put it this way—they used to drive my dad around back in the day," says Elena, but instead of taking Manny home to sleep it off, he and the officers would end up having dinner back at El Tepeyac. "He probably told them they looked hungry."

A veteran who served in Okinawa at the age of fifteen (using a fake ID), Manny grew up in the business; his father, Salvador Rojas, opened El Tupinamba in 1942 and, later, La Villa Café in Lincoln Heights. When Salvador passed away, Manny's mother asked if he would help her out at the family's hot dog and hamburger joint in Boyle Heights. He'd already owned three Mexican restaurants that didn't work out, so he jumped at the chance to add some Mexican flair to his mom's burger joint, which they named El Tepeyac. By then, a new style of Mexican American cuisine was flowing from Boyle Heights and East L.A. This wasn't Olvera Street or a "Spanish" restaurant (what restaurants like El Cholo and El Torito called themselves so they'd be accepted by gringos). Manny cooked for Chicanos and others who lived in Boyle Heights, which was ethnically diverse because of the lack of restrictive covenants that kept minorities out of other neighborhoods. Every ethnic group got roasted while waiting in line for a table, and if you'd been eating at El Tepeyac since you were a baby, Manny would announce, "I used to change his diapers!" Japanese customers would be startled by wisecracks in their native tongue, which he'd learned while stationed in Okinawa.

"He treated everyone the same," says Elena. "Our restaurant is about people, and the customers who have been coming here for years know each other. It's like a big reunion of friends, so when I took over I didn't want to change things." There's still always a line, especially on weekends. Manny wanted to make sure everyone got fed, so he used to tell his customers to stop talking and hurry up, because he had friends to feed.

The menu was born from Manny's sense of hospitality. The formidable Hollenbeck burrito is covered in enough spicy pork to make a whole other burrito, and the Manny's Special was big enough to feed the original lineup of Cannibal and the Headhunters (a Chicano rock band from the '60s). When his white customers couldn't take the heat, he created the Original Okie, a Hollenbeck-size burrito with a milder salsa verde. The chilaquiles come with rice, beans, and a cup of sour cream; combo plates are made with more than a dozen burrito fillings and the Holy Trinity of Mexican American stews: chile verde, chile colorado, and steak picado. It's impossible to leave El Tepeyac hungry.

El Tepeyac represented a new breed of Mexican American cuisine that reflected the flavors and appetites of blue-collar Chicanos on the eastside. It was followed by El Arco Iris (1964), Al & Bea's Mexican Food (1966), Los Cinco Puntos (1967), and Lupe's No. 2 (1972). Unlike the pocho restaurateurs who entered hostile territory off Olvera Street and out of the barrio, like Casa Vega (1956) and La Cabaña (1963), Manny's was free of kitsch, margaritas, and the clichéd décor of the Mexican restaurant scene in Dan Gilroy's 2014 thriller *Nightcrawler* (which was filmed at El Compadre on Sunset Boulevard).

The food served at these places used what ingredients were available and created an authentic cuisine—not Tex-Mex or a bastardized version of Mexican cuisine—that reflected L.A.'s Mexican American community. Manny's has fed three generations of pochos and has cooks and waiters who have been around since the beginning, like Lidia, who started when she was twenty and retired at sixty-five.

Elena worked as a cashier while in high school but set out to find a job after graduation outside the restaurant, dressing up and applying for a stock girl position downtown. Once she got the job, Manny said he didn't want her taking the bus late at night, so she's been working the business side of El Tepeyac ever since. In 2013, when her father died, she assumed full responsibility for his house, his customers, and his recipes. Honoring his culture of community, Elena established a way to appreciate longtime customers ninety-five or older, a club that currently has four members: Mami (101), Madre (104), Roy (98), and Uncle (101). They get food on the house for the rest of their lives.

Manny's El Tepeyac is a unique restaurant that third-generation burrito empress Elena Rojas is not interested in duplicating. "But I'd like to have some small takeout places just for the burritos," she says. The only goal is to share her father's food with a larger audience. "My dad taught me that it's not about fame, money, or anything like that—this is his house, and everyone is our guest."

HOLLENBECK BURRITO
In honor of Manny Rojas, El Tepeyac Café

This recipe is my tribute to the generosity and creativity of a Boyle Heights legend, Manuel "Manny" Rojas, who passed away in 2013. For decades, he treated every customer as a guest in his home at El Tepeyac. Manny's chile rojo is a cross between a chile verde, with tomatoes substituting for tomatillos, and a chile colorado. He poured this stew over his famous Hollenbeck burrito, making what might have been L.A.'s original wet burrito, and every guest has always left full and happy. They still do—daughter Elena carries on the spirit today.

A tip: Rolling a big burrito takes practice, so if it's your first time, watch a video online first. If you're a beginner, you can also use two tortillas to hold your ingredients in place. It only needs to make it as far as the plate anyway—you'll be eating this wet burrito with silverware.

HOLLENBECK BURRITO
Makes 1 burrito

1 large flour tortilla
¼ cup refried beans (*see recipe page 25*)
1 cup Mexican rice (*see recipe page 26*)
¼ cup guacamole (*see recipe page 27*)

2½ cups Chile Rojo (*recipe follows*), divided
¼ cup Eastside Pico de Gallo (*see recipe page 48*)
¼ cup cheddar cheese, finely shredded

Warm the tortilla on a griddle or skillet and place it in a towel to steam for a minute or two. Spread tortilla with beans, then layer the rice, guacamole, 1½ cups Chile Rojo (spoon on mostly meat and just a little sauce—too much sauce will just get soaked up by the rice), and pico de gallo.

Fold over the left and right ends of the tortilla, roll the burrito, and set it on a plate. Top with cheese and pour remaining 1 cup of Chile Rojo over everything. Enjoy with a fork and a knife—and a big appetite.

CHILE ROJO

3 medium tomatoes
6 California or guajillo chiles
3 chiles de árbol
½ onion, cut into chunks, plus ¼ cup chopped onion
3 cloves garlic

1 teaspoon oregano
1 teaspoon ground cumin
Sea salt and freshly ground black pepper to taste
Vegetable oil
2 pounds pork butt, cut into small cubes
¼ cup chopped bell pepper

Bring a saucepan of water to boil, add a pinch of salt, and add the tomatoes. Cook until tender, just a few minutes. Remove tomatoes from the water, peel, and set aside.

Toast chiles in a pan or on a comal until they change color, taking care not to burn them. Remove from the heat and remove the stems. Put chiles into a blender or food processor and add tomato, ½ onion, garlic, oregano, and cumin. Blend until the salsa is smooth. Taste and add salt as desired. Set salsa aside.

Place a large nonstick saucepan over medium-high heat and swirl in some oil. Add pork and about 2 teaspoons salt. Cook, stirring occasionally, until browned, about 8 minutes. Add ¼ cup chopped onion, bell pepper, and salsa. Bring to a boil, lower the heat, and simmer until the meat is tender and the dish has reduced to a thick stew, about 40 minutes. Taste and add additional salt and pepper to taste.

CHILE RELLENO BURRITO, LA AZTECA STYLE

One of the popular burritos from the Mexican American table is the burrito de chile relleno, a northern Mexican version done with a poblano chile, which makes for a thick and hearty dish. In Chihuahua, they use a thinner chile chilaca, but in East L.A. and Boyle Heights, this hefty version is meant to be a full meal. I modeled this recipe after the award-winning one from La Azteca Tortilleria, but you'll find this pocho favorite at many Mexican American burrito joints.

Note that in many supermarkets, poblanos are mislabeled as pasilla chiles. If you see pasillas, they're likely poblanos.

Makes 4 burritos

4 poblano chiles, roasted and peeled
1 cup (4 ounces) shredded Monterey Jack cheese
Toothpicks
2 eggs, separated
1½ cups all-purpose flour, more as needed
Sea salt and freshly ground pepper
Vegetable oil
4 large flour tortillas, preferably from La Azteca Tortilleria
1 cup refried beans (*see recipe page 25*)
2 cups Eastside Pico de Gallo (*recipe follows*)

Use a paring knife to make a lengthwise slit along the poblanos, stopping short of the top and bottom, and carefully remove the seeds and membranes. Pat the peppers dry with a towel and stuff each with ¼ cup cheese. Thread 4 toothpicks through the seams in a pair of X patterns to snugly close the chile rellenos.

Use a stand mixer or electric mixer to beat the egg whites on high speed until soft peaks form. You should be able to hold the bowl upside down without the egg whites falling out. Stir in 1½ of the yolks and mix on high speed for another 3 minutes. Set aside.

Pour flour in a shallow dish for dredging, and season with salt and pepper. Spread the flour evenly throughout the bottom of the dish.

Line a baking sheet with paper towels. Heat about 2 inches of oil in a large Dutch oven or frying pan over medium-high heat until oil reaches about 375° (check with a thermometer). Dredge a pepper lightly in flour, coating evenly, then in the beaten egg mixture. Use a spoon to help fully coat the pepper in egg batter. Holding the pepper by the stem, gently slide it in the hot oil. Fry the pepper for 1 to 2 minutes and use a long-handled spoon or ladle to spoon hot oil over the top as the pepper cooks. Flip the pepper by the stem with tongs and cook until golden brown, about 1 minute. Transfer the pepper to the paper towels and repeat with the remaining peppers. You can fry two at a time in the pan.

Use a knife to slice off the thicker, top end of each chile relleno to prevent having a lopsided burrito. Warm a tortilla on both sides until it's pliable and place it on a work surface. Spread ¼ cup refried beans on the tortilla, arrange the chile relleno in the middle, and top with ½ cup pico de gallo. Fold over the left and right sides of the tortilla and roll up the burrito. Toast the burrito evenly on all sides on a comal or griddle and wrap it in foil or butcher paper immediately—this will make it easier to eat while keeping the burrito together.

EASTSIDE PICO DE GALLO

4 roma or other tomatoes, diced (about 2 cups)
¼ cup chopped cilantro
2 jalapeños, roughly chopped
1 medium onion, chopped (about 2 cups)
¼ cup fresh lime juice
Sea salt

Combine tomatoes, cilantro, jalapeños, onion, lime juice, and salt in a container with a lid and place in the refrigerator for 30 minutes so the flavors combine. Remove the salsa from the fridge and sauté over medium heat, stirring occasionally, for about 5 minutes. Season with salt to taste and set aside at room temperature until needed.

JOHN ANTHONY

In the fall of 2012, my friend Jair Téllez, the chef behind the seminal Baja California wine-country restaurant Laja and Mexico City hotspots Merotero and Amaya, was in L.A. for an event I'd curated at the yet-to-be-opened Bestia. He was asking me about Mexican American food, so we went to East L.A. to discuss the finer points of pocho gastronomy. I took him to Lupe's No. 2 on 3rd Street for bean and cheese burritos just a little thicker than the ones he'd grown up eating in Hermosillo and, later, Tijuana. "This is great—I fucking love it," he said then. "I'd really like to bring this food to the people's attention in Mexico."

The style of burrito served at Lupe's No. 2, founded in 1972, first appeared on the eastside sometime in the 1950s and was popularized at El Tepeyac, then later delegitimized by white cookbook authors like Diana Kennedy and Rick Bayless, who were seeking to impose their own dominance over Mexican cuisine. In recent years, L.A.'s Mexican American chefs started getting invited to culinary events in Mexico, while Mexican masters headed to El Norte to cook with those same chefs, acknowledging the dishes that some had dismissed and mocked as inauthentic and Tex-Mex trash.

These burritos aren't the same bags of slop favored by mainstream America, filled with a buffet of starches, bland stews, salsas, and cream. The mere mention of putting rice in a burrito elicits a sharp side stare of displeasure not unlike the one your tio (uncle) makes when the wedding band doesn't know any oldies. East L.A. burritos are filled with simple stews, creamy refried beans, and yellow cheese in a coarse, crackly flour tortilla with a residue of noble grit from leftover flour. For old-timer Mexican bikers, OG cholos, and vintage car club members, this is real Mexican food; for John Anthony, it's a shrine to his beloved abuela, Adeline Portillo. They shared a bond that's quite common in Mexican families—the boys, especially first-borns, can do no wrong in the eyes of their grandmothers (I have some experience with that). As a kid, John helped his grandparents out, and many customers thought he was their son, but Adeline didn't want him to go into the family business. She wanted him to get an education.

"I attended college, worked at a trading company, and did some stuff with marketing, and traveled," says John. "But I always had a desire to be a part of Lupe's; it was always a passion to follow my grandmother and help the business continue to be a staple in the community." And then in 2010, Adeline went to the emergency room. She had stage-four cancer. Without hesitation, John stepped in to keep her legacy alive.

Lupe's No. 2 serves a hearty taste of nostalgia of a very personal nature, spanning generations of Mexican Americans—some of whom now return on the weekends in BMWs and Mercedes to enjoy a chile relleno burrito, pastrami fries (popular on the eastside), or taquitos covered in lime-green guacamole. Grandparents are now introducing their grandchildren to the regional flavors of East Los, recalling tales of John's charismatic and feisty grandmother, who suffered no fools when the line was long—you either knew what you wanted to order, or you might get a few choice words. Because of her spirit and her popularity with the customers, John has been careful not to upset the gods. "After she passed away," he says, "people were skeptical, wondering if I was going to change anything—but the place needed a lot of work." So he made changes little by little, adding dishes that appealed to next-gen East L.A. He also had to survive the five-year construction of the Gold Line, which drove out many businesses and forced him to reach into his own pocket to keep the place running. It's definitely a different scene than it was back in the day; in the 1970s and '80s, the area was brimming with business, and Lupe's was open until 2 a.m. Back then, 3rd Street was a main drag, but it eventually went from two lanes to just one, and now it's quieter than other nearby streets.

"Truth is," John says, "we couldn't have survived without the hard work of our employees, Gloria Parrera and Cinthia Avila, who've both been with us for around thirty years—they're a part of our family." In the last five years, things have picked up, and John has added social media and online ordering. "We've gotten some press in *LA Weekly* and other places, which has brought in a more hipster crowd, and people who've moved out of the neighborhood are starting to come back around."

"I love all of what we do here—when the lunch rush is three rows deep, as well as later in the afternoon, when there's just a handful of customers at the counter," says John. Like some of the new breed of Mexican American chefs who have stayed in the barrios, Adeline made food that was legitimately Mexican but adapted for Mexican Americans in El Norte who were disconnected from the edicts and ingredients of their hometowns. She catered to a Chicano audience whose Mexican dining habits had been altered by long hours at work and mainstream American dinner-table conventions, giving them simple, delicious food that they could call their own, with pride that's one-hundred percent East Los.

REGIONAL MEXICAN CUISINE

It's an American tradition to dismiss the contributions of minorities and immigrants and instead recognize the first efforts of Anglo imitators. Elvis Presley was crowned the king of rock 'n roll, hoisted above the African American performers he imitated. Bill "Bojangles" Robinson inspired Fred Astaire, but it was Astaire who achieved greater success and mass appeal. For Mexican American restaurateurs, the hundred-year struggle to gain mainstream acceptance was hijacked by Rick Bayless, who opened Chicago's Frontera Grill in 1987, and it's only now that the culinary reconquista happening in L.A. is returning the focus to the rightful care-takers of Mexican food in America—including all the trailblazers in this chapter. They have gifted the City of Angels with the complex, richly flavorful dishes, techniques, and ingredients of their hometowns, in many cases working hard for decades before even getting a chance to have their own places. From tacos and tortas to moles and ceviches, they have enriched Los Angeles in ways too numerous to count.

PEOPLE

Vicente, Connie &
Bianka Cossio 52
Jimmy Shaw 55
Soledad Lopez 61
Alberto Bañuelos 66
Rocio Camacho 70

Esdras Ochoa 76
Ramiro Arvizu &
Jaime Martín del Campo . . . 80
Zeferino Garcia 84
Gilberto Cetina Jr./Sr. 88
Francisco "Paco" Perez 92

Cindy, Gloria &
Adrian Estrada 97
Maria Ramos 101
Marc and Annie Burgos . . . 104
Roberto Berrelleza 108

RECIPES

Shrimp Ceviche 54
Huevos Divorciados 57
    Salsa Ranchera 59
    Salsa Verde 60
Tlayuda 63
    Refried Black Beans 65
    Soledad's Salsa 65
Tinga (Chicken Chipotle)
Burritos 68
Mole Negro Oaxaqueño 73

Carne Asada Vampiros 78
    Vampiro Sauce 79
    Salsa Tatemada 79
Chicken with Pipián Rojo . . . 82
Huevos Ahogados 86
Cochinita Pibil Tacos 90
    Recado Rojo
    (Achiote Paste) 91
    Pickled Onions 91
Lamb Barbacoa with
Consommé 94
    Salsa Borracha 96

Shrimp Tortas Ahogadas
Gemma Style 99
    Chipotle Cream 100
Enfrijoladas 103
Chicken Relleno Negro
(Chirmole) 106
Crab Huarache on
Cactus Paddle 110
    Salsa Mexicana 111
Papaya Cream Soup 111
    Sofrito 112

VICENTE, CONNIE & BIANKA COSSIO

In 1968, twenty-three-year-old Vicente "Chente" Cossio arrived in California from Acaponeta in the state of Nayarit and made his way to Manhattan Beach, a place where surfer boys and girls played in the post–Summer of Love era. The Bay 90s was a popular steakhouse in that beach-volleyball capital, serving steaks named after such ninteenth-century pugilists as John L. Sullivan and Jim Corbett, as well as the Duke (chopped sirloin and mushroom), named after John Wayne, and the Can Can (steak on a sizzling plat-ter), perhaps a nod to the boudoir painting hanging over the bar that caught generations of young Man-hattan Beach boys sneaking a peek over their creamy mashed potatoes.

Vicente started there as a bus-boy and worked just about every job including cook. With the aero-space boom in the 1980s came lots of cash and more competition, so the Bay 90s owner decided to change things up a bit. "They asked us to wear thongs and no shirts to work," says Vicente. "I mean, maybe in my twenties, but I was already in my mid-forties, and one lady who worked there had a belly hanging down to her legs—we were a mess," he says, laughing. "So I needed to find another job."

A job wasn't easy to find, how-ever, so in 1987 he started selling seafood out of his house in Lennox: ceviches, seafood cocktails, aguachiles, and other dishes from Acaponeta. "I hadn't worked in seafood restaurants back home, but I grew up eating the food and watching the cocktailers. It was food that I knew."

L.A. has a long history of unlicensed street vendors and home restaurants (Mexicans in L.A. did pop-ups long before it became a thing), and seafood from Nayarit and Sinaloa was flooding into the city. Fortunately for Chente, he didn't have to rely just on South Central's sizable *culichi* (people from Culiacan) and *nayarita* (people from Nayarit) immigrants—everyone from Mexico respects the oceanic gastronomy of these regions, and word spread quickly about Chente's flavors. Word also spread about the party atmosphere at his underground restaurant, complete with banda music, a BYOB policy, sassy girls from Sinaloa, and a Mexican narco subculture. "It was wild," he says. Among the regulars were Mexican celebrities, including traveling members of Banda Recodo, Chalino Sanchez, and local Mexican stars. The party came to an end when the health department caught up with Chente, his wife, and their kids, forcing them to close their illicit operation.

Fortunately, he had saved up enough to open a legit place in 1995: Inglewood's Mexican seafood paradise, Mariscos Chente's. It was a classic *barra fria* (cold bar) and *barra caliente* (hot bar), mixing fresh shrimp sourced from Mexico into cocktails, bright ceviches, and fiery aguachiles, and then adding classic, rich coastal stews: camarones a la diabla (spicy "devil style" shrimp), camarones al mojo de ajo (garlic butter shrimp), and camarones borrachos (drunken shrimp).

Mariscos Chente's most famous dish, pescado zarandeado, came later. Translated as "shaken fish" (it's shaken in a grill basket), pescado zarandeado is a Nayarit specialty that you can only get at the beach, traditionally cooked over manglar wood (which is now endangered). Vicente would make it for special occasions. "Whatever I put on the menu had to be like what we had in Acaponeta," he says, so to make this pre-Hispanic barbecued whole fish dish, he had to bring in róbalo (snook) from Nayarit or Sinaloa. Even though Imperial Highway isn't exactly the Riviera Nayarit, Chente led the way for L.A.'s Mexican seafood restaurants to bring the beach experience to their menus, and his success came at a time when L.A. was growing more interested in regional Mexican flavors.

The bawdy steakhouse that had wanted Chente to shake his ass for tips was now gone, the beach cities were filling up with chef-driven restaurants, and the local press began to recognize regional Mexican restaurants, bringing in new customers. Chente didn't want his most dedicated employee to strike out on her own, and he was slowing down anyway, so he decided to hand over the reins to his daughter, Connie Cossio, who'd long been his right-hand woman. She changed the name to Coni'Seafood and, with the support of her daughter, Bianka Córdova, has worked hard to preserve her father's cuisine. But Chente didn't exactly retire—he opened another Mariscos Chente's, a divey, nautical-themed joint in Lennox, where you can still get the best shrimp ceviche in L.A.

"I do everything my dad does when I make his shrimp ceviche," says Connie. "I've trained for years with him. But there's something about his touch—the flavor is just better when he makes it." But you won't catch him making pescado zarandeado anymore. "You'll have to go to Connie's for the zarandeado," he says, laughing. "I'm too old for that."

SHRIMP CEVICHE
Vicente Cossio, Mariscos Chente's

This Nayarit-style ceviche, ideally made with fresh Mexican shrimp from the Pacific, is simple but full of vibrant flavor. It's a staple in Don Chente's hometown of Acaponeta in the state of Nayarit. Nayarit is famed for its raw bars (ceviches, cocktails, snacks, and tostadas), its spicy shrimp stews, and its grilled whole fish, known as pescado zarandeado. The true measure of a master cocktailer is how he or she prepares ceviche, a simple dish that relies on striking just the right balance between quality ingredients and technique. These cocktailers are Mexico's sushi masters. In the United States, the patriarch of the Cossio family is the best ceviche maker I know.

A note about the shrimp: You're not likely to find fresh Mexican shrimp in California, so quality frozen shrimp is fine. White shrimp is preferred, because of the resulting color after the lime marinade, but if you're only buying sustainably caught seafood and can't find white shrimp, that's fine.

Serves 4

10 jalapeños, washed, dried, and stems removed
10 to 12 limes, divided, plus 4 whole limes for garnish
Sea salt to taste
2 pounds white Mexican shrimp, or other large shrimp, peeled and deveined

½ red onion, diced
2 large cucumbers, peeled and diced
3 medium tomatoes, drained, seeded, and diced
Tortilla chips, for serving

First, prepare a Nayarit-style salsa verde. Place jalapeños (remove seeds and devein if you want the salsa milder) into a blender with the juice of 5 limes, purée until blended, and add salt to taste. Set aside.

Combine shrimp, red onion, and juice of 5 to 7 limes in a nonreactive bowl and set aside to marinate for 5 minutes. Add salt to taste. Add cucumber and tomato, then stir in the salsa verde. Taste and add salt or a little more lime juice if needed. Arrange on a plate with chips and extra lime wedges and serve.

JIMMY SHAW

Growing up in Mexico means that some of your most significant social interactions involve taco stands; it's where you go after hitting the clubs, after the movies, after church, and of course, on a date. In Mexico, taco stands run the spectrum from street carts on poorly lit, post-apocalyptic streets to taquerias with valet service and uniformed staff. This was the pitch Jimmy Shaw made in 2001 to Hank Hilty of the Gilmore Company, owner of the legendary Farmers Market. For the first time, Jimmy told Hank, a couple on a date could meet at 3rd and Fairfax for tacos—at his taqueria—just like they do in Mexico City.

Jimmy doesn't fit the profile most Americans have of Mexicans, but even an hour waiting for a flight at Benito Juarez Airport will show you how multicultural the country is—Mexicans come in all colors and sizes. Tall, fair, and as Irish looking as his name suggests, Jimmy was in fact born in Mexico City and is 100-percent chilango (a person from Mexico City), from his accent to his willingness to put anything in a torta.

The kitchen was the biggest room in their house. "We had twelve burners, and something was always cooking, so there were plenty of opportunities to help—it inspired a love of good food," says Jimmy. And good food meant Oaxacan food from his grandmother, who lived with the family. The skills he picked up at home in Mexico came to good use when he went to the US to study film at UPenn, right around the time of Mexico's economic crisis, when the peso took a nosedive. "I worked in restaurants because I wanted to be able to cook for dates, but I also needed the money," he says. He put an ad out for a personal chef and was hired by husband-and-wife producers Ellen Shire and Garret Brown. Jimmy wasn't a chef, so he called his mother, who suggested some books and helped him write the menu, incorporating a few family recipes. Through Ellen and Garret he started catering film shoots, and after graduation, he found production work on commercials. In the evenings he'd cook for his friends, scrounging for Mexican ingredients. "I'd get my tortillas from an Amish guy who had them canned, but if I wanted cilantro, I'd have to drive to New York."

The friends at his dinner parties hadn't experienced real Mexican food before and urged him to open a restaurant. He only had a temporary visa, though, and jobs in film production or food were not paths to a green card. The only way to get long-term legal status was to work in a field where his bilingual skills were essential. So in 1989, Jimmy headed to Los Angeles to work for an ad agency targeting a Spanish-speaking audience. "The very first day I arrived in L.A. planted the seed for Lotería Grill," he remembers. "I was on Pico and Sawtelle where a friend had taken me for tacos, and everything about them was disappointing." As he worked in advertising and got his green card, he continued in vain to find a place to take a date for tacos. Standing next to a dirty gutter in Highland Park eating $1 tacos made from dubious ingredients wasn't how you wooed women back in Mexico's capital.

Jimmy had written up a business plan for his taqueria, and one day a friend unexpectedly introduced him to Hank Hilty as "the guy who has a great idea for a taco stand." Within three months Jimmy got a call about a space at the market, and he enlisted help from his brother, Andrew, a successful restaurateur in Mexico City, who arrived in L.A. with a stack of Mexican lotería cards. Lotería, similar to American bingo, is played with colorful cards depicting folk art pictograms and is an iconic staple in Mexican culture. Andrew thought Jimmy could do something with them.

And he did. On July 1, 2002, he opened Lotería Grill at the Farmers Market, complete with lotería cards as the décor and a menu of tacos filled with stews (L.A.'s original tacos de guisado concept), sopes, tostadas, enchiladas, and Mexican breakfasts.

Angelenos had never seen this style of taqueria, with beef tongue in salsa verde, stewed chicharrón, zucchini, corn, and tinga—a dish made of spicy meat that would become a citywide fascination by 2010 (one restaurant was even named after the dish).

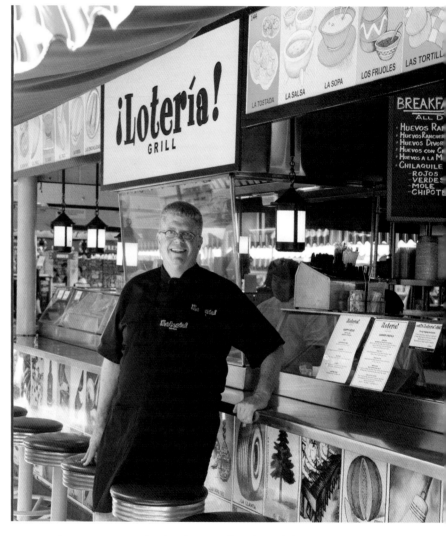

Jimmy started to do more catering, where he could serve alcohol (which isn't allowed at his Farmers Market stand), and people began to say how much more they enjoyed his food with a nice margarita or a shot of tequila. His wasn't the first Mexican restaurant to serve tacos, tequila, and mezcal, but when he opened the Hollywood Lotería Grill, complete with a full liquor license, he laid down a blueprint for others to follow. Angelenos had always been able to count on combo plates covered with orange cheese to go with a margarita made with a mix so sugary-tart you'd suffer from facial spasms all night, but traditional Mexican food and top-shelf tequila were starting to appear more. In 2008, the Lotería Grill in Hollywood ushered in a new era of taqueria, and by 2012, everybody was opening a hip taqueria stocked with mezcal and rare Mexican spirits.

Jimmy Shaw was a decade ahead of L.A.'s taco boom. And as a new generation of chef-turned-taqueros eschews the brick-and-mortar life (or prefers the street aesthetic), Lotería Grill at the Farmers Market remains a great place to take a date for tacos.

HUEVOS DIVORCIADOS

Jimmy Shaw, Lotería Grill

Jimmy Shaw's "divorced eggs" marry the salsas from two of his favorite childhood dishes in Mexico City, huevos rancheros and enchiladas verdes, so you get three recipes in one: the eggs and the two salsas. Of course, these salsas are divorced from each other on the plate, separated by beans. Use a serving plate large enough for space between the two divorced eggs.

Make the salsas in advance; the recipes make plenty to keep on standby in the fridge or freezer. You can use them later to serve with quesadillas or to make enchiladas. The huevos recipe makes a single serving, but it's easy to scale up for more people.

Serves 1

Canola or other vegetable oil, for cooking
2 corn tortillas
2 large eggs
About ½ cup Salsa Ranchera (*recipe follows*)
About ½ cup Salsa Verde (*recipe follows*)

Generous scoop refried black beans
  (*see recipe page 65*) or pinto beans
2 tablespoons crema mexicana, for garnish
Crumbled queso fresco or queso cotija, for garnish
1 teaspoon each finely chopped onion and cilantro,
  mixed together, for garnish

Preheat a medium skillet over medium heat and add enough oil to generously cover the bottom (about ⅓ cup). Once oil is hot, fry corn tortillas, one at a time, until lightly browned and they begin to crisp, 10 to 15 seconds on each side. Drain the tortillas over the skillet and transfer, with tongs, to paper towels and carefully blot on both sides (tortillas will be very hot) to remove excess oil.

To prepare the eggs, pour off most of the hot oil from skillet. Reduce heat to low (unless you prefer toasted edges on your eggs). Crack each egg separately into skillet and add salt and pepper. Cover skillet with a lid or another pan and cook eggs as preferred, checking them often. (For sunnyside-up eggs, don't flip; for over-easy, medium, or firm eggs, carefully flip after a minute or two to cook yolks as desired before flipping eggs back over.) While eggs cook, warm up both salsas and refried beans in separate small pans on the stovetop or in the microwave.

To serve, dip one of the tortillas into the Salsa Verde and the other into the Salsa Ranchera and arrange side-by-side on a large serving plate. Slide an egg on top of each tortilla. Cover one egg and tortilla with Salsa Ranchera and the other with Salsa Verde, then arrange refried black beans or pintos between the eggs, down the center of the plate. Garnish beans with crema and queso fresco, then sprinkle onion and cilantro over eggs.

SALSA RANCHERA

Salsa ranchera is a daily staple in many Mexican households, made with ripe tomatoes, onion, and serrano or jalapeño chiles (Jimmy prefers serranos). Here is his family recipe.

The fresh vegetables can be used raw, or quickly toasted on a comal or in a cast-iron skillet to help boost the flavors.

Makes about 2 quarts

4 pounds roma tomatoes, quartered
½ medium onion, quartered
5 cloves garlic
4 to 6 serrano or jalapeño chiles, stemmed

3 teaspoons kosher salt, more to taste
2 to 3 cups water
Canola or other vegetable oil, for cooking

Place tomatoes, onion, garlic, chiles and 2 cups water in a blender or food processor and blend on low for about 10 seconds and then on high for another 30 seconds to 1 minute (do this in batches if needed). Add a little more water if it seems to need it. After about 30 seconds, the salsa will be chunkier; at 1 minute, it will be smoother.

Place a large saucepan over high heat and add a little oil (about 2 tablespoons). Once oil is hot, pour in about ⅓ cup of salsa to "kiss the pan." After a minute or two, when salsa has begun to turn a deeper red, add remaining salsa to pan. Stir, bring salsa to a boil, reduce to a low simmer, and cook for 30 to 40 minutes, stirring occasionally. The tomatoes should be fully cooked and the sauce nicely thickened. Use salsa immediately, while hot, or cool and refrigerate. Keep any leftover salsa in the fridge for use through the week, or in the freezer for use in the future.

MEXICAN MOTHER SAUCES

In their many varieties, salsa ranchera and salsa verde are practically mother sauces for an infinite number of favorite platillos and antojitos in the Mexican kitchen. The recipes vary according to the cook, but all can be simply made with only a few ingredients. You can roast the ingredients or add a selection of aromatics to deepen the flavors of the salsa or whatever dish you are serving, and purée them to be chunky or as smooth as you like.

Jimmy advises making these salsas in advance to give them time to rest and build flavor—but if you don't have the time, no problem. They can both be made in less than an hour. The fresh ingredients in these recipes are readily available at most supermarkets.

SALSA VERDE

Growing up, Jimmy knew from the aroma of salsa verde that a special meal was being prepared. When his mother served enchiladas verdes, it was usually as part of a bigger family meal. When he came to the US to study and went back to Mexico on breaks, she'd serve enchiladas verdes for his first lunch at home.

You can find good tomatillos in many grocery stores in the US, but sometimes they seem over-fed, too large, causing them to have little flavor. For this reason, I prefer the smaller "criollo" strain, so look for those.

Making this salsa is similar to the Salsa Ranchera with one main difference: you simmer the vegetables before blending.

Makes about 2 quarts

3 pounds fresh tomatillos

3 to 4 jalapeño chiles, stemmed, seeded, and
   roughly chopped

4 cloves garlic

1 medium onion, quartered

1 bay leaf

1 quart water

½ teaspoon dried oregano

½ teaspoon dried thyme

½ teaspoon ground white pepper

3 teaspoons kosher salt, more to taste

Canola or other cooking oil

In a large bowl, clean and shell the tomatillos in plenty of water. Place tomatillos, jalapeños, garlic, onion, and bay leaf in a heavy stockpot and cover with the water (it should fully cover vegetables; if not, add a little more water). Bring water to a boil and simmer for about 15 minutes. Discard bay leaf and transfer vegetables with a slotted spoon to a bowl or pan to cool for about 30 minutes, reserving the cooking liquid. When vegetables have cooled, purée in a blender or food processor with some of the cooking water, the oregano, thyme, white pepper, and salt (do this in batches if needed). Blend on low for about 10 seconds and then on high until smooth, about another minute. Season with additional salt to taste.

Place a large saucepan over high heat and add a little oil (about 2 tablespoons). Once oil is hot, pour about ⅓ cup of salsa into the pan to "kiss the pan." After a minute or two, when it has begun to turn a deeper green, add remaining salsa to the pan. Bring to a boil for a minute or two, reduce to a low simmer, and cook for 10 to 15 minutes, stirring occasionally. Taste and add salt if needed. Use salsa immediately, while hot, or cool and refrigerate for up to 1 week. This salsa stores well in the freezer.

SOLEDAD LOPEZ

Sin Maiz, No Hay País—"Without Corn, There Is No Country"—is part of a campaign in Mexico against transgenic corn in favor of the country's native breeds, because corn and the tortillas made from corn are fundamental to Mexican culture. But Oaxacans cannot flourish on corn alone—without mole, Oaxacan cheese, mezcal, tlayudas, and chapulines there is no Oaxacan cuisine. That was the reality in 1982 in Los Angeles when Soledad arrived—Oaxacan food was a hallucination that tormented the souls and bellies of Oaxacan immigrants.

Soledad's parents had both died by the time she was thirteen, and after seven years of taking care of her brothers and feeling like there was nothing left for her in her hometown of Santiago, Matatlán, she headed north. At the time, only Oaxacan men and their wives made the journey to the US. Soledad was the first woman to leave her town all alone.

She soon found domestic work in L.A. and also labored in a factory and a laundry room. Most importantly, she felt at home. Many Oaxacans lived in L.A. in the early '80s, and when they gathered, a constant theme was how much they missed their food. In Oaxaca, food and mezcal are not just sustenance, they are the spirit of a land and a people—a people who consider themselves first Oaxacan and then Mexican. Because they had one of the most difficult Mexican culinary traditions to replicate away from home, they began to test the vigilance of LAX customs, one tlayuda at a time. When the ingredients made it past customs to the homes of wistful Oaxaqueños, every taste of mole made time stop and each sip of mezcal burned with memories of the Guelaguetza, the indigenous cultural festival held in July in Oaxaca.

Soledad didn't know it at the time, but she was about to change the history and course of Mexican cuisine in Los Angeles. In the late 1980s, she decided to visit Oaxaca and bring back foodstuffs to sell. Her house had already become an underground restaurant serving dishes from what few ingredients she could find around L.A. At that time, Oaxacans were selling tamales and atole out of their homes and on the streets, but many of her friends had been without tlayudas, Oaxacan cheese, and mole paste for many hopeless years. She returned from her trip with 200 tlayudas, five kilos of mole, and ten large balls of cheese. Waiting for her was a line of twenty women ready to buy anything and everything she had.

With just a small piece of Oaxaca, an industry was born. "I had no idea what to charge, and I couldn't fly back to Oaxaca every week," says Soledad. "So I called my sister Teresa, who was living in Chiapas, to help me figure out a way to get the products to Los Angeles." Tijuana—always at the ready to satisfy L.A.'s every whim, whether keeping us wet during Prohibition or dazzling us with cheap trinkets—would now fuel the emerging Oaxacan food frenzy in Oaxacalifornia (the Oaxacan nickname for L.A.).

With her supply chain in place, Soledad, who came to L.A. to leave Oaxaca behind, found herself moving a couple of tons of Oaxacan foodstuffs, even making house calls in the white van she'd purchased—like an Avon lady selling crickets and fragrant chiles de agua. Now a businesswoman, she was free of the constraints she had in Oaxaca—Oaxaca now bent to her will, and an entire restaurant industry was soon to follow.

"I was always analyzing the market based on what people asked for, and I paid attention to the seasons," she says. "For Dia de los Muertos it was chocolate; during Lent, mullet and dried shrimp. And I looked for quality brands that others couldn't get." With these pre-Hispanic goods and the sizable Oaxacan community, the table was set for a feast of mythical dishes: mole, tlayudas, barbacoa enchilada, atoles, tejate, and memelas.

The next logical step for Soledad was to open a restaurant, a place where Oaxaqueños could come to remember the flavors of mercados, celebrations, and their moms' kitchens. Tlapazola Grill, opened in 1992 by four brothers from San Marcos Tlapazola, Oaxaca, served Cal-Mex moles. El Texate opened in 1994, but it was more of a place for multi-colored chips and margaritas. That same year, Soledad took $2,000 she had saved up and opened L.A.'s first truly authentic Oaxacan restaurant, the original Guelaguetza on 8th Street.

"On the first day I wasn't sure what to cook, so I made a cazuela de arroz, and of course I had mole negro oaxaqueño, tamales with mole, and tlayudas," she says. She was thrilled to make $400 dollars that first day, and in a short time the Oaxacan customers were joined by non-Latinos from the emerging foodie scene, as the mainstream media took notice—ironically, more than a decade before the Spanish-language press showed up.

Soledad's brother Fernando, who had arrived in 1993, had come on board to help, gradually taking a larger interest in the business, and together they opened a second Guelaguetza in Palms before a rift developed, ending their business relationship. Soledad took the Palms location, and Fernando took 8th Street. The ambitious older brother expanded his Guelaguetza brand, first to Olympic Boulevard and then to multiple branches, before having to close all except the larger, very profitable Olympic location in the heart of Koreatown. Today, the iconic L.A. restaurant has rebounded, earning a James Beard Classic award in 2015 and adding a hip mezcal bar and a line of Oaxacan products, including mole paste and a michelada mix that's served from a customized VW bus outfitted with beer taps and a DJ booth.

Soledad's Guelaguetza Palms location was a hit, earning praise from Ruth Reichl and a TV spot with Martha Stewart, but she ran into some bad luck, or rather, it ran into her. A woman who was learning to drive in the parking lot plowed right into the kitchen, literally driving her out of business. Without skipping a beat, however, she returned to the hustle she'd pioneered, selling Oaxacan products to more than forty restaurants and markets around the greater L.A. area. She remains in high demand on the Oaxacan festival circuit, where she sells exceptional tamales with mole negro, tlayudas, and more, and where she's affectionately addressed by her followers as La de la Guelaguetza: the woman from Guelaguetza.

TLAYUDA
Soledad Lopez

Sometimes called a Mexican pizza or Mexican flatbread, this is one of the most important Oaxacan dishes served at markets and over barbecue grills in the evenings. It features the Oaxacan trinity of meats: cecina (salted, dried pork), tasajo (a soft beef jerky), and chorizo. This was a favorite of Soledad's customers at Guelaguetza, because only someone who has mastered the grill can get this dish right. (In Oaxaca, tlayudas are cooked over mesquite, but in L.A., Oaxacan restaurateurs prepare this on a griddle.) Be careful not to overcook the meats, and enjoy shopping at one of L.A.'s many Oaxacan markets to gather your ingredients (including the very large tlayuda tortilla) for the dish that founded Oaxacalifornian cuisine. Note that sometimes you'll see tlayuda spelled clayuda.

TLAYUDA

Makes 2 tlayudas

½ pound cecina enchilada
  (cured pork cutlets in adobo)
½ pound tasajo (soft jerky)
½ pound Oaxacan chorizo
2 tlayuda tortillas
2 cups refried black beans (*recipe follows*)
⅓ pound asiento (unrefined pork lard)

2 cups quesillo (queso Oaxaca),
  torn into thin strips
¼ head green cabbage, shredded
½ large onion, thinly sliced
2 roma tomatoes, cut into medium slices
1 large avocado, thinly sliced
Soledad's Salsa to taste, optional (*recipe follows*)

Remove cecina, tasajo, and chorizo from the refrigerator 30 minutes prior to cooking or until they are at room temperature.

If your range doesn't have a griddle, use a flattop attachment or a large electric skillet on low heat to warm your tlayuda tortillas. Meanwhile, warm the beans in a saucepan over low heat. Using a spatula, apply a thin layer of asiento to cover each tlayuda. Add a layer of refried beans, leaving a thin strip of the tortilla's circumference exposed. Add a layer of quesillo strips and set the tlayudas aside.

Place a medium skillet over medium-high heat and cook the tasajo, turning once to brown both sides. Remove and cook cecina until cooked to medium, 1 to 2 minutes per side. The goal is to brown the cutlets and just cook them through while being careful not to overcook; these thin-sliced cured meats cook up quickly. Remove skillet from heat and cover to maintain the meat's temperature. Cook the chorizo in another skillet over medium-high heat until it is cooked through, 4 to 5 minutes.

Return the tlayudas to the griddle or flattop with heat at the lowest setting. Add a patchy layer of cabbage on each, then onion, then tomato slices on top, and, finally, avocado slices. Drizzle with salsa if you want a little more heat.

Arrange each cut of meat on one-third of each tlayuda, so it has its own territory. Remove from the griddle and place them on platters for sharing with family and friends. In Oaxaca, the tortillas are fresher, so they fold over tlayudas (like a calzone), making them easier to eat, but you're better off keeping them open-faced, letting guests tear off pieces. Hopefully, someone will have remembered to bring the mezcal!

REFRIED BLACK BEANS

It's best to prepare these the day before you need them. This recipe makes a lot, so refrigerate or freeze the leftovers and you'll be ready to use them in more dishes, like Huevos Divorciados (page 57).

Makes about 12 cups

2 pounds (about 4 cups) dried black beans
1 medium onion, quartered

6 cloves garlic
Sea salt to taste

Sort and rinse beans to remove all impurities and broken or brittle beans. Place beans, onion, and garlic in a large pot, add water to cover with about 2 inches above the beans, cover, and cook over medium heat until soft, about 1½ hours. To test, remove one bean and press it with the back of a spoon. If it presses into a smooth paste, the beans are done. During the cooking process, add water if needed to keep beans from drying out. Salt beans to taste (taste the bean broth, not just the beans).

Discard the onion and garlic and drain beans, reserving the cooking water. Purée beans in batches in a food processor or blender with a few tablespoons of reserved cooking water until smooth enough to spread. If beans seems too thick to spread easily, add a little more cooking water. Cool, cover, and refrigerate until needed.

When it's time to make the tlayuda, warm beans over low heat and adjust the consistency by either adding water if too thick or cooking it down if too thin. The bean purée should be smooth so it spreads easily but doesn't run off the tortilla.

SOLEDAD'S SALSA

If you want less heat, remove the seeds and membranes from the chiles before toasting.

Makes about 1 cup

10 dried chiles de árbol, stems removed
3 cloves garlic
¼ medium onion

¼ cup water
Sea salt to taste

Toast chiles in a dry, preheated cast-iron skillet over high heat until beginning to color, about 1 minute, stirring constantly with a wooden spoon. Be careful not to burn the chiles. Place toasted chiles in a blender with garlic, onion, and water and purée to the consistency you prefer. Season with salt to taste.

ALBERTO BAÑUELOS

In many parts of the United States, supportive enclaves provide immigrants with a safe landing: Filipinos populate the "Pinoy capital" in Daly City, California, for instance, and the Lebanese community is strong in Dearborn, Michigan. For the many Mexican immigrant communities in L.A., it's not a question of country but of state. For Alberto Bañuelos, the state is Zacatecas, so when he was opening the first US branch of his family's Mexico-based burrito chain, Burritos La Palma, he chose the town of El Monte, strategically equidistant from Zacatecan communities in the San Fernando Valley, the Inland Empire, Orange County, and Los Angeles. He knew his first and primary customers would be Zacatecans from Jerez, and he imagined that his food wouldn't find acceptance from a mainstream audience—at least not right away.

Alberto was born in Baldwin Park, where his father, Jose, worked as a cook at a steakhouse. When he was thirteen, the family moved back to their ranch in Tepetongo, about thirty kilometers southwest of Jerez de García Salinas, Zacatecas. "It was tough going from being a teenager in the US to living on a ranch with no running water, and where you had to go to shit in a corral," says Alberto with a laugh.

The food, of course, was different. "Flour tortillas were not a thing in Jerez—it's a corn tortilla town," he says. "But in some towns and other states nearby, they were creeping in." His father had loved the flour tortillas in the States, so in 1980 he opened a tortilleria, the first of its kind in Jerez. "For lunch, we'd eat burritos while sitting on flour sacks in the shop," he remembers, and those burritos would elicit hungry stares from patrons. Their northern Mexican–style burritos were filled with Zacatecan guisados, or stews, though the bean and cheese burritos were inspired by the kind Alberto's father, Jose, had enjoyed during his time in Los Angeles, bringing a bit of pocho cookery to small-town Zacatecas. Before that, flour tortillas had only been used in the area for flautas. Burritos La Palma changed that, becoming part of the region's gastronomy. The business grew, eventually totaling nine branches in Mexico. Then, in 1986, Reagan's amnesty program lured Alberto back to the US, where he found work as a truck driver before being recruited into the hospitality industry, which he'd studied in school back in Zacatecas.

Alberto became part of the opening front-of-house team for all of the new Wolfgang Puck Cafés, working alongside Wolfgang himself, from whom he learned a lot about excellence. He also worked as a manager for other regional chains, but he kept dreaming of opening a Burritos La Palma in L.A.—he just wasn't sure how it would play there. Then, while working at Pei Wei in 2010, he started noticing the "handcrafted this, handcrafted that" movement around the country. "This is what we do, so I asked for my father's blessing, and he loved the idea."

El Monte might as well be another planet to most Angelenos, especially the craft-hungry hipsters who'd inspired Alberto, but that didn't matter, because he knew that the generations of Jerezanos (people from Jerez) who'd grown up eating their burritos would sustain the business when he opened its doors in 2012. L.A. was already crazy for burritos, but the ideal was a starch bomb the size of an airline pillow, or breakfast burritos stuffed with a greasy spoon's slop bucket. The city had yet to experience the smaller, skinny ones brimming with flavorful northern stews of slow-cooked meats and hearty vegetables wrapped in delicious, springy flour tortillas. (Burritos like this are a regional style of taco popular in Sonora, Chihuahua, and Nuevo León.) At last, however, L.A. hipsters have caught up—Alberto has gotten good press, has opened a food truck, and has even won the Vendy Cup. Most recently, he's begun participating in food events.

Here in the City of Angels, you may be able to get kombucha, green juice, and fancy doughnuts in just about every neighborhood, but it's really all about the Mexican food—and the burritos at Burritos La Palma might be the greatest single expression of that. They're simply unforgettable. And now they're an institution back in Zacatecas, something Alberto's family has a special way of reminding him. "To this day, when I go home," he says, "even though I have my own branch of my family's business, my mom still brings me our burritos when she greets me at the airport."

TINGA (CHICKEN CHIPOTLE) BURRITOS

Alberto Bañuelos, Burritos La Palma

This recipe is truly an L.A. Mexicano dish: small and simple burritos de guisado, flour tortillas filled with fla-vorful stews and rolled up snugly. When this offshoot of a famous chain in Zacatecas opened in El Monte, it featured its well-known pork and beef burritos, most notably the signature birria de res, a slow-cooked, spiced, shredded beef stew. But their Angeleno customers kept asking for chicken, so Alberto and team cre-ated the tinga (chipotle chicken) burrito. Popular in many parts of Mexico, tinga has now become one of the most essential burritos at this most essential of burrito joints. The best way to enjoy this tinga is wrapped in one of Burritos La Palma's handmade flour tortillas, available for purchase at their restaurant, but any quality, smaller flour tortilla will work fine.

Makes 12 small burritos

2½ pounds boneless, skinless chicken breasts
2 bay leaves
4 cloves garlic
3 medium chipotle chiles in adobo
  (roughly 3 tablespoons)
Extra-virgin olive oil, for cooking

1 medium onion, sliced into matchsticks
1½ pounds russet potatoes, peeled and
  diced into ½-inch cubes
1 to 2 cups chicken stock
2 to 3 teaspoons sea salt, to taste
12 medium flour tortillas

Place chicken and bay leaves in a medium Dutch oven or pot. Add water to cover. Bring to a boil over medium-high heat, reduce heat to simmer, and cook until chicken is cooked through and tender, about 20 minutes. Transfer to a bowl to cool. Discard bay leaves and set aside the chicken stock to use later in the cooking process.

While chicken is cooking, place garlic cloves and chipotle chiles in adobo sauce in a food processor or blender, cover, and pulse until a thick paste forms, adding chicken stock a few tablespoons at a time, up to ½ cup. Set aside.

When chicken is cool enough to handle, finely shred by hand or with two serving forks to pull apart the meat.

In a medium saucepan, heat 1 tablespoon olive oil over medium heat and sauté onions, stirring occasion-ally, until golden brown, about 10 minutes. Add enough reserved chicken stock to cover onions and bring to a boil. Stir in garlic-chipotle paste. Reduce heat and continue to cook over medium to low heat, stirring occasionally, about 15 minutes.

Meanwhile, in the pot or Dutch oven you used to cook the chicken, add 2 to 3 tablespoons olive oil and sauté diced potatoes over medium-high heat until they begin to brown, about 10 minutes. Add enough

Birria de res burrito at Burritos La Palma, a close cousin to the tinga burritos

reserved chicken stock to cover the potatoes; you might have to augment it with a cup or so of additional stock. Bring potatoes to a boil, reduce heat to low, cover, and simmer until tender, 15 to 20 minutes. Add shredded chicken, salt, and onion mixture to the potatoes. Stir well. Cover and cook over medium heat until guisado thickens, 10 to 15 minutes.

To make the burritos, place a fresh flour tortilla onto a preheated griddle or comal, watch for it to begin to puff up, flip, and cook a few more seconds until warm. Place tortilla on work surface and spoon 3 to 4 tablespoons of the chicken mixture into center. Fold about 1 inch of the left and right edges of the tortilla over the chicken, then roll up the little burrito. Place the whole burrito, seam side down, on the comal and lightly toast it, then flip it over and toast the other side. Serve immediately. At Burritos La Palma, two to three of these small burritos typically serve one person.

ROCIO CAMACHO

In the town of Huahuapan de Léon, Mixteca, one of Oaxaca's eight regions, Rocio Camacho, owner of Rocio's Mexican Kitchen in Bell Gardens, grew up with the scent of toasting chiles, handmade tortillas, and guisados like chileajo, a reddish-brown stew of pork spine, chiles, spices, and roasted garlic. By the time she was nine years old, she was cleaning chiles, creating cazuelas of colorful stews, and making tortillas for her mom, who catered large events, serving such local gems as mole dulce, a mole with pork sweetened by raisins and cacao.

Her prep kitchen had neither gas nor electricity, "We'd make mole, rice, beans, and tortillas only using a metate [a mealing stone] and mano [a stone tool], a clay comal over an open fire, and molcajetes—and a lot of smoke," says Rocio, whose voice is always on the verge of laughter. If happiness can be attained through cooking, she has achieved a state of nirvana.

By the age of twelve, Rocio was already a culinary professional in one of Mexico's most exalted traditional kitchens, working for Silvina Cruz at 3 Flores, helping her make atole, white pozole dressed in a red salsa, and plates employing the aromatic hierba santa (sacred leaf). She took culinary classes from the age of thirteen through sixteen, learning knife skills and the exhausting list of Oaxacan ingredients. A few years later, she married a teacher who shared her dream of getting out of their small town and seeking more opportunities. And so in 1986, a nineteen-year-old Rocio and her husband, Javier, arrived in Bell Gardens, a city destined to be a nerve center of excellent Mexican food. Rocio would have stunned L.A. with her cooking in '86, but family came first, so she transitioned from chef to stay-at-home mom while Javier worked in construction. A few years later, one of Javier's jobs was at a new restaurant in Bell being built for Jaime Martín del Campo and Ramiro Arvizu. "That's how I first heard about them; I brought food to the job site for my husband and brother, so the chefs tried my food, too," says Rocio. For the next five years, she was the "right hand" for the chefs at La Casita Mexicana.

Rocio returned to her domestic responsibilities in 1995 after her tenure at La Casita, once again leaving L.A. without one of its most promising Mexican chefs. By now, Babita, La Casita Mexicana, Chichén Itzá, and Lotería Grill, along with some prominent Oaxacan places, were raising the bar for Mexican food in L.A. Still, when she returned to cooking, too many restaurants were still serving a questionable cuisine rooted in outright disdain for Mexican American customers unversed in their own regional foods. At Premier, the Mexican seafood place where she worked after La Casita, "I was asked to clean shrimp, and after a month they put me in charge of the kitchen," she remembers. "They were using a big can of dried chiles and adding water and flour to make enchilada sauce." Not afraid to speak her mind, Rocio told them it wasn't any good. Little by little, they let her change the menu and improve the ingredients.

Next up was a job as chef de cuisine at La Huasteca in Lynwood's Plaza Mexico, one of L.A.'s most respected Mexican fine-dining restaurants, known at the time for its haute cuisine classics and its inspiration from Mexico's Huastec region. Under her direction, the kitchen expanded its regional offerings. To her credit, the petite Oaxacan chef ventured beyond her roots. "I was reading books from Patricia Quintana, Martha Chapa, and anyone else who was exploring the cuisine," she says. "I got into the Purépecha [the Purépecha native Americans]. I just love all the names of the dishes in their language."

Rocio still flew somewhat under the radar until she was pegged to be chef de cuisine at Moles La Tia in East L.A., where she quickly gained a reputation for creating moles with rose petal, pistachio, tequila, lime, and coffee. It was the golden age of the blogger, and the self-appointed culinary kings and queens organized mole tastings with Rocio, who also earned the title for Best Mole Negro in L.A. at the 2009 L.A. Taste of the Nation event, over tough competitors Guelaguetza and Tlapazola Grill. Despite the accolades, Rocio was destined to be her own boss and left Moles La Tia, which still serves the menu she created back in 2009.

After a brief return to La Huasteca, she opened Mole de los Dioses in Sun Valley in 2012, but sadly, it was destroyed in an arson fire in 2015. After all her experiences, and the lasting impact she'd had on many restaurant menus, L.A. still hadn't seen the full brilliance of her cooking. But the fire that ended her role as chef ignited a fire that now burned in her soul: to finally own her own place.

"It was always my dream to have my own place. I was taking care of my children and working to take care of my parents," she says, beaming from the small, Oaxacan-themed dining room at Rocio's Mexican Kitchen. Handmade tortillas come with snips of chaya leaf in the masa, tacos are made with Oaxacan stews, and the rest of the tight menu showcases traditional moles, classic chiles rellenos with tomato sauce and chileajo, and a rapturous chile-based pork stew reminiscent of the ones served at the central market in Huahuapan de León. And all it takes is a trip to Bell Gardens—the city where Rocio's journey in the US began, where she could finally cook with passion. It's a homecoming banquet of moles, guisados, and salsas to celebrate the liberation of a great culinary mind. "I feel free here," she says. "This is where I live."

MOLE NEGRO OAXAQUEÑO

Rocio Camacho, Rocio's Mexican Kitchen

No two moles are alike, and Oaxaca's most famous dish, mole negro oaxaqueño, has survived for generations of weddings, quinceñeras, and birthdays as Oaxaca's favorite party dish. When the time comes for such an occasion, a brigade of women from each pueblo show up to share the intense work of putting together a mole, a dish that's often misunderstood in the United States. Patricia Quintana once said, "We shouldn't call mole a sauce—mole is mole." It's the dish, and it's what you're eating.

Rocio Camacho is the L.A. goddess of moles, and while mole's reputation is that it's difficult to make, once you've learned the routine, it's not all that hard. Just don't assume it will be perfect the first time out, and have a friend (or two) on hand so you can take turns with the constant stirring required. Note that you can make the chicken stock, chile paste, and nut-seed paste a day in advance, and the hours of continuous stirring (necessary so the mole doesn't burn) is a lot easier if you have friends to help.

Serves 12

MOLE

10 chilhuacle negro chiles (may substitute mulatos)

12 mulato chiles

8 pasilla chiles

6 guajillo chiles

3 dried chipotle chiles

3 cups lard or vegetable oil

2 plantains, peeled and cut on the diagonal into ½-inch slices

¼ cup almonds

¼ cup peanuts

¼ cup walnuts

¼ cup pumpkin seeds

¼ cup sesame seeds

½ medium onion, quartered

1 head garlic, peeled

4 whole cloves

1½ teaspoons chopped fresh oregano

1½ teaspoons chopped fresh thyme

3 sticks cinnamon

3 dozen corn tortillas

1 tablet Mexican chocolate (like Ibarra), broken into pieces

3 tablespoons sugar

1 tablespoon sea salt

2 avocado leaves

5 quarts chicken stock, with chicken (recipe follows)

12 cups cooked white rice, for serving

Rinse all the chiles under cold water, removing veins, stems, and seeds. Pat dry and lightly toast chiles in a heavy skillet or comal (no oil needed) over medium heat until they are browned but not blackened. Place the browned chiles in a plastic container, cover them in lukewarm water, cover container, and set aside to steep for 2 hours.

Heat a thin layer of lard or vegetable oil in a skillet over high heat and fry plantain slices until just cooked through, flipping once to brown both sides. Set aside.

Now it's time to toast many of the ingredients. The goal here is to add complexity to the mole—under-toasted ingredients will not shine through, and burnt ingredients will add bitter flavors that will overwhelm your mole. The key is to practice and make adjustments as you learn; watch the pan closely and turn whatever you're toasting with a pair of tongs to keep it from burning and to toast evenly. In a dry skillet or comal over medium heat, toast the almonds, peanuts, and walnuts until lightly browned and aromatic. Set aside in a bowl. Next, toast, the pumpkin and sesame seeds and add to the bowl with the nuts. Next, sauté the onion and garlic in a little dab of oil until lightly blackened, and add to the nuts and seeds. Next, toast cloves, oregano, and thyme and add them to the nut mixture. Finally, toast the cinnamon sticks, grind them in a coffee grinder or spice mill, and set the ground cinnamon aside separately.

Burn two tortillas over a direct flame until they are firm like a tostada and just blackened. Place in a food processor and add the reserved nut-spice mixture and plantains. Blend until combined into a paste and set aside. Save the remaining tortillas for serving.

Drain chiles and save the chile water. Place chiles and cinnamon into a food processor or blender and blend, adding a little chile water if necessary to make a paste. Coat a large Dutch oven with lard or vegetable oil and place the chile paste in the pot. Cook over medium heat, stirring, to blend the flavors, about 10 minutes. Add chocolate, stir, and cook over low heat until the mixture darkens to almost black, about 40 minutes, stirring frequently. Add sugar and salt and stir to combine.

In small batches, slowly incorporate reserved nut-seed mixture into the chile paste, stirring constantly and cooking for 15 more minutes. Add 2 quarts chicken stock and whole avocado leaves, increase heat to medium, and continue to cook, stirring constantly with a wooden spoon, for 4 hours. Add more chicken stock (preferably hot) and lard or oil as the mole thickens, until the 5 quarts stock and remaining lard are used. The resulting mole should have the consistency of heavy cream.

Warm tortillas on a griddle or comal and wrap them in a towel to keep them warm and pliable.

To serve, place 1 cup warm white rice and a chicken leg or thigh on a plate and cover the chicken and rest of the plate with mole. Remember, mole is the star—the chicken and rice are supporting actors. Tear off small pieces of tortilla to scoop up the mole.

CHICKEN STOCK

6 bone-in chicken leg/thighs
1 onion
5 cloves garlic, peeled

3 bay leaves
1 tablespoon sea salt

Place 10 quarts water in a large stockpot and add chicken, onion, garlic, bay leaves, and salt. Bring to a boil, reduce heat to medium, and cook, uncovered, for 30 minutes. Remove chicken pieces, separate legs and thighs (carefully cut through the joint to keep each whole), and save to serve with the mole. Strain stock and set aside until needed.

Next page: Mole Negro Oaxaqueño

ESDRAS OCHOA

In L.A., dull flour tortillas have mostly served as edible casings for burritos crammed with under-seasoned ballast. Those of us who had experienced the pleasures of carne asada in artisanal tortillas and other northern Mexican "burritos" (the regional name for tacos) could only grumble about every insult hurled at the flour tortilla, or get on a plane and devour them at the source. All that changed in the spring of 2009, when an amateur taquero and aspiring fashion designer named Esdras Ochoa set up a stand at 1st and Beaudry in downtown L.A. His goal was simple—to share the Mexicali-style tacos he'd grown up eating with Angelenos. He ended up ushering in a northern-Mexican revolution that has spread as fast as chisme (gossip) at your cousin's wedding.

As with most Mexicans, life had always revolved around the kitchen table for Esdras. "My mom was always making dishes like entomatadas, enfrijoladas, and mole verde for dinner," he says proudly. His family was from Mexico City, where he was born into the business of tacos, as his

grandfather and uncle sold carnitas in the state of Mexico before heading north, where they enjoyed a cross-border life between Mexicali on the Baja side and Calexico on the California side. In Mexicali, Esdras lived and breathed carne asada tacos in the carne asada capital of the Baja peninsula.

After finishing school, Esdras, a Mormon, went on his mission to Cle Elum in Washington, a town with fewer than two thousand people, ninety-five percent of whom are white. "It was hell for me at first to make the adjustment, but people sort of took a liking to me—I was exotic," he says with a grin. Of course, his new friends wanted to take the Mexican to the town's best Mexican restaurant, which was one tableside guaca-mole short of an El Torito. He just couldn't hide his sentiments, which baffled his hosts—wasn't Mexican food just chips, salsa, nachos, and spicy buffalo wings? They might have left a little disappointed, but the good-natured Esdras saw an opportunity. "I kind of shattered their image of what Mexican food was when I offered to cook carne asada for them," he says, and that turned into a regular thing, so much so that it was starting to interfere with his missionary work. "But that's when I got the idea that I could cook for non-Mexicans." After completing his mission, he returned to L.A. to study fashion design and merchandizing at the Art Institutes, but something had clicked back in Cle Elum, and he became increasingly dissatisfied with L.A.'s taco scene, a leitmotif that has driven so many Mexican émigrés in L.A.

Thankfully for us, Esdras was unable to find work in the fashion industry, other than at a Victoria's Secret, and as the dream of headlining Paris Fashion Week withered, he saw a local fashion trend blossoming—in America's largest Mexican city, tacos were becoming haute couture. So he took a road trip to Mexicali, traded in his Honda Civic to get startup money, and bought all his taco-making supplies there. His parents thought he was crazy, and on that first night of doing business in downtown L.A., he served only eight people. Mexicali Taco Co. continued on like that for a while. "The only thing that kept me going," he says, "was that the people who came said they were the best tacos they'd ever had."

Finally, after about a year, bloggers had helped spread the word about Mexicali's carne asada and grilled chicken served in flour tortillas that Esdras brought in each week from Mexicali, and business was booming. He made up names for his tacos, like cachetadas (little slaps), the Zuperman (a giant meat-filled quesadilla), and vampiros (flour tortillas filled with meat, melted cheese, and a very garlicky aioli). It turned out that his merchandizing education came in handy after all. With their sharp black uniforms and hip tacos, Mexicali was the height of street-food chic that year, but alas, after two years of success, the health department shut him down, a common fate for so many of L.A.'s talented vendors. Luckily, one of his fans stepped in, becoming an investor in a brick-and-mortar place in Chinatown. Here, Esdras cemented his status as a restaurateur and landed front and center in the Los Angeles food world. By the spring of 2016, he was ready to open Salazar.

Esdras had gone from being an inexperienced taquero to opening one of L.A.'s hottest new restaurants of 2016: Salazar, a Sonora-inspired steakhouse with fine cuts of meat cooked on a Santa Maria grill, beautiful salads, complex bean dishes, and flour tortillas machine-made on site. He's not just one of the new flour-tortilla players changing L.A.'s culinary landscape—he started the trend, all from a humble sidewalk cart illu-minated by campfire lamps set in the pitch black of a downtown L.A. night.

CARNE ASADA VAMPIROS

Esdras Ochoa, Mexicali Taco, Salazar

Esdras Ochoa's vampiros aren't what people call vampiros in Mexico—they're actually quesatacos or quesadillas. But it's one of the many reasons we love his Mexicali Taco in downtown L.A. He tops his northern-style carne asada "taco" with a spoonful of humor: a garlic aioli to ward off the vampires at the taco stand.

So many cookbooks offer taco recipes that you'd never actually find at a taqueria, or failed attempts to reconstruct the secrets of a cagy taquero, but this is the real deal, from one of L.A.'s greatest taquerias. Make these for your next Taco Tuesday party and be a rock star.

Makes 4 quesadilla-style vampiros

1 pound skirt steak
Sea salt and freshly ground black pepper to taste
Canola or vegetable oil for cooking
4 8-inch flour tortillas

2 cups shredded Monterey jack cheese
½ cup Vampiro Sauce (*recipe follows*)
Salsa Tatemada (*recipe follows*), sliced red onions, and/or guacamole, for garnish

Salt and pepper the skirt steak on both sides and heat a cast-iron skillet over high heat. Once the pan is hot, pour in a little oil and cook the steak until medium rare, about 2 minutes per side. Let the meat rest for at least 5 minutes on a cutting board, then cut into ¼-inch cubes and set aside.

To assemble each quesadilla, pour a bit of cooking oil into a large skillet set over medium heat. Place a flour tortilla in the pan and top with ½ cup shredded cheese and 2 tablespoons Vampiro Sauce. Add one-fourth of the reserved steak and fold over the quesadilla without closing it up tight. Cook until the cheese is melted and the tortilla is slightly crisp and golden brown on both sides. Repeat for the other 3 quesadillas. Garnish with Salsa Tatemada, red onion, and/or guacamole.

VAMPIRO SAUCE

This is Esdras's version of a garlic aioli, a great staple to have on hand.

2 medium potatoes, peeled and quartered
¼ cup chopped fresh garlic (about 12 cloves)
Juice of 1 lemon

2 cups mayonnaise
Sea salt to taste

Place the potatoes in a pot and add water to cover and a pinch of salt. Bring to a boil, reduce heat to medium, and cook at a gentle boil until soft, about 20 minutes. Remove from the water and set aside to cool. When cool enough to handle, place them in a food processor or blender and add garlic, lemon juice, mayonnaise, and salt. Process or blend until smooth. Use immediately or store, covered, in the refrigerator for up to a week.

SALSA TATEMADA

4 tomatillos
4 roma tomatoes
¼ onion
4 cloves garlic

5 dried chiles de árbol (up to 15 if you like it
   really hot)
Sea salt to taste

Remove and discard tomatillo husks. Rinse tomatillos and pat dry with a towel. Place tomatillos and tomatoes in a hot, dry pan and toast them, turning with a wooden spoon, until they get a nice, even char. Place tomatoes and tomatillos in a bowl and then toast the onion and garlic, taking care not to burn the garlic (some char on the onion, however, is nice). Add those to the bowl. Toast the chiles for just about a minute. Remove stems and add chiles to the bowl.

Transfer onion, garlic, tomatillos, tomatoes, and chiles to a food processor or blender. Pulse for a chunkier texture or blend on a high setting if you prefer a smoother salsa. You can make this just before cooking or a few days in advance; it will keep, covered, in the refrigerator for a week or two.

RAMIRO ARVIZU & JAIME MARTÍN DEL CAMPO

It's been a challenge for Southern California's Mexican chefs to capture the attention of national media. Fortunately, the local press is on top of it, frequently acknowledging Mexican chefs and chronicling Mexican cui-

sine as one of the city's brightest stars since El Pueblo de Nuestra Señora la Reina de los Ángeles del Río de Porciúncula was founded in 1781.

For many Americans who'd never been to Mexico (or had just been sequestered in luxury resorts), the first knowledge of regional Mexican cuisine came through television programs and non-Mexican cookbook authors in the 1970s and '80s. But if you'd asked the Mexican community back then, you'd know that regional Mexican cuisine already existed here in L.A., segregated to the barrios, invisible to an indifferent mainstream press. Most traditional cooking was found at street stands, bakeries (Flor de Yucatán had opened in 1971), and underground restaurants. But in the mid '80s, a pair of charismatic, animated chefs with TV-star looks, Jaime Martín del Campo and Ramiro Arvizu, both of whom worked for airlines, met at a party in Bell. It was a fortuitous meeting that ultimately led to the founding of La Casita Mexicana, one of L.A.'s most treasured institutions.

"There was a beautiful display at the party, with every detail just perfect—I had to find out who the culprit was," says Ramiro.

"It was a buffet, and I had to use colors—it was black, white, and yellow," adds Jaime. The event was a gathering of mutual friends in the airline industry, and that night they found out they were both from small towns in Jalisco: Ramiro from Tecolotlán and Jaime from Tototlán, which practically made them brothers.

Jaime learned to cook from his mom and grandmother back home, where they also made cheeses: queso fresco, adobera, requesón, and jocoque. "They kept trying to push me out of the kitchen, and finally they gave in and started to show me the steps," he says. In Mexican families, men aren't supposed to be in the kitchen. Ramiro's mother, however, didn't push him out of her domain. Quite the contrary: He learned to make pozole rojo, chiles rellenos, tamales, and tortillas at her restaurant, La Fonda de Doña Chuy. In fact, his chiles rellenos were so good that they beat Bobby Flay's on the hit show *Throwdown*.

The new friends began to cook together at L.A. restaurants, while hatching their plan to bring real Mexican cuisine to Bell, a difficult market in which to do such a thing—the Mexican American locals were used to burritos, yellow cheese, and sour cream. In 1990 they opened La Casita Mexicana, serving moles, pipianes, and quesadillas filled with huitaloche (corn smut) and squash blossoms, the kind of regional Mexican cuisine that was entering the national discussion—but not the Bell discussion.

"One day, a woman threw red enchiladas at me, saying that this wasn't Mexican food," says Ramiro. "She later came back and apologized, and she's still a regular customer at our other restaurant, Mexicano." What crime had the pair of clean-headed chefs committed? They'd refused to put cheddar cheese on the enchiladas. Even more shocking: When Ramiro suggested they consider adding tacos and burritos because people were asking for them, Jaime angrily replied, "Better to close than to sell a burrito."

After two years, the locals who had made the effort to understand their own culture better came to see that La Casita Mexicana was for real. Ramiro and Jaime decided it was the perfect time to venture deeper into Mexico's regional cooking and haute cuisine, which had become popular in Mexico thanks to Patricia Quintana, Susana Palazuelos, and Martha Chapa. They'd taken some classes at L.A. Trade Technical College, but decided to go deeper and head to Tijuana's Culinary Art School, one at a time, before traveling all over Mexico to research recipes from other regions.

Soon they'd add such Mexican haute cuisine classics as chiles en nogada to their culinary arsenal, and their presentations were stylish enough to appear on the top TV food shows, but it was Spanish-language television that first embraced them. Univision asked them to do a cooking segment, and Ramiro said yes. "I was so scared that I never even looked at the camera," he says, blushing. The second segment featured a merrier and more spirited duo together, and that worked like a charm. Today, Jaime and Ramiro are the stars of the Mexican American Top Chef franchise, *Top Chef Estrellas*, and they've been on the *Today Show*, *Throwdown*, a Chase commercial, and *The Best Thing I Ever Ate* with Giada De Laurentiis.

In 2015, they opened Flautas, a deep-fried taco spot, and Mexicano, a regional restaurant in the Baldwin Hills mall. Meanwhile, their flagship continues to pack in the crowds for upscale fonda fare. "We've stayed in Bell because Bell has been good to us," says Ramiro. They're a perfect example of how the country's best Mexican chefs, who start out cooking for the L.A. Mexican community in modest, lesser-known neighborhoods, end up attracting a diverse audience to parts of the city they never knew existed. It's as if the L.A. freeways were built just to bring people to good Mexican food.

CHICKEN WITH PIPIÁN ROJO
Chicken with Red Pumpkin-Seed Mole
Ramiro Arvizu & Jaime Martín del Campo, La Casita Mexicana & Mexicano

When Ramiro Arvizu and Jaime Martín del Campo first opened their doors at La Casita Mexicana, they gave moles the greatest attention and care, even if their Mexican American customers were begging for burritos. To promote their moles, the chefs served it on their chips and came up with such fun dishes as tres moles (my personal favorite), a trio of chicken enchiladas covered in mole poblano, green pipián, and red pipián. Pipianes, a group of pumpkin-seed-based dishes, are among the more than 300 moles that exist in Mexico.

I recommend this pipián dish as your gateway dish into the rich world of moles—it's delicious and it has fewer ingredients than more complex moles and is quite versatile—try it with almost any protein.

Serves 4 to 6

1 whole chicken, cut into pieces, skin on
½ medium onion, quartered
3 cloves garlic, peeled
1 bay leaf
1 teaspoon sea salt
2 California chiles
1 chile de árbol
1 ancho chile
¼ cup peanuts
⅓ cup pumpkin seeds
¼ cup sesame seeds

1 clove garlic
1 whole roma tomato
½ small onion
2 allspice berries
2 cloves
Corn or other vegetable oil for cooking
Sea salt and freshly ground pepper to taste
6 cups cooked white rice (*see recipe page 26*)
1 dozen corn tortillas

Place chicken pieces in a large, sturdy pot, add water to cover (about 8 cups), and set over high heat. Add ½ onion, 2 garlic cloves, bay leaf, and salt. Bring to a boil, reduce heat to barely a simmer, cover, and cook over low heat until the chicken is almost but not quite cooked through, about 50 minutes. Remove chicken pieces and set aside. Strain the stock through a fine-mesh sieve.

Put 2 cups of the strained chicken stock into a large bowl. Toast chile peppers over medium-high heat on a comal or in a skillet for about 15 seconds per side. Remove and discard stems, seeds, and membranes and place chiles in the bowl with the chicken stock. Toast peanuts, stirring constantly with a wooden spoon, until golden brown, about 3 minutes, and add them to the stock. Toast pumpkin seeds, stirring constantly, until they take on a golden color and start to jump; do not overcook. Add to the chicken stock. Toast sesame

seeds for only a few seconds, taking extra care not to burn these tiny seeds. Add to the stock.

Toast 1 tomato, onion, and remaining garlic clove on the comal, turning occasionally to obtain an even char. Add them to the chicken stock. Toast allspice and cloves and add them to the stock.

Place saucepan over medium-high heat. When it's hot, add about 2 tablespoons oil and pour all of the bowl's contents into the saucepan, stirring to combine. Cook for 8 minutes, stirring occasionally. Remove from heat and set aside to let all the ingredients soften for about 15 minutes.

When softened, pour pipián mixture into a food processor or blender and process (in batches if necessary) until you have a smooth blend. Pour sauce into a large skillet over medium-high heat, add chicken pieces, and cook, stirring occasionally, until chicken finishes cooking through, about 10 minutes. The sauce consistency should be that of a milkshake; if it seems too thick, add more stock. You might need to add as much as 2 cups. Taste and add salt and pepper as desired. Serve with white rice and warm corn tortillas.

ZEFERINO GARCIA

Oaxaca isn't known for its tacos, and the guardians of Oaxacan culture won't promote tacos when entertaining American media, which has instead settled on dishes like mole and tlayudas to define one of Mexico's most esteemed gastronomic regions. But I've found Oaxaca City to have great tacos, especially the taco de cazuela: a large corn tortilla called a blandita is given a healthy spread of refried black beans, guacamole, salsa, and a stew served from a clay casserole, and then it's rolled into a long, cylindrical "taco." Let us never take seriously the claim that there are no burritos in southern Mexican cuisine, because this delicious taco is a damn burrito. (The al pastor is really good in Oaxaca, too, with lots of creative alambres, which is al pastor meat sautéed with onions, peppers, bacon, Oaxacan cheese, and more.)

The taco de la abuela is one of the signature items at Zeferino Garcia's Expresión Oaxaqueña restaurants. It resembles that Oaxacan taco de cazuela in its shape, but it's filled with a silky purée of black beans, salsa, guacamole, onions, cilantro, cabbage, and one of Oaxaca's most popular meats: tasajo, cecina, or chorizo. "Sometimes I laugh at how luxurious this taco is—we were very poor when I was a kid, and my grandmother would just fill a handmade tortilla with salsa," says Zeferino.

Zeferino was born and raised in San Francisco Yateé in the Sierra Norte region of Oaxaca, where he studied to be a teacher but never quite made it to the classroom. "I knew people from my town who were working in the United States, and within a short time they were pouring concrete for their new homes back in our village," he says. "I knew I couldn't achieve success like that as a teacher in Oaxaca." So at just twenty-one, the young man who'd subsisted on salsa tacos left his hometown, destined to become the most successful Oaxacan restaurateur in Los Angeles.

When he arrived in L.A. in 1986, it had no Oaxacan cuisine, but Oaxacans were spilling out of their pueblos and heading to El Norte to seek economic opportunity, creating a community known as Oaxacalifornia. (One of the greatest myths of migrant labor is that Mexicans are cheap labor—in the restaurant industry, Oaxacans are some of the most sought-after employees for their culinary skills and fierce work ethic.) He found work cleaning restaurants after hours and then as a dishwasher for Hamburger Hamlet. Later he moved to line cook, which he did for five years. Well versed in American cuisine, Zeferino cooked at downtown L.A.'s Engine Co. No. 28 until an encounter with a hot dog vendor in Beverly Hills encouraged him to become his own boss. In 1992, he set up a hot dog cart at Pico and Veteran in front of a Department of Social Services office, where he scored customers picking up their checks, which was good business while it lasted.

The success came to a halt when customers switched to check-cashing places, a situation made more difficult by the divorce he was going through. Alone and out of work, he crashed on a friend's couch, where he noticed lots of vacant spaces on Pico Boulevard, which had been hard-hit in the years following the L.A. riots. "I got a great deal on a place at Pico and Western," he says, "and I started selling CDs, curios, and, later, Oaxacan food products." He was on his way, but there was one problem—no place to live.

"I grew up taking cold showers—we had no hot water—so to this day I still take cold showers," he says. That toughness helped him manage without a residence for five years, a frugality that helped ensure the success of his business, Expresión Oaxaqueña. Let's just say the shop never needed a night watchman. In the adjoining space, he added a café, where he served his grandmother's tacos de la abuela. Later came an Expresión Oaxaqueña on Pico and Van Ness, where a Saint Bernard–size chapulín (grasshopper) mounted on a pole acts as both a sign of things to come on your plate and a sentry for nearby Country Club Park.

There were tough times, but Zeferino, a fit and serene man who seems far too relaxed for someone who takes cold showers every day, always had a positive outlook. "I came from nothing and had nothing," he says, smiling. "On a month when I don't make money, I'm content to know I don't owe anyone any money." He found a true partner in his second wife, Maria, who understood his business in ways he'd never thought of, and they now have six locations, including markets, restaurants, and two stores called Mayordomía, which make blanditas (Oaxacan-style corn tortillas), import tlayudas and quesillo, and have onsite chocolate production and milling services, features that grew not from his ambition, but from his customers' demand.

"In my pueblo, people have their own recipes for chocolate, they are very particular about it, and they need to grind ingredients for moles they prepare for baptisms, quinceañeras, and other events for the community," he says. And when he says "community," he means it—today L.A. is home to more than 400 Zapotecs from San Francisco Yateé, more than the number of Zapotecs still living there.

Until recently, his clientele was eighty percent Zapotec, but now it's more diverse. But his ties to the community remain strong. He, his wife, and their children are musicians in Banda Filarmonica Grandeza Oaxaqueña, which performs sones and jarabes from the Sierra Norte; a few days after we spoke, the family was headed back to Oaxaca to perform—music has made their family stronger. "My wife was tired of our kids always on the electronics, so she made us all take music lessons together and join a banda oaxaqueña group," he says. "She wants them to be educated and to have the life we didn't have growing up in Oaxaca." Music keeps them connected with L.A.'s Zapotecs, but it is their moles, guisados, antojitos, and Oaxacan products that have become a testament to the vibrancy of Oaxacalifornia and regional Mexican cuisine in L.A.

Any chef on television can claim that he or she has spent time and studied in Mexico, but L.A. has entire transplanted villages whose culinary talents are evident everywhere from fine restaurants to taco trucks. "These recipes are from our towns, our grandparents," Zeferino says. "It's important to have our hand in all the details, to take care of the cuisine so it lives on."

HUEVOS AHOGADOS
Zeferino Garcia, Expresión Oaxaqueña

One of the things I crave the most in Los Angeles is the spectrum of egg dishes that you can find in Mexico. It's easy to find huevos rancheros (although, too often, they just use a house salsa instead of a real ranchero sauce) and huevos a la Mexicana, and sometimes even huevos divorciados (*see page 57*). However, at Mexico's grand breakfast spots like El Cardenal, you can order a dozen different styles of eggs, and El Bajío serves many Veracruz-style egg dishes. Everywhere you go, eggs are freshly prepared in the local style.

Expresión Oaxaqueña is one of only three places I've seen in L.A. that make drowned eggs poached in a spicy tomato sauce. Making these eggs at home makes me feel like I'm at a grand hacienda in Mexico, which is why I especially love this recipe.

Serves 5

10 eggs
2 cactus paddles, cut into long strips
Sea salt
8 roma tomatoes, quartered
8 guajillo chiles, stemmed
2 cloves garlic
2 sprigs fresh epazote

To serve:
1 onion, finely diced
8 to 10 serrano chiles, stemmed, seeded, and
  finely diced
1 cup chopped cilantro
5 limes, cut into wedges
1 dozen blanditas (Oaxacan corn tortillas)

Take the eggs out of the refrigerator to bring to room temperature and decrease the cooking time.

Put sliced cactus paddles into a medium pot with enough water to cover, add a pinch of salt, and bring water to a boil. Boil, uncovered, until cactus paddles are soft and turn dark green, about 10 minutes. Strain cactus strips and rinse under running water to remove the sticky residue. Set aside.

Put tomatoes, guajillo chiles, garlic, and 1 cup water in a food processor or blender and purée until smooth. Pour tomato mixture into a large, wide-mouth pot (a Dutch oven works well), stir in 7 cups water, and bring to a boil. Reduce heat, add epazote, and simmer sauce, uncovered, for about 15 minutes. Season sauce with salt to taste.

When the sauce is ready, set out 5 wide, shallow serving bowls. Crack one egg into a small mixing bowl and whisk it a few times with a fork before sliding it into the hot tomato sauce. Leave the egg undisturbed as it sets. Repeat with the remaining eggs, placing each in separate areas of the pot. Scatter the cactus strips all over the sauce and eggs (do not stir). Cook eggs uncovered until well done, about 8 minutes, and sprinkle with a little salt to taste. This is the way the restaurant does it, resulting in a very well-cooked scrambled egg. If you prefer poached eggs, do not whisk the eggs and let them cook for no longer than 4 minutes, or until the whites are just set.,

To serve, use a ladle or large spoon to carefully scoop two eggs into each serving bowl. Ladle plenty of sauce over the eggs so they are well covered, and add a couple of cactus strips. Set the chopped onion, serrano chiles, cilantro, and lime wedges on the table in separate bowls to use as condiments (add to your personal taste). Enjoy this classic breakfast with a warm blandita.

GILBERTO CETINA & GILBERTO CETINA, JR.

The first big television shows featuring Mexican food didn't feature Mexicans, and the first talk of alta cocina, or modern Mexican, by the mainstream media didn't even consider Mexican Americans. When Rick Bayless, for example, won *Top Chef Masters* for his dishes inspired by Oaxaca, Veracruz, and the Yucatán, a panel that included no Mexicans (some hardly even knew Mexican cuisine) rewarded his mastery over someone else's cuisine. If they had spent any time in Mexico, they'd have understood that what Bayless and others who followed him were cooking were the traditional recipes of others—they weren't rescuing or elevating Mexican cuisine, save for a few haute classics like chiles en nogada.

In fact, that very same level of cuisine had been in L.A. since 1985, complete with rectangular plates and elegant garnishes, at places like Chichén Itzá, run by Gilberto Cetina and his son, Gilberto Jr. The setting (in Mercado La Paloma near USC) might not be fancy, but the food is sophisticated and among the best Mexican cooking in the nation.

Gilberto Sr. learned to cook in his hometown of Colonia Yucatán in the municipality of Tizimín, where his mom had a fonda (a mom-and-pop restaurant). "My first kitchen job was to clean an entire stomach of a cow for mondongo (tripe soup)," he says. "We'd practice our baseball swings trying to knock off the hooves." After he married, Gilberto moved his family to Mérida, one of Mexico's famed culinary cities, where he worked in construction. When peso troubles killed a big project, his brothers in L.A. invited him to head north. Construction work was hard to find, so he took a job cooking at Sea Cliffs Country Club in Huntington Beach, where he delighted his fellow cooks with staff meals featuring his family's Yucatán recipes. From there, he worked his way up the restaurant-chef chain. His wife grew tired of the US and wanted to return to Mexico, but then he was lured by a new project called Mercado La Paloma, whose owner knew about Gilberto Sr.'s culinary talents. Gilberto was intrigued by the complex and its potential; in fact, it later became the home of Mo Chica, the first restaurant by Peruvian-born chef Ricardo Zárate, as well as a place known for its active, community-based events (it's a nonprofit community center).

Gilberto Jr. arrived from Mérida to help open the new place while working at a couple of restaurants to learn about the business. He didn't plan on staying beyond the opening, intending to return home to his girlfriend and his computer studies program in Mexico, but all bets were off when the relationship ended. With nothing tying him to Mérida, he joined his father at Chichén Itzá on the business side. Then in 2003, he found himself unhappy with the performance of one of the cooks. "I started to butt in and spend more and more time in the kitchen," he says. In 2005, the father-and-son team opened a second location at MacArthur Park, and the challenges of the expansion pulled Gilberto Jr. into the hot flames of the kitchen. On his twenty-sixth birthday, the father gave the son more than a gift. "His present was a knife kit," says Gilberto Jr. "I was like, 'What is this for?'"

"It's for your new career," said his father with a huge grin.

In 2008, they closed the MacArthur Park branch and the sous chef at their first place quit, so Junior stepped in; for a while, it was just father and son cooking together. Chichén Itzá had earned a citywide reputation for its cochinita, papadzules, huevos motuleños, and fresh agua fresca made with chaya. The recados (marinades) are all made from scratch using locally acquired bitter orange, and chaya leaves are often foraged by industrious gardeners—the same ones who run the pre-Hispanic ingredients racket in L.A. (maguey leaves, chaya, yucca flower, etc.). And whenever they got stuck on a recipe, the secrets of the Yucatán kitchen were just a phone call away. "There's always an aunt who knows what's missing in a recipe," says Gilberto Jr.

There was room for modernity, too, and the chefs introduced innovations where it made sense. "I started buying books, including the Culinary Institute of America curriculum," says Gilberto Jr. "I saw a recipe from El Bulli and didn't understand what they were doing, but I wanted to learn." So he studied up on sous vide and making foams and found ways to improve dishes. The turkey in the US, for example, is drier than the turkey in Mérida, so he discovered that a little sous vide made the salbutes and panuchos moister and tastier.

The Cetinas aren't ones to advertise that sort of thing, however—humility often goes unrewarded in an industry that glamorizes brash and boisterous chefs. The Yucatán crowd, however, sustains their business, especially on weekends, when they roll out the suckling pig tacos and tortas. Evenings bring a more diverse crowd who've read about Chichén Itzá or have discovered the Cetinas's cookbook, *Sabores Yucatecos: A Culinary Tour of the Yucatán*. It's only a matter of time until more food writers catch on to these trailblazers, who have been giving Los Angeles a superb culinary experience for many years.

COCHINITA PIBIL TACOS

Chichén Itzá
Courtesy of Sabores Yucatecos:
A Culinary Tour of the Yucatán,
by Gilberto Cetina, Katarine A. Diaz, and Gilberto Cetina, Jr.

Yucatán's signature dish is steeped in tradition as well as chiles and spices. Pibil (which means "buried" in Mayan) refers to the peninsula's pit style of cooking meats marinated in achiote paste, or recados—in this case, a red recado. If you've visited Mexico City's best restaurants, you'll have seen chefs using recados. And you see them at L.A.'s Yucatán places, too.

The habanero pepper is an essential flavor in this regional cuisine, and while you may think it to be too hot, using it as a chaser with controlled bites is the best way to moderate the burn. Don't worry, if you do get stung, the habanero's bite is fast and furious but dissipates quickly—and the best cure is another bite of your taco de cochinita pibil.

Serves 8 to 10

2½ tablespoons Recado Rojo (*recipe follows*)
1½ cups bitter orange juice or lime juice
1 tablespoon sea salt
5 pounds pork (loin, butt, cushion, or boneless shoulder), cut into large pieces

Banana leaves
2 dozen corn tortillas
Pickled Onions (*recipe follows*)
5 habanero chiles (optional), sliced into rings

Combine the Recado Rojo, citrus juice, and salt in a large, nonreactive bowl and stir to blend. Add the pork and rub the mixture all over the meat. Set aside in the refrigerator to marinate for about 4 hours, or overnight.

Preheat the oven to 350°. Pass the banana leaves over the flame of a burner, being careful not to burn or tear them, until they are soft and pliable. Line a Dutch oven or casserole with the leaves, overlapping them to cover the bottom and sides. Place the pork atop the leaves, pour over remaining marinade, and fold the leaves inward to completely cover the pork. Cover and seal the baking dish with heavy aluminum foil.

Roast until pork is tender to the point of falling apart with a fork, 3½ to 4 hours. When it is cool enough to handle but still warm, shred meat with a pair of forks or by hand.

It's time to taco! Heat tortillas on a comal, griddle, or electric skillet and wrap them in a towel or place them in a tortilla basket to keep them warm. Place a warmed tortilla in your hand and spoon in about 2 heaping tablespoons of the cochinita pibil. Top with pickled onions and, if you like, as much of the habaneros as you can tolerate—or put the chile slices on a plate and do it the Yucatán way, by taking a bite of your taco and chasing it with a small bite of habanero.

RECADO ROJO
Achiote Paste

You can use this marinade on other meats—there's a reason it's a "mother paste" of Yucatecan cooking.

Makes 1 cup

½ cup ground annatto seeds, toasted
1 tablespoon ground white pepper
¼ cup sea salt
1 tablespoon garlic powder
Pinch of ground cloves

Pinch of ground allspice
Pinch of oregano
¼ cup white vinegar
¼ cup water

Place all the ingredients into a nonreactive bowl and stir until the marinade is well blended. Store it in a sealed container in a cool, dry place until needed. It will keep for a long time.

PICKLED ONIONS

1 medium red onion, chopped
¾ cup white wine vinegar

¾ cup water
1¼ teaspoons sea salt

Place onion in a large bowl and add vinegar, water, and salt. Chopped onion should be completely covered with the mixture; if it's not, add a little more. Cover with plastic wrap and let stand for at least 15 minutes in the refrigerator. This will keep up to 2 weeks in the fridge.

FRANCISCO "PACO" PEREZ

To experience Mexican lamb barbecue, called barbacoa, in its hallowed centers of Hidalgo and the state of Mexico, especially the city of Texcoco de Mora, is a superlative breakfast ritual as breathtaking as the Sistine Chapel and as memorable for me as seeing Van Halen in 1980. Other places do fine barbacoa, including Tlaxcala, Guerrero, Puebla, and Oaxaca (goat barbacoa). In Mexico City, you can find plenty of stands representing the various regional expressions, but I can't even entertain the thought of it—barbacoa is far better at its source.

Alas, Los Angeles is too far for trips to Actopan or Texcoco for weekend barbacoa, but happily, we now have more regional styles of barbacoa than Mexico City, even if they are often flawed. The health department and its culture-strafing codes, the offal-skimming meat suppliers, and nosy neighbors are cohorts in a conspiracy to extinguish the underground pits that burn in L.A.'s barrios. If only someone could design a special oven to solve this problem—which is exactly what industrial engineer and barbacoa master Francisco "Paco" Perez did.

Paco, who studied engineering in college, was twenty-one when his uncle opened the first Aqui es Texcoco in Tijuana's Otay Mesa neighborhood. Paco was in charge of the consommé, the prized lamb broth that's a companion to the barbacoa; soon he and his mother operated the barbacoa pit by themselves, because Paco's uncle was often too hungover to work. In 1995, his uncle retired to Texcoco, leaving the business to his sister and brother-in-law, allowing the young engineer to accept a job offer in Madrid at Stejasa Agregados Industriales, where Paco worked for the next seven years. The money was good, but the food was even better.

"The work was the same all the time, so when I traveled to places like Beijing, Warsaw, and Munich, I was more excited about where I was going to eat," he says, and that meant street food. Trying new foods from new vendors felt like he was back in Tijuana, where every street corner offers the chance of a rapturous bite. Meanwhile, a friend had invented an apparatus to shoot three-dimensional video, and he offered to fabricate the prototype in Tijuana, but the $200-million project came to a halt when another engineer got involved, leaving Paco without work. "I moved on to help my brother build 120 houses, but then insecurity in Tijuana from the war on the drug cartels hurt our sales."

Still, being in Tijuana meant working with his mom at the barbacoa stand, where he came to realize that people were driving all the way from L.A. just to get their barbacoa to go. The light bulb turned on. "I told my mom that I thought the barbacoa could be successful in Los Angeles, but first I'd have to perfect our product in a legal kitchen in Chula Vista," Paco says. L.A. had good barbacoa, but it was either made in unlicensed pits and brought into restaurants or sold illegally at backyard events, food trucks, and street stands—mostly by weekend warriors—and the condiments lacked regional authenticity. The fact that Mexicans were willing to drive three hours for an artisanal product had Paco smelling barbacoa gold.

Paco designed his oven to mimic the conditions that exist in the ground. "It's the closest I can get to the real deal and still have the approval of the health department," he says with a smile. He spent the next six years in Chula Vista perfecting his barbacoa and regional menu, which includes pit-roasted lamb, pancita (offal-stuffed stomach), consommé, whole lamb heads, lamb-brain quesadillas, and mixiotes (meat cooked in parchment), before coming to Los Angeles—more precisely, to Commerce—in 2014. Two times a year, he heads back to Mexico to research barbacoa in Hidalgo, Texcoco, Tlaxcala, and other small towns in the state of Mexico. He's the best regional barbacoa specialist in the United States, and he's available in Los Angeles all week long.

Barbacoa is a weekend breakfast tradition, but in L.A., you can get it on a Tuesday night with Mexican craft beer, pulque, and grasshoppers. This year, Aqui es Texcoco participated in dineLA, the city's restaurant week hosted by the Los Angeles Tourism and Convention Board. I'm pretty sure it was also the first time lamb skulls were enlisted to attract tourists to the City of Angels.

LAMB BARBACOA WITH CONSOMMÉ
Paco Perez, Aqui es Texcoco

Texcoco-style barbacoa, complete with consommé is one of the most revered traditions in Mexico, usually cooked on weekends in an earthen pit or an above-ground brick or clay oven. It's a celebratory breakfast feast to share with friends and family, but the pre-Hispanic cooking technique can be a real challenge to replicate in a conventional restaurant or home kitchen. Paco Perez, the engineer-turned-owner of Aqui es Texcoco, solved this problem. His ingenious method to cook this dish at home? A giant fifty-quart vaporera (steamer pot for tamales) produces the same steam cooking that happens when meat is cooked underground. They're available at all Latino supermarket chains and, of course, easily purchased online.

Avocado leaves add a nice aroma; if you can't find them on a neighborhood walk (they're everywhere!), they're sold at Mexican markets. Also known as maguey or *Agave americana*, the century plant has long, prickly-edged leaves. Not only do they add flavor and aroma to the barbacoa, but the leaves protect the meat from excessive heat from the vaporera's walls. You can find them at nurseries and at stalls in the Mercado Olympic; ask them to cut them into four pieces. You'll need to remove the spines, including the very sharp ones at the tips—use gloves and be careful!

For the lamb, if you can't order a whole lamb from a butcher, you can use the equivalent in various cuts (leg, shoulder, and so on).

If you want to go all in, start cooking this dish around 3 o'clock in the morning and invite your guests to arrive at breakfast time. As this is L.A., if you'd rather get a good night's sleep and a lamb dinner is more practical, that'll do just as well.

Serves 20 to 25

2 pounds dried chickpeas
6 dried guajillo chiles
4 large onions, divided
2 heads garlic, 1 whole and 1 with cloves peeled
2 teaspoons freshly ground pepper, more to taste
½ cup kosher salt, more to taste
1 whole lamb, about 30 pounds, trimmed and cut
    into body-part pieces (legs, spine, etc.)
1 cup uncooked rice

3 dried chipotle chiles (not canned)
3 century plant (agave) leaves, spines removed
20 avocado leaves
5 medium bunches cilantro, for garnish
20 limes, for serving
5 dozen good-quality yellow corn tortillas,
    from a tortilleria, for serving
Salsa Borracha, for serving (*recipe follows*)

The day before cooking, soak the chickpeas in enough water to cover by a few inches, cover, and refrigerate overnight. Drain and let chickpeas come to room temperature before using.

Rinse the guajillo chiles with cold water to remove dirt and impurities. Place whole chiles in a medium pot with 1 quartered onion and peeled garlic cloves, and add enough water to cover. Bring to a boil over medium-high heat and cook until soft, about 20 minutes. Drain half of the water, snip the stems off the chiles, and place cooked chiles, onion, garlic, and remaining chile water in food processor or blender. Add pepper and salt and purée into a very smooth, thick paste. Rub paste generously all over the pieces of lamb (if you have any leftover paste, save it for the steamer).

Preheat the oven to 375°. Remove steamer insert from vaporera and put chickpeas, rice, whole garlic head, and chipotles into vaporera along with any leftover chile paste. Place steamer insert on top of ingredients and add enough hot water to cover about 1 inch above the insert. Arrange century plant leaves with open sides facing up to form a cradle for the pieces of lamb, so the pointy ends face the top of the pot and the open, pulpy sides of the leaves face the internal part of the steamer. Set pieces of lamb onto the agave leaves, beginning with bigger pieces such as legs and shoulders, then add the spine and ribs. Scatter the avocado leaves evenly on top of the lamb. Enclose meat like a package by folding ends of the agave leaves toward the center to fully encase lamb. Cover vaporera with a lid and roast until meat easily separates from the bones, about 5 hours.

Once the lamb is cooked, unwrap the agave leaves and use tongs to remove the lamb parts from the vaporera (be careful; the steam will be very hot). Pour the consommé into another pot, skim off excess fat with a large spoon, and keep warm. Place meat back into the vaporera and cover to keep warm.

To serve the barbacoa, finely chop the cilantro, quarter the limes, and finely dice remaining 3 onions, placing each in separate serving bowls. Preheat a comal, electric skillet, or flattop, warm (but do not toast) the tortillas, and place them in a container wrapped in a towel to keep warm. To serve, place a piece of lamb on each plate (or let guests serve themselves) with a cup or small bowl of consommé on the side. Add some chickpeas and rice to each soup bowl. (In some regions, the consommé is more pure, but in Texcoco-style barbacoa, the consommé is closer to a hearty soup.) Place chopped cilantro, quartered limes, diced onion, and Salsa Borracha on the table. To make tacos, tear off enough lamb to fill a warm tortilla and then dress with cilantro, onions, salsa, and a finishing squeeze of lime.

SALSA BORRACHA
Drunken Salsa

Drunken salsa is traditionally made with pulque, a milky looking, rather sour fermented agave drink from central Mexico. You can find pulque at Aqui es Texcoco, at the Mercado Olympic, or at other Mexican markets, or you can substitute beer if you'd rather. Make the salsa a day or two before serving for the best flavor.

Makes about 2 cups

8 pasilla chiles, stems removed
5 cloves garlic
1 teaspoon kosher salt, more to taste

1 cup pulque or beer, like Mondelo or Tecate
½ medium orange

Put chiles in a medium pot, add enough water to cover, and boil until chiles are tender, about 20 minutes. Transfer chiles to a blender, add garlic and salt, and pulse until you have a very thick paste, adding a tablespoon or two of cooking water only if needed. Add pulque or beer and blend until the salsa has consistency of a milkshake; if needed, add a little more cooking water. Finish by squeezing orange juice into salsa and seasoning with additional salt to taste. Transfer to a bowl if serving immediately, or cover and refrigerate.

CINDY, GLORIA & ADRIAN ESTRADA

There has never been a greater time in L.A. to explore Mexico's regional sandwiches, tortas—the city is now blessed with skilled torteros (sandwich makers) from Puebla, Mexico City, and Jalisco. We also have a quality pocho hand in the torta game at Monterey Park's Cook's Tortas, not to mention the Alta California creations of Wes Avila at his famed Guerrilla Tacos truck. And while New York City gets called Puebla York because of

all the Pueblan immigrants serving street food, L.A.'s Puebla-style cemitas poblanas are far superior. We've even gained a few veteran sandwich makers from Mexico City who work the plancha with the command of well-seasoned sous chefs.

But most of all, L.A. has always reigned supreme when it comes to tortas ahogadas.

Rooted in Jalisco, tortas ahogadas are drowned tortas, in which a birote salado (a hard roll) is doused with a liquid fire of chile de árbol salsa and packed with rich, fatty Mexican confit-style pork or carnitas and a garnish of pickled purple onions. L.A.'s Jalisco natives have led to a spicy trail of torta ahogada shops and stands descending southeast from Pacoima to Paramount. Many got their start selling out of hot dog carts, like Huntington Park's Tortas Ahogadas Guadalajara, founded by tapatíos (people from Guadalajara) Adrian and Gloria Estrada in 2001.

Adrian and Gloria's children, Cindy, Jose, and Jacob, were born in the US but grew up in Guadalajara. "It was amazing growing up with my mom's cooking in Mexico," says Cindy. "We always had dishes like chiles rellenos and albondigas for lunch, and my mom also made pozole—sometimes even for the teachers." She also remembers visiting her grandfather in Santa Maria, where they'd go out for barbacoa and tortas ahogadas. It's something they'd miss when the family moved back to Los Angeles in 1996 so Cindy's brother could attend an American school.

Cindy found work in the fashion industry, while her father worked as a painter. But it didn't take long for Adrian reach the conclusion that given all the tapatíos in L.A., there must be an untapped market for tortas ahogadas, one of Jalisco's most iconic dishes. So he got a recipe for the salsa from back home and started selling tortas ahogadas from a hot dog cart on the corner of Florence and McKinley in South Park, five years before Guadalajara-based Chago Tortas Ahogadas opened in East L.A. By 2008, Adrian had found a bread maker to supply him with birotes just in time for the opening of his first brick-and-mortar location in Huntington Park. The same craft-food-and-drink movement that was incubating in Brooklyn, Silver Lake, and Portland was happening in L.A.'s Mexican enclaves—today, for example, many of the city's top torta ahogada shops source their own bread, and this sandwich is all about the bread.

When Tortas Ahogadas Guadalajara moved to its current location in Huntington Park in 2010, Cindy joined the team to add social media and marketing strategies to help her parents reach a broader audience. "I also added a full menu of our family recipes to offer a more complete dining experience," she says. In 2012 they opened Pika Tortas Ahogadas in Paramount (pika is an incorrect spelling of pica, which means spicy).

The growth in traditional Mexican cuisine that began in the '90s has been sustained by access to ingredients—without quality birote salado bread, for instance, there are no drowned tortas. Skilled cooks, artisans, and access to regional products are what give families like the Estradas the ability to share their unique culinary traditions. But there's more to it than ingredients and technical skills—there's also the Estradas' ability to capture a sense of nostalgia on the palate. "We're always tasting the food, especially the salsa, to make sure it's coming out the way we want," says Cindy. "And we *always* keep a good relationship with our birote man."

SHRIMP TORTAS AHOGADAS GEMMA STYLE

Estrada family, Tortas Ahogadas Guadalajara

The state of Jalisco is famous for its drowned sandwiches, known as tortas ahogadas, where some of the best rolls in Mexico are filled with carnitas or pork loin and covered in a fiery salsa. For those looking for a milder salsa, the well-known Lonches Gemma, a Guadalajara institution, came up with a chipotle-cream torta that's almost as famous as the original torta ahogada. Shrimp tortas ahogadas are another traditional style of Mexican sandwich, and this recipe from L.A.'s original torta ahogada vendor, the Estradas, brings these two great flavors together.

Note that you'll need to get birotes salados or comparable long rolls with a firm, crunchy crust for this dish to work. If the rolls are too soft, they'll fall apart when they're drowned with sauce.

SHRIMP TORTAS AHOGADAS GEMMA STYLE
Makes 6 tortas

48 medium shrimp, peeled and deveined
  (8 shrimp per torta)
½ medium onion, quartered
1 tomato, quartered
1 chipotle pepper in adobo

Sea salt to taste
Mayonnaise for the rolls
6 birotes salados
Chipotle Cream (*recipe follows*)

Place saucepot over medium-high heat and add shrimp, onion, tomato, chipotle, and a pinch of salt and cook until shrimp cooks through, 2 to 3 minutes. Remove shrimp and set aside, covering them to keep them warm; you can discard the rest of the mixture in the pot.

To serve, apply a thin layer of mayonnaise to each roll and fill with 8 shrimp, arranged evenly. Place each torta on a plate and pour Chipotle Cream over the whole torta to "drown" it—about 1 cup of sauce per torta.

CHIPOTLE CREAM
Makes 6 cups

5 dried California chiles
1 pound roma tomatoes
½ cup chipotle peppers in adobo
½ cup mayonnaise
1 cup crema mexicana

¼ cup chicken bouillon powder
2 tablespoons ketchup
1 bay leaf
Sea salt to taste
½ cup (1 stick) butter

Place chiles in a saucepan, cover with water, and bring to a boil over high heat. Pour water and chiles into a container with a lid, seal, and set aside. Remove chiles after 20 minutes, reserving the water, and remove and discard stems, seeds, and membranes.

Prepare an ice-water bath. Fill a stockpot with water, add salt, and bring to a rolling boil over high heat. Add whole tomatoes and cook until soft, about 1 minute. Shock tomatoes in the ice-water bath and peel off the skins. Place tomatoes in food processor. Add chipotles, mayonnaise, crema, bouillon powder, ketchup, and bay leaf and pulse until blended to a smooth consistency.

Melt butter in a large saucepan. Add chipotle mixture and cook over medium heat, stirring frequently, until flavors are blended, about 15 minutes. Pour chipotle cream through a strainer. The sauce is now ready for torta-drowning. You can make the sauce up to 4 days in advance and store in the refrigerator.

MARIA RAMOS

If you visit Oaxaca City, you're going to go to the Tlacolula market on Sunday. It's one of Mezoamerica's oldest running markets, where women plunge their hands into large bowls of tejate (a maize and cacao drink), people dress colorfully in the styles of their pueblos, and shoppers nosh on empanadas stuffed with yellow mole, molotes, grilled Oaxacan meats, tacos filled with carne enchilada, and of course, the main attraction: barbacoa enchilada, or goat barbecue in a red chile paste.

Unlike barbacoa in other regions, the Oaxacan version is distinguished by its use of goat and its exclusively female chefs; in Oaxaca, women rule the kitchen, the barbecue pit, and the grill, while the men butcher and prep the goats. Like her mother and grandmother before her, Maria de los Remedios Ramos Jimenez, a third-generation barbacoa master, learned her craft in Tlacolula. She was making tortillas by the age of ten for her grandmother's eatery, Comedor Lety, and later she learned how to make the family's barbacoa—a recipe that will live on in her family for generations. Comedor Lety sold their barbacoa in the famed Tlacolula market (where Maria's father was acclaimed for his skill in butchering and prepping goat), and her grandparents made chito (goat jerky) to help feed US troops during World War II. Her family was practically Oaxacan royalty in a state that values gastronomy and mezcal above all.

As the Mexican economy sank, Maria and her husband, David Padilla, decided to give L.A. a chance in 1992. They'd hoped to leave the labor-intensive days of cooking behind in their new American life, but Maria's reputation as a skilled barbacoa master preceded her, and besides, few jobs could offer an immigrant such adoration. So for the next eighteen years she and David catered two to three private events every weekend, preparing goat barbacoa for the growing community of Oaxacalifornia, as well as for Central Americans who also craved the rich, aromatic blend of spices and mild chiles in barbacoa enchilada.

In 2010, Maria and David opened Gish Bac, which means "sacred place" in Zapotec. Besides their weekend barbacoa, they serve Oaxacan classics: mole negro, tlayudas, atoles, chile de agua relleno, yellow-mole empanadas, and more. The food media's penchant for gushing over a famous Neopolitan pizzaiolo or Tokyo-based ramen franchise while ignoring a specialist like Maria right in the heart of L.A. (Washington and Crenshaw) remains a formidable challenge for Mexican cooks, especially when her barbacoa is just as distinguished as those dishes.

Gish Bac goes through four or five whole goats on a weekend, cooked in a proprietary blend of chiles and spices until it's a tender, crimson pile of meat and consommé, using the same process Maria's family has practiced for more than seventy-five years.

While an appreciation of regional Mexican cuisine has slowly grown among L.A.'s food lovers, Gish Bac has long survived on the patronage of Oaxacans longing for a taste of the Tlacolula market. But now, with a little social media presence (thanks to David and Maria's kids) and word of mouth, their customer base has broadened. Yet mainstream appeal is not what drives them. "It's all about the love and passion we have for our business," says Maria, beaming. "It takes two days to prepare our barbacoa, and six hours to cook. It's a recipe that's highly guarded by our family, because it's more than a recipe—it's our heritage."

ENFRIJOLADAS
Maria Ramos, Gish Bac

Just as in the City of Oaxaca's fondas, enfrijoladas are always on the menu in Oaxacalifornia, because it's hard to do any better than this simple dish of fresh, quality corn tortillas and flavorful beans. Gish Bac is my favorite place in L.A. to get this dish. When I bring friends there, they often ask why we'd bother ordering beans when the menu is rich with moles, antojitos and other famous dishes—but once they've had a taste, it's pure bliss all around, then apologies for doubting me.

To make this dish shine, get some really good yellow-corn tortillas from a trusted tortilleria, or buy hand-made tortillas from a restaurant or street vendor. Any place that presses its own tortillas will usually be more than happy to press a batch for you to go. If using regular, old, or storebought tortillas, fry them in lard or oil for about 10 seconds on medium-high heat, to add some flavor and pliability.

Serves 4

2 cups refried black beans (*see recipe page 65*)
Lard or vegetable oil for cooking
¼ white onion
2 tablespoons ground avocado leaves

Sea salt to taste
1 dozen good-quality corn tortillas
½ cup grated Oaxacan cheese
½ cup crema mexicana

Purée the beans in a blender or with an immersion blender until you have a smooth blend. Set aside.

Place a skillet over medium heat. Add lard or oil to coat the bottom of the skillet, and after it has heated, add onion quarter and cook, stirring occasionally, until browned to flavor the fat, about 5 minutes. Discard onion, reduce heat to low, add bean purée, and cook for about 10 minutes, adding the ground avocado leaves for the last 2 minutes. The goal is to have a sauce consistency, so if the beans are too thick, stir in enough water (up to a cup) to attain a smooth sauce. Add salt to taste.

Warm tortillas on a comal or griddle at medium heat for about 10 seconds per side. Dip a tortilla into the bean sauce and fold in half, and then fold it in half one more time to make a triangle. Set onto a plate, and repeat the process with 2 more tortillas. Arrange the 3 folded tortillas in a circle on the plate and top with another tablespoon of bean sauce. Crumble 2 teaspoons cheese over the top and finish with 1 tablespoon of crema. Repeat the process for the remaining 3 servings.

MARC & ANNIE BURGOS

For just about every rebellious Mexican American kid who ever told his or her parents, "You can't spank us here in America," the response has always been, "Oh yeah? Wait till I get you back to Mexico, then we'll see!"

While it was never a real threat in most households, taking a kid back to live in Mexico to teach them some manners and their heritage was always a possibility—and that's just what Antonio and Rosa Ana Burgos did in 1986. The founders of La Flor de Yucatán bakery took their children, Marc and Ana (Annie), back to live in the town of Mérida. "I was sort of a know-it-all," says Marc, "and I refused to speak Spanish—having to go to school in Mexico gave me no other choice."

Back in the Yucatán, Marc went to work in a bakery at the age of twelve, and he ended up gaining the same appreciation his father had for Mexico. Antonio was born in Kantunil, Yucatán, and came to L.A. in the late '60s, working as a dishwasher at the Pasadena Sheraton and buying flour on credit so he could make some extra money by baking. By the time Marc was in his teens, he was working with his dad, baking conchas, hojaldras, pastelitos de atropellado, and other regional Mexican sweet breads.

"My father would bake in our small apartment, sell from his car, and pay off the flour while also doing odd jobs," says Annie. He also bought the bakery back in Mérida where he used to work, and made trips back and forth to check on the business.

What Antonio really wanted, though, was his own "flower" (flor in Spanish)—there was already a Flor de

Michoacán and a Flor de Jalisco, but Antonio's dream, Flor de Yucatán (1971), would blossom into an L.A. institution. In 1975, they moved to their current location in L.A.'s culturally rich Pico-Union neighborhood, and the business thrived by selling special products to the Yucatecan community, including recados (aka recaudos), ground pumpkin seeds, El Gallo Azul (Dutch edam cheese used in the Yucatán and Belize), and baked goods. After returning from the Yucatán, with Annie and Marc now completely fluent in Spanish, the family assumed full control of La Flor (Antonio leased out the business while they were back living in the Yucatán), and were busier than ever before.

Marc was working as a supervisor for the Alta Dena Drive-Thru Dairy, but the bakery was getting busy and his parents kept asking him to come visit. They were workaholics, so seeing them always meant wrapping tamales and working at the shop. "Little by little, I got absorbed by the business and started liking it—my mom is a cake decorator, so I ended up taking some classes on advanced cake decorating."

Marc began to add a menu of Yucatecan antojitos, tacos, tamales, and plates, which became so popular that La Flor de Yucatán was catapulted into a busy catering business. Annie joined the operation in 2007 after she earned a business management degree—and it was painfully clear that her family needed to modernize their books. "Uh, that meant actually keeping books," she says with a sly smile.

La Flor de Yucatán is perhaps the oldest business in L.A. from Mexico's revered Yucatán peninsula, whose generations of Yucatecos have grown up eating relleno negro (turkey in a black recado), cochinita pibil, and weekly specials. One of those is frijol con puerco, or Yucatán-style pork and beans, a Monday dish cooked in homes, and every Monday, it's on the menu at Flor. Weekends bring tacos and tortas filled with roast suckling pig.

This delicious food has been respected in L.A. for generations, and a new generation is carrying it forward. Marc, the once-wayward son, now works alongside his sister and their parents as part of the small but impactful Yucatecan restaurant community. La Flor represents everything that has always been great about Mexican cuisine in Los Angeles—even before anyone really knew about it.

CHICKEN RELLENO NEGRO

Chirmole

Marc & Annie Burgos, La Flor de Yucatán

One of La Flor de Yucatán's most famous dishes is chirmole, also known as relleno negro. This savory soup of the gods is a very popular Mayan dish that's found at many street food stands and restaurants in the Yucatán. The most striking feature of the soup is its distinctive black color, which comes from the use of black recado, a paste made from charred peppers, annatto seeds, and spices. You can find black and red recado at Mexican markets and specialty stores—including, of course, La Flor de Yucatán.

Serves 8 to 10

2 whole chickens, cut into quarters and
    trimmed of excess fat
2 bay leaves
1 sprig epazote or 4 epazote leaves
1 head garlic, chopped
1 large onion, chopped
1 sweet pepper, seeded and chopped
1 banana pepper, seeded and chopped
2 tomatoes, chopped
5 to 6 whole cloves allspice or 1 teaspoon
    ground allspice
1 teaspoon ground cumin
1 tablespoon oregano
3 small bricks black recado
½ small brick red recado
Sea salt and freshly ground black pepper
    to taste
¼ cup flour dissolved in ¼ cup of
    warm water
2 to 3 cups chicken stock, as needed
Chirmole Stuffing (*recipe follows*)

Place chicken pieces in a very large stockpot with bay leaves and epazote and add enough water to cover. Bring to a boil over high heat, reduce heat, cover, and simmer for 30 minutes.

Place garlic, onion, sweet pepper, banana pepper, tomatoes, allspice, cumin, oregano, black recado, red recado, and salt and pepper to taste in a food processor or blender and purée (in batches if necessary), adding just enough water to make a smooth paste. Set aside.

After chicken has simmered for 30 minutes, stir in recado mixture and cook until chicken is tender, about another 30 minutes. Add more water as needed to keep the chicken covered. Slowly stir in flour and simmer for another 10 minutes. Remove chicken from the pot and set aside. Pour recado negro liquid through a sieve to remove any pieces not liquefied, and return liquid to the stockpot.

Set stockpot over medium heat. Add Chirmole Stuffing loaf to the pot and cook for 1 hour. When the chicken is cool enough to handle, shred it by hand into thin strands and discard the bones. Return chicken to the pot for the last 5 to 10 minutes of cooking to heat it through. Taste the soup, and if it's too intense and/or reduced, stir in chicken stock until you have a flavor balance you like.

Remove chirmole loaf from the pot, remove cheesecloth, and cut loaf into thick slices. Place a slice in a soup bowl and ladle over with the black chicken soup. Serve hot.

CHIRMOLE STUFFING

½ pound ground pork
½ pound ground beef
½ onion, finely chopped
1 dulce yucateco chile or green bell pepper, finely chopped
1 clove garlic, minced

Sea salt and freshly ground black pepper to taste
1 egg
½ small brick black recado
3 hard-boiled eggs, whites and yolks chopped separately
1 sprig epazote, finely chopped

In a large bowl, mix ground pork and beef with chopped onion, chile, garlic, salt, and pepper. Add egg and black recado and mix well. Add chopped egg whites and epazote.

Lay out a piece of cheesecloth on a large plate and form the meat mixture into a loaf. Make a valley across the middle of the loaf and fill with chopped egg yolks, closing up the meatloaf afterward, so the yolks are in the middle of the loaf. Wrap and bind the loaf in the cheesecloth and set aside until needed to add to the soup.

ROBERTO BERRELLEZA

It was easier to find a formal French restaurant than a formal Mexican one in Mexico City in the 1970s and '80s, and the same held true then in Los Angeles, when a young chef named Roberto Berrelleza began

his career in fine dining. He was raised by a family of cooks in one of Mexico's top seafood towns, Los Mochis, Sinaloa, near the beaches of Maviri and the touristy Topolobampo. But cooking wasn't his first love. "I really wanted to be a musician, and I studied guitar and learned solfeggio," he says, and later he joined Los Cristales, a popular band in the '70s. While a student at Universidad Autónoma de Baja California (UABC), he opened up for Los Frevis, Los Solitarios, and other top acts in Tijuana, and then he hit the big time playing a gig at the Grandia Room on Melrose in L.A. "When it was time to head back to Tijuana, I just couldn't stop thinking about the club and L.A.," says Roberto. Los Cristales returned to Tijuana light one guitar player. Seduced by L.A.'s charms, Roberto stayed to begin a new chapter of his life.

He found work as a busboy at the Tower, one of L.A.'s most exclusive French restaurants at the time, a place where he became well versed in the wines of France, Italy, and Napa Valley. Known to the staff as El Capitano, he was promoted to waiter, "where the big bucks were," and then maître d' before moving to François at 6th and Flower, where he'd spend the next eight years. "Back then, the maître d' was the most respected job in the house," he says. He had to know everything about each dish, and he had to finish dishes like whole duck at the table. Back then, the idea of Mexican fine dining wasn't even a consideration. "All the restaurants were staffed by Europeans, and that was the restaurant culture, but some of us [Mexicans] made it," he says.

With the '80s came chef culture, California cuisine, and a Mexican cuisine that was moving from combo plates toward street food and regional cuisine. Roberto remained at his post, though, serving as the opening maître d' at the Pasadena Brown Derby and then working at such classics as the Castaway in Burbank and San Pedro's Port O'Call, biding his time until he could find his own place. He did just that in 1990, when he took over La Moderna, a Mexican restaurant in Whittier, the kind of place that served the typical orange-cheese-covered standards—beans, rice, and something drowning in a sauce. One night, he threw a steak au poivre on the menu. "I called it bistec a la pimienta, or pepper steak—the customers loved it and thought I'd invented it," he says.

His experiments with French-Mexican cuisine didn't go unnoticed by critic Jonathan Gold, who drew attention to Roberto's chiles güeritos with salmon and a strawberry habanero sauce in a 1992 review. Soon, customers began to request those dishes, like his shrimp Topolobampo and shrimp Elba. Then, in 1999, he opened Babita in the old Emperador Maya space in San Gabriel, after owner Felipe Cabrera had tired of the restaurant business and offered it to Roberto, inviting Cabrera's loyal customers to give shrimp Topolobampo a try. Babita joined La Serenata de Garibaldi, Guatemalan chef Hugo Molina's eponymous restaurant, and La Casita Mexicana in the growing club of Latin American fine-dining restaurants, a trend that could be traced back to Mexican American chef John Sedlar's groundbreaking modern place, St. Estèphe in Manhattan Beach.

Roberto's white tablecloths and sophisticated service are in stark contrast to the dining room—a plain, smallish corner space that more resembles a hideout than a restaurant. Babita's walls have no pictures of famous clients or family members adorning its walls. Instead, Roberto tells tales through his chiles en nogada served with fried tortilla cups filled with black beans, two-toned soups with Mexican flavors, and shrimp cocktails in martini glasses. His Mexican wine selection is broader than many of the acclaimed restaurants in Baja, boasting producers from Paso Robles, Burgundy, Mendoza, and, of course, Valle de Guadalupe. Plates come with vegetable garnishes from a bygone era, and enchiladas are dressed in a lattice of cream, with matchstick-cut radishes neatly arranged on top.

As the city welcomes a new breed of Mexican American chef, there's no one to follow in Roberto's footsteps, except maybe Danny Godinez of Orange County's Anepalco's Café, and making a regular pilgrimage to Babita is a requirement for all Mexican food devotees. Roberto's career has encompassed the passing of the baton from maître d' to chef, as well as the transition from French cuisine to modern Mexican American. As L.A.'s Eurocentric culinary past fades away, it is becoming apparent that the city's future is being made by Mexican chefs like Roberto—El Capitano—a man who has steered us toward an appreciation of Mexican cuisine as among the best in the world.

CRAB HUARACHE ON CACTUS PADDLE

Roberto Berrelleza, Babita Mexicuisine

There may be no more noble and nutritious ingredient in Mexican cuisine than the nopal, or cactus paddle, and it holds a celebrated place among L.A.'s top Mexican chefs. In this dish, a street food classic, the huarache, gets the Babita treatment with a cactus paddle in place of the traditional sandal-shape masa boat, and it's topped with crab instead of squash blossoms or huitlacoche. Enjoy this dish with a Mexican white wine (Roberto has an extensive list from Baja California) for an elevated antojito experience.

Makes 2 huaraches

1 tablespoon plus 1 teaspoon vegetable oil,
   plus more
2 teaspoons red wine vinegar
Sea salt to taste
2 nopales (cactus paddles), washed and
   patted dry
¼ cup refried black beans (*see recipe page 65*)
½ cup finely shredded lettuce
6 ounces lump crab meat, cooked
Salsa Mexicana (*recipe follows*)
¼ cup crema mexicana
Pinch of chopped cilantro, for garnish

In a small bowl, briskly whisk together 1 tablespoon plus 1 teaspoon vegetable oil and vinegar and add salt to taste. Set the vinaigrette aside.

   Heat a grill or cast-iron skillet over medium-high heat. Rub cactus paddles lightly with vegetable oil, apply a pinch of salt to each side, and cook until tender, 8 to 10 minutes. Arrange each cactus paddle on a plate and apply a thin spread of refried black beans, then layer each with half the lettuce and crab. Sprinkle vinaigrette on the crab and add an even layer of Salsa Mexicana. Spoon some crema on top and garnish with cilantro.

Right: Roberto likes to serve his soups half and half—here he pairs the payaya soup with a cilantro soup.

SALSA MEXICANA

⅓ cup diced tomato
⅓ cup diced onion
⅓ cup diced jalapeño chiles

⅓ cup finely chopped cilantro
Juice of 2 key limes
Sea salt to taste

In a nonreactive bowl, gently mix all the ingredients. Transfer to a container with a lid, cover, and keep in the refrigerator; the salsa will keep for a week or so.

PAPAYA CREAM SOUP
Roberto Berrelleza, Babita Mexicuisine

In Mexico, the grand masters of Mexican haute cuisine have made way for modernist chefs using Mexican techniques and ingredients. But in L.A.'s San Gabriel Valley, Roberto Berrelleza is keeping classic haute

Mexican flavors alive. This style of soup was a typical starter in Mexico City's fine dining restaurants, marrying French technique with Mexican flavors—in this case, papaya. I always order the soup of the day at Babita, not for nostalgia's sake, but because, as is the case with this one, they are simply delicious.

Makes eight 1-cup servings

1 papaya, about 3 to 4 pounds, peeled and
  cut into chunks
½ carrot, peeled and cut into chunks
¼ cup Sofrito (*recipe follows*)

½ cup sugar
5 cups chicken stock
1 cup half and half
Sea salt and white pepper to taste

Preheat the oven to 450°. Wrap papaya and carrot in aluminum foil with a tight seal and roast in the oven until both ingredients are cooked through, about 30 minutes.

In a medium saucepan, combine papaya, carrot, Sofrito, sugar, and chicken stock. Bring to a gentle boil and cook for 10 minutes, stirring occasionally. Pour soup into a blender, blend for a minute, and then pour through a strainer back into the saucepan. Whisk in half and half and return the soup to a gentle boil for another 5 minutes. Season with salt and pepper to taste and serve.

SOFRITO

This flavor base is useful for many soups, stews, and sauces. Consider doubling the recipe to keep more on hand.

2 tablespoons vegetable oil
½ onion, diced
½ stick celery, diced
½ green bell pepper, diced
1 garlic clove, minced

Pinch of thyme
Pinch of oregano
1 bay leaf
½ cup white wine

Set a medium saucepan over medium heat and add oil, onion, celery, bell pepper, garlic, thyme, oregano, and bay leaf. Cook, stirring, until onion turns translucent, about 5 minutes. Add wine, increase heat to simmer briskly, and cook until the sauce reduces, about 5 minutes. Discard bay leaf. This will keep in the refrigerator, covered, for a week or more.

ALTA CALIFORNIA CUISINE

An original, modern Mexican American cuisine is emerging in Los Angeles, one that is seeing innovative pocho chefs elevating tacos, tamales, pozoles, and ceviches to fine-dining status. Angelenos who have grown up eating the best Mexican food in the US are found buying foie gras tacos from a truck in front of Silver Lake Wine to pair with a flight of sauvignon blanc, or brunching on wild boar chilaquiles, or slurping up bowls of fideos served with queso fresco and cilantro chutney. Alta California cuisine is a colorful, boldly flavorful blend of Mexican and California cuisines, with international influences for good measure, and with a devotion to the wealth of fresh, seasonal ingredients that Californians take for granted.

PEOPLE

Josh Gil 114

Carlos Salgado 118

Ray Garcia 122

Eduardo Ruiz 128

Wes Avila 132

Ricardo Diaz 136

Josef Centeno 140

Thomas Ortega 144

Andrew Lujan 148

RECIPES

Seafood Cocktail 116

  Charred Habanero Salsa 117

  Cocktail Sauce 117

Scallops in Aguachile 120

Corn & Summer Squash Tamales 124

  Corn-Poblano Sauce 125

  Masa 125

Wild Boar Chilaquiles 130

  Homemade Tortilla Chips 131

Tuna Tostada 134

  Raw Tomatillo Salsa 135

Fideos 139

Steak Fajitas 142

Puerto Nuevo Lobster 146

  Roasted Tomatillo Salsa 147

Squash Tacos with Pumpkin Seeds & Avocado-Tomatillo Salsa 150

JOSH GIL

Outsiders, even professional food journalists, often misunderstand Los Angeles. To get great food, a devoted L.A. diner travels from the San Gabriel Valley to Huntington Park and from to Venice to Downtown L.A.. These journeys across our urban sprawl are frustrating and sometimes overwhelming for visitors used to exploring the world's other great food cities without a car. That was the challenge met by the writers of the first L.A. *Michelin Guide* in 2008, which was panned by locals who found it limited in scope and in understanding of the vast city.

One of the few places to earn a Michelin star in that first edition was Joe's Restaurant in Venice, owned by chef Joe Miller. The very week after the book came out, while L.A. was droning on about whether the *Michelin Guide* was finished in this town or if the town even cared, Joe's chef de cuisine, Josh Gil, quit. The Michelin star awarded to this (now-shuttered) Abbott Kinney institution had been achieved with a Mexican American chef de cuisine, who was running an all-Oaxaqueño crew.

L.A.'s rejection of the *Michelin Guide* caused the once-infallible name in guidebooks to leave town within a few years. Meanwhile, Josh Gil was rebelling against the ironed tablecloths and fine china so cherished by the esteemed French tire peddlers. After earning one of the highest honors in the culinary world, he chose to retreat from a business and a customer base that respected neither Mexican cuisine nor the army of Mexican line cooks that assembled the plates being placed on pedestals.

But Josh Gil had always been an iconoclast. Born in Riverside, he lived in Rosarito, Baja California, from the age of seven to fifteen, where his Sonoran mother and Sinaloan father had roots; Sinaloans and Sonorans comprise the largest groups that have settled in Baja. In Baja, he was surrounded by seafood, from fish tacos to ceviches with geoduck clams and sea urchin. Artisans shucked fresh and luxurious oysters, and nearby Puerto Nuevo and Popotla made a trade in deep-fried lobster and spider crabs, while an emerging wine region northeast of Ensenada was accompanying a local modern Mexican-food revolution.

When his family moved back to Riverside, Josh joined his mother in working at a care facility for mentally disabled women. That's where his cooking career began, making salads, main courses, and even a baked potato with vegetarian chorizo, inspired by his grandmother. By twenty-two, he was married, had survived a short-lived career as a punk musician, and had landed the chef de cuisine spot at the Ontario Hilton.

For the next few years, he bounced around various hotels, sharpening his skills by doing massive banquets and spending his free time reading about the philosophies of Adrià, Escoffier, Brillat-Savarin, and Waters. All the while, he was pissing off his bosses, once failing a drug test for weed and always challenging his critics in the kitchen. "I was a sous chef at the restaurant in the Hotel Laguna, and my boss didn't feel that Chinese or Mexican food had any place in his dining room," he says. "So I'd trick him and wouldn't tell him until later that a dish was Mexican. He was always making racist cracks, typical kitchen bullshit, so I constantly pushed his buttons." The first boss who learned how to deal with Josh was Joe Miller, who let him do his thing. A general manager at another place where Josh had worked once asked Joe, "How do you control this guy?" He answered, "You don't!"

After he left Joe's, Josh worked at pop-ups, sold foie gras, did a stint at the Inn of the Seventh Ray (where he made the owner's head explode by cooking their macrobiotic food to punk music instead of Zamfir or Kenny G), and laid low for a while at the Jonathan Club. He wasn't just burned out by the establishment, he was also going through a divorce and needed time with his kids, and he had to find a way to cook the way he wanted without having to listen to "Songbird." So he and a friend, Daniel Snukal, formed a pop-up called the Supper Liberation Front, giving the incorrigible chefs a place where they could just cook.

At Santa Monica's Utopia in 2012, they were given an unusual condition for their event. "The owner said, 'You can pop-up here, but why don't you buy the place?' " recalls Josh. "After smoking about five joints, we said, 'What the fuck are we going to put in here?' We'd been thinking of a Japadogs concept. But we were spending all our time going to Ricky's Fish Tacos and 4 Vientos, and in a brief moment of sobriety it dawned on us that there was nothing like that on our side of town." Josh had also been cooking in Mexico City and Baja California, which was pulling him back to his early teens and his love for Mexican beach cuisine. "We came in the day before opening and put the menu together: fish and shrimp tacos, tostadas, a cauliflower ceviche, and a few other ceviches." This was a cuisine he'd grown up with, both in Baja and L.A.

Tacos Punta Cabras, named after a surf break in Baja, opened with the same counterculture attitude that drove them out of the fine dining world, and without PR (they both hated food writers and PR companies) to help bring in customers, they mostly played chess that week; that Friday, Daniel bailed to go play soccer. "By the time he got back, we were crushed," he says. "*Eater LA* had come in a day before and had written about us, followed by *LA Weekly*. So I'm starting to think maybe food writers aren't so bad."

Tacos Punta Cabras has since added seafood cocktails, and it offers such specials as miso beef tostadas, mapo tofu tacos, and roasted pumpkin tacos with vadouvan and Sichuan French beans, all of which reflect the growing aesthetic of Alta California cuisine.

Perhaps it's because he's matured, or maybe it's because he and Daniel are cooking Mexican food their way—but whatever the reason, Josh is finally in a comfortable space and is even enjoying his success. It's a sign that L.A. is entering a new age for Mexican American chefs, one in which cooking high-quality Mexican food has become the new criterion for mainstream acceptance.

SEAFOOD COCKTAIL
Josh Gil, Tacos Punta Cabras

Josh Gil spent a good part of his childhood in northern Mexico, where the finest seafood products are served at carretas (seafood carts) and mariquerias (seafood restaurants). These dishes became part of the Baja chef culture that emerged around 2001. Josh honors the Baja tradition with flavors from Alta California in this refreshing, contemporary seafood cocktail, which goes well with a nice lager and friends.

Serves 8 to 10

5 Persian cucumbers, diced
Sea salt and freshly ground black pepper
1 pound peeled shrimp (31-40)
1 pound bay scallops
1 small red onion, diced
3 small roma tomatoes, diced
2 bunches cilantro, minced

6 avocados, diced
Charred Habanero Salsa (*recipe follows*)
Cocktail Sauce (*recipe follows*)
8 to 10 key limes
Salsa Huichol, for garnish
14.7-ounce box Saladitas crackers or
    14-ounce package tostadas

First, cure the cucumbers. Place diced cucumbers in a bowl and cover with salt for 15 minutes, then rinse and gently press out the excess liquid, completely removing the salt. Set aside until needed.

Prepare an ice bath and set aside. Place 3 quarts water and 2 teaspoons salt in a pot and bring it to a mild boil. Poach the shrimp until cooked through, 30 seconds to 1 minute, then shock in the ice bath. Repeat for scallops. Reserve the cooking liquid and chill until needed.

In a nonreactive bowl, combine cooked shellfish, onion, tomatoes, cucumbers, and cilantro. Stir to combine. Place eight to ten 12-ounce serving glasses on a table. Fill each glass ¾ full with the seafood and vegetable mixture. Add ½ teaspoon each salt and pepper, applying an even layer of seasoning over the mixture, then cover with 2 heaping tablespoons diced avocado and 1 to 3 tablespoons Charred Habanero Salsa, depending on your heat tolerance (the salsa is fiery!).

Pour in reserved cooled seafood stock about ½ inch above the seafood cocktail and gently fold with a spoon. Add 2 tablespoons Cocktail Sauce, folding it in until the cocktail is evenly colored by the sauce, then squeeze in the juice of 1 lime. Have a bottle of Salsa Huichol handy to add more heat, and extra Cocktail Sauce if you want a little more sweetness. Use the Saladitas as mini-tostadas for spooning on the mixture, which is the best way to eat a Mexican seafood cocktail.

CHARRED HABANERO SALSA

2 teaspoons grapeseed oil
10 habanero chiles
Juice of 2 oranges (about ½ cup)
Juice of 4 Persian limes (about ½ cup)
1 teaspoon dried oregano
Sea salt to taste

Heat a skillet over high heat. Add oil and habaneros and cook, stirring, until they are evenly charred. Remove from skillet and chop off the stems. Place chiles, orange juice, lime juice, and oregano into blender or food processor and mix well on a high setting. Taste and add salt as desired. This will keep in the refrigerator for a week.

COCKTAIL SAUCE

3 cups ketchup
1 cup fish sauce
1 cup fresh lime juice
1 tablespoon sea salt

Stir together ketchup, fish sauce, lime juice, and salt in a bowl until it is well blended. Set aside until needed. This will keep in the refrigerator for a week.

CARLOS SALGADO

Traditional corn tortillas, the foundation of Mexican cuisine, have seen increased industrialization for years on both sides of the border, due to large-scale production by the Gruma Corporation (Mission, Maseca, and Guerrero brands), which uses commodity corn and is now pushing for GMO corn. In 2015, the Colectivo Mexicano de Cocina, an association of Mexican chefs, started resisting this, and now, north of the Rio Grande, chef and maize activist Carlos Salgado has declared an all-out war.

Carlos grew up helping out at La Siesta, his family's Mexican American restaurant in the city of Orange. It's a crunchy-taco-and-burrito joint that's been around since 1986, long enough to have melted a sufficient amount of yellow cheese to cover the Channel Islands. "I worked as a dishwasher, fried chips, folded crispy beef tacos—our best seller—and worked the front," he says. But Carlos was a curious and ambitious soul who became fascinated with the world of tech startups while attending community college, which led to San Francisco in 2001, where he landed a job with a video-game company.

He settled in the Mission, which was in the throes of gentrification, but its historic Mexican and Central American restaurants still filled the air with the scent of fresh corn tortillas, chicharrones, and pan dulce. "Being a Mexican American kid in the Mission rekindled my love for Mexican food," he says. "When I visited the La Palma Tortilleria and La Victoria bakery, I'd always grab carnitas, tortillas, locally made queso fresco, corn, and cal."

Cal, or calcium hydroxide, is mixed with water to convert corn into hominy, a process called nixtamalization that was invented in Mesoamerica thousands of years ago. This was how Carlos learned to make tortillas, as well as pozole, sopes, and perfect quesadillas, with Harold McGee's great book *On Food and Cooking* guiding each fold of the tortilla.

This inspired him to study cooking at the California College of the Arts, after which came an internship at Winterland under Vernon Morales, an early practitioner of modernist techniques. "They asked if I had experience in pastry," says Carlos. "I lied and was offered the job, so I read books, researched, and began my career as a pastry chef." Hungry for knowledge, a bespectacled Carlos then hiked over to Daniel Patterson's celebrated Coi on a rare hot day and wouldn't take no for answer. "I straddled the savory and pastry line," he says. "The experience was very broad, and it was a time of reinventing myself."

Daniel Patterson was a great mentor, and they earned two Michelin stars during Carlos's time at Coi, raising his profile and making him prime for the picking. None other than James Syhabout poached him to be opening pastry chef at Commis, where he fell in love with his girlfriend, Emily (they are now married), and matured as a chef at what today is a Michelin two-star restaurant. "I used to think cooking was all about techniques and ideas," he says, "but thanks to Emily and James, I realized I was cooking for people." He further concluded that Mexican food was in his blood, and it was what he loved to cook for himself.

Then an urgent call came. Carlos's grandmother was in poor health, forcing his parents to attend to her in Mexico, and they needed Carlos to help out at La Siesta. He moved back to Orange County, and soon his parents returned with his ailing grandmother in tow. He loved talking with her about food, especially her recipes, like mole dulce (sweet mole), a dish from her hometown, Tonalá, Jalisco's artisanal center on the outskirts of Guadalajara.

Turning his worry for her into action, Carlos opened his own modern Mexican food truck, using the La Siesta kitchen as the commissary. He named the truck Taco Maria after his mom, both grandmothers, and most of his aunts—a roaming tribute to the women who had fed and cared for him. In 2011, he hit the streets of Costa Mesa, serving bone marrow quesadillas, fish al pastor, and chicken mole tacos. "It was Mexican flavors driven by the California cuisine I'd learned from my mentors," he says. "I was trying to operate on their same level in terms of a love for simple, rustic foods." The Taco Maria truck wasn't another odd attempt to elevate Mexican cuisine—it came from the heart, with respect for his family's roots. In 2013, it became a proper restaurant inside Costa Mesa's upscale SoCo Collection mall. Other than a quick trip to Mexico City to see and taste what its exciting young chefs were doing, Carlos's prima materia would be California ingredients, the California melting pot, and the Mexican American perspective.

Alta California cuisine at Taco Maria means sunchokes with chorizo, abalone pozole, and duck with a mole sweetened by dates, all paired with wines from Santa Barbara County, the Willamette Valley, and the Loire. Unlike the fancy Mexican restaurants created by non-Latinos who boast of having better products and technical superiority but mostly achieve bland cultural appropriation, Carlos has focused on traditional Mexican methods to produce his very modern cuisine. "Our food doesn't need anyone to rescue it," he says.

The strong-willed chef took the tortilla-making skills he'd gained in San Francisco to the next level, learning how to make them from Mexican heirloom corn (brought in by Masienda) cooked in a traditional alkaline solution. He has initiated a new age of corn tortillas in L.A., where masa is now ground with non-GMO heirloom corn varietals—the kind of leadership that won him the *Food & Wine* Best New Chef award in 2015.

Before chefs like Carlos, the city's major food events, like the Los Angeles Food & Wine Festival, snubbed Mexican chefs. But now, Taco Maria serves Alta California bites that are bringing prestige and excitement to the country's food scene. Even Mexico's star chefs, like Enrique Olvera, are taking notice—Carlos recently cooked with Enrique at Manta in Cabo San Lucas.

As the stature of Mexican food continues to grow in this country, Carlos's journey has come full circle—like the tortilla, which represents his ideology and heritage, and which serves as a vessel for a cuisine that is now being returned to its owners.

SCALLOPS IN AGUACHILE

Carlos Salgado, Taco Maria

In the Pacific states of Sinaloa and Nayarit, aguachile de callo de hacha (scallops in chile water) is the Rolls Royce of ceviche dishes, in which the luxurious scallop is bathed in a fiery solution of lime and fresh green chile. Traditionally, only two vegetables—cucumber and purple onion—serve as a garnish, so the dish shines with just a finish of sea salt and pepper. Not surprisingly, the elegantly simple aguachile has become a favorite of modern Mexican chefs like Carlos Salgado, who is slowly evolving the flavors in his versions.

TWO NOTES: Poached shrimp, sliced in half down the middle, will substitute beautifully for the scallops if you prefer that. And if you can't find anise hyssop leaves (they are uncommon), fresh mint makes a delicious variation.

Serves 6

6 large Hokkaido scallops

2 Persian cucumbers

2 teaspoons sugar, plus more if needed

30 anise hyssop leaves, plus a few more
   (with flower) for garnish

1 cup grapeseed oil

2 serrano chiles, stemmed

¾ cup Bearss or key lime juice

¼ cup Meyer lemon juice

¼ cup mandarin orange juice

Sea salt to taste

Place 6 flat bowls in the refrigerator or freezer to chill.

Remove the foot from each scallop, rinse under cold water, and pat dry. With the flat side of the meat down, slice each scallop in half, making two disks, then dice both into ½-inch pieces. Place in a container lined with a clean linen towel and refrigerate until needed.

Wash and dry the cucumbers and chop into ½-inch pieces, leaving the skin on. Place into a bowl, add 2 teaspoons sugar, and macerate until the sugar dissolves and the cucumber softens and releases its liquid. Set aside in the refrigerator to keep cold.

Prepare an ice water bath and, separately, bring a pot of water to a roiling boil. Add a pinch of salt. Drop in the anise hyssop leaves (or mint) and blanch until they are soft, 20 to 30 seconds. Remove with a fine-mesh skimmer (called a spider) and shock the leaves in the ice water. Drain the leaves, squeezing out any excess moisture. Purée in a blender with grapeseed oil until completely smooth.

Refresh the ice water bath and have a small stainless steel bowl ready to rest in the bath. Working swiftly, pour the hyssop oil into a saucepan and quickly bring to a simmer. After just a few seconds, remove from the heat and pour into the metal bowl over the ice bath. Stir to cool quickly. When cooled, strain through a coffee filter to obtain a clear, green-tinted aromatic oil.

Rinse chiles and drain them well. Place chiles and the 3 citrus juices into a blender and mix on high until fully combined. Add salt to taste. If the liquid is too spicy, add a bit of sugar to tone it down. Strain the aguachile liquid into a nonreactive container.

To serve, divide chopped scallops among the 6 chilled bowls. Spoon some macerated cucumber around the scallops, being sure to include some of the cucumber liquid. Spoon a few tablespoons of aguachile liquid around the scallops, then spoon a few beads of hyssop oil into the liquid. Finish by tearing some hyssop leaves and spreading the sweet flowers over the bowl. Garnish the scallops with a few grains of coarse salt and serve immediately.

RAY GARCIA

The irony was not lost on Ray Garcia that he'd won *Esquire*'s Chef of the Year award in 2015 for Broken Spanish by cooking food based on his childhood as an L.A. pocho, instead of the elite French-inspired cuisine that usually receives such an honor. He'd grown up poor—but rich in food memories—in the Latino barrios of Cypress Park and in the San Fernando/ Pacoima area. "There were always chiles roasting, and nopales, menudo, tamales, braised meats, and salsas," says Ray. "Most of the protein we had were beans, bologna—yes, bologna tacos are a thing for us pochos—hot dogs, and sometimes ground meat."

While he was at San Fernando High School, he worked as a busboy at a Tex-Mex place called Chuy's in Glendale. ("Tex-Mex" is a legit regional cuisine from Texas, but in the US it's often used as a derogatory term to describe inauthentic Mexican food.) There was something about working in restaurants that attracted Ray as he transitioned from high school to college, but it certainly wasn't the money.

While pursuing a BA in both political science and business economics, Ray chose campus food service for his work-study job, making pizzas and sandwiches and serving as a cashier. But there was no money in food, and he was looking to leave his impoverished past behind, so he looked into joining the FBI. "I was a twenty-year-old intern at the Department of Justice, assisting prosecutors at the US Attorney's Office," he says. But food was always on his mind, distracting him from his pragmatic ambitions. If he were to pursue cooking, however, it would have to be a cuisine that's respected—not Mexican. Mexicans were lavaplatos or line cooks, not chefs at top restaurants.

"I took a year off to decide what I wanted to do—I took the LSAT and got jobs waiting tables at Olive Garden and Gladstone's, among other places," he says. Meanwhile, he also enrolled at the Southern California School of the Culinary Arts. Talk about hedging your bets. It all came to a screeching halt one evening when a sleep-deprived Ray, who was interning for long hours at the Belvedere inside the Peninsula Hotel while attending culinary school, was involved in a costly auto accident.

Any thoughts of making a splash in the culinary world were blunted by shattered glass and twisted metal. He had to make money to pay off the debt caused by the accident, so he took a job at the Belvedere as an executive sous chef while also managing the hotel's six food outlets. "It taught me the business side of cooking, the art of fine dining, and the challenges of dealing with a particular kind of guest," says Ray with a grin. It was good work, but he was now even further from doing the kind of cooking that inspired him, at a time when the flavors of his ancestors were at last gaining prominence. That would all change at his next job.

In 2008, Ray was the opening executive chef at Fig at the luxurious Fairmont Miramar Hotel in Santa Monica, also managing the hotel's seven food-service operations. It's where Angelenos first discovered his cooking, and where he emerged as a StarChefs Rising Star—and where we first got a taste of his chilaquiles. "Once I learned the basics, I started to branch out, both as a chef and as a person," he says. That meant upscale chilaquiles, huevos rancheros, and a parade of tacos. He added Mexican flavors because he could, unsure of how westsiders would take to chilaquiles served on the same menu as duck magret and tuna niçoise. To his surprise, they became popular, and people started dropping major cash for a romantic oceanview suite with tacos and a nice country wine from the Côtes-de-Gascogne. Admirers (including myself) began rooting for Ray to open his own place.

A turning point came in 2013 at Cochon 555, the renowned annual pork battle waged between the country's best chefs to promote heritage pig producers. He decided to make everything Mexican; he and his crew stayed up late cleaning out Pelon Pelon Rico (a popular Mexican candy) push-ups and filling them with tamarind pork in a fortified glaze for dessert. Ray was connecting with his memories, and it felt amazing to kick some ass with Mexican food. "Note to self," he said back then, "my next restaurant has to be Mexican." He won Cochon 555 that year and the next before retiring from that competition—so as not to be a hog, I suppose. In his last week at Fig, he served a small group of friends and supporters a menu that would later become the inspiration for Broken Spanish.

In 2015, Ray opened Broken Spanish and Broken Spanish (B.S.) Taqueria, adding a powerful voice to the Alta California culinary movement, where bologna tacos on heirloom blue corn tortillas with dots of lardo, lamb neck tamales, and bread smeared with foie gras—a savory version of rebanadas de mantequilla (a traditional sweet bread)—are sketches of Chicano technique in an overture for an original cuisine.

Like his Alta California peers, Ray cooks food that is anchored to a place, Los Angeles, where Mexican American traditions run deep, fresh ingredients are plentiful, and multiculturalism challenges our palates. As he says, "When you can connect with your food in that way, it transcends any style or technique."

CORN & SUMMER SQUASH TAMALES

Ray Garcia, Broken Spanish & B.S. Taqueria

"It hadn't occurred to me to try to change the tamal until chef Guillermo Gonzalez of Pangea was in my kitchen cooking for an event when we first opened," says Ray Garcia. Inspired by one of modern Mexican cuisine's founding fathers, Ray had the confidence to use his chef skills to create a few fine-dining tamales for Broken Spanish, including this sweet California-style tamal that pairs well with white wine.

Makes 25 to 30 tamales

30 dried corn husks
2¼ pounds summer squash
3 large onions
12 to 15 serrano chiles
Vegetable oil

6 cups fresh sweet corn kernels (about 8 ears)
6 cups heavy cream
Sea salt

Place dried corn husks in an 8-quart pot or very large bowl and cover completely with hot water. Make sure the husks stay submerged for about an hour. This process can be done 1 day ahead. Refrigerate the husks in the soaking liquid until you are ready to make the tamales.

Chop squash and onions into small pieces, about ½ inch thick. You should have roughly twice as much squash (about 8 cups) as onions (4 cups). De-stem and slice enough serrano chiles into rings to equal roughly 2 cups. Heat a thin layer of vegetable oil in a large Dutch oven or other heavy-bottomed pot over low heat. Add the chopped squash, onion, serrano rings, and corn kernels, and cook until onions are translucent and squash begins to soften, stirring occasionally, about 5 minutes.

Pour cream into the pan, bring to a simmer, reduce heat to low, and cook, stirring occasionally, until the squash has completely broken down and the cream thickens slightly, 15 to 20 minutes. Season with salt to taste, remove from the heat, and set aside to cool. When cooled, the consistency should be that of mashed potatoes.

You'll have about 4 cups filling left over, which you can use for a second batch of tamales, or refrigerate or freeze to use later.

CORN-POBLANO SAUCE

Vegetable oil
1 medium onion, diced
3 medium poblano chiles, diced

6 cups fresh sweet corn kernels (about 8 ears)
1 pound unsalted butter, cut into chunks
Sea salt

Heat a thin layer of vegetable oil in a large Dutch oven or other heavy-bottomed enamel or stainless steel pot over medium-low heat. When the oil is shimmering, add the diced onions, poblanos, and corn kernels. Cook slowly, stirring often, until the onions are translucent but not browned, about 5 minutes.

Carefully transfer the hot vegetables to a blender. Partially cover the blender (so no hot liquid escapes) and blend the vegetables on low speed, slowly, adding the unsalted butter little by little. The sauce should gradually emulsify. Season the sauce with salt to taste. The sauce can be made up to 3 days ahead and gently rewarmed over low heat before serving.

MASA

3 pounds prepared (storebought) corn masa
3 teaspoons baking powder

3 teaspoons sea salt
1¾ cups vegetable oil

Combine the masa, baking powder, and salt in a stand mixer (divide the amounts evenly and mix in batches) fitted with a paddle attachment. Wrap a kitchen towel over the top of the stand mixer to cover the mixer bowl (this helps keep the dry ingredients from flying out). Turn the mixer to low speed and with the mixer running, slowly pour in the oil.

Once the oil is well incorporated, mix the dough on medium speed until the masa is soft and moist, 1 to 2 minutes longer. If the dough still appears dry, add a small amount of water, 1 tablespoon at a time.

PREPARING THE TAMALES

Soaked corn husks
Masa
1½ cups grated queso Oaxaca or Chihuahua
Corn & Summer Squash Filling

To serve:
Corn-Poblano Sauce
1 bunch chives, chopped (optional)
1 to 2 small summer squash, shaved in thin strips (optional)

Strain the husks from the soaking liquid and rinse well under running water. Shake off the excess water and lay the husks out flat on a table or large work surface that has been lined with plastic wrap.

Scoop about ¼ cup of masa onto the center of each husk. Use a rubber spatula to spread the masa into a smooth rectangle about 4 inches long by 3 inches wide. Leave a gap of about 1 inch between the masa and both ends of the husk.

Sprinkle about 3 tablespoons of grated cheese all over the masa in each husk. Spoon about 3 table-spoons of the squash filling directly in the center of a tamal. The vegetable filling should be placed in a straight, vertical line of even thickness so the tamales can be rolled properly.

To roll a tamal, fold the filled husk over itself vertically so the masa completely covers the filling in the shape of a log. Fold in the husks lengthwise over the filling then fold the unfilled bottom toward the top into a rectangular shape

Work quickly so that the masa and filling stay in place. Set up a large pot or pasta pot with a steamer insert, or use a vaporera (special pot for tamales). Add water to just below the steamer insert line so that water doesn't touch the tamales. Stack the tamales in an upright position, to make sure that they stay closed, around the perimeter of the pot. Work quickly so that the masa and filling stay in place, making several circular rows working from the outside in.

Cover the tamales with a damp kitchen towel, place the lid on the pot, and steam the tamales over medium heat for about 1 hour, or until the masa sets. If the masa is set, the tamales will be firm and easily peel away from the husk. If not, continue to cook, checking every 15 minutes. Throughout the cooking process, be sure to add more water to the steamer whenever needed.

Remove the tamale-filled steamer insert from the pot. Allow the tamales to cool slightly (leave them in the steamer insert) and serve, or cool completely and refrigerate for up to 1 week.

To serve, place the tamales on serving plates and open the husks so the masa is exposed. Rewarm the corn-poblano sauce, if needed, and spoon the sauce over the tamales. Sprinkle each tamal with a little chopped chives and thinly shaved squash, if you'd like.

EDUARDO RUIZ

In the summer of 2012, Eduardo Ruiz was cooking at Corazón de Tierra, a Latin America's 50 Best restaurant, during the wine harvest festival set in Baja's Valle de Guadalupe. Chef Diego Hernandez had enlisted a who's who of modern Mexican cuisine—Enrique Olvera, Guillermo Gonzalez, Edgar Nuñez, and others—to celebrate the anniversary of his renowned Mexican farm-to-table restaurant. Olvera and Gonzalez, the founding fathers of modern Mexican cuisine, cooked alongside their former student, Diego Hernandez, who represented a new breed of Mexican chef, a product of Mexican technique and Mexican masters. These new chefs have turned away from European influences to embrace the ingredients and dishes of their regions, a philosophy that's also followed by a handful of young Mexican American chefs like Eduardo, whose recipes are shaped by the terroir of South Gate, East L.A., and Pacoima.

Cooking has always been essential to Eduardo. "My family's life was centered in the kitchen, and when I wasn't separating beans or chopping cilantro, my mom and I were watching cooking shows," he says. He grew up making the tasty foods of his Salvadoran and Mexican heritage: fideos, barbacoa made by his grandfather, menudo, pozole, and some really good refried beans. And pan con pavo, a Salvadoran turkey sandwich that would later become a signature dish, was a favorite of his father's.

As a teenager, Eduardo worked as a dishwasher and busser at one of the OG Mexican grills in Covina, La Parrillada, a family restaurant popular for fajitas as well as for steaming molcajetes overflowing with chicken, beef, cactus, and panela cheese, and hissing braziers covered with the grilled meats, chiles, and vegetables of a Mexican backyard cookout. Ruiz worked his way up to assistant manager before heading to Pasadena's Cordon Bleu to become a chef.

After working at Animal, Vinny Dotolo and Jon Shook's L.A. institution, Eduardo immersed himself in Baja California, where Mexico's wine country was making headlines for both its world-class street food and its chefs, who were changing the way people perceived Mexican dining. Eduardo wanted to do the same for Los Angeles, where contemporary Mexican cuisine was incubating among a few chefs and restaurateurs.

"I was checking out stands in Ensenada like La Guerrerense and El Güero," he says, "and I was getting ready to open my first restaurant." Called Corazón y Miel, it was a joint venture created with Travis Hoffacker and Eduardo's childhood friend Robin Chopra, located in Bell, a Latino neighborhood that had no trend-setting restaurants. "When we opened, I didn't think elevated Mexican food would be accepted, so I went pan-Latin," says Eduardo. Watching the emergence of such pocho contemporaries as Carlos Salgado and Wes Avila has since inspired Eduardo to move his cooking toward his Mexican flavors.

Corazón y Miel was a hit with critics for its bold, original approach to modern Latin flavors, but it struggled to reach Bell's Mexican American residents; he had to give away food at first to get people to stay. "Bacon dates were the gateway dish—they changed people's perception and the locals dug it," he says. The place was a collaborative effort between first-time restaurateurs; the ceviches, for instance, reflected Eduardo's memories of eating Peruvian cuisine at Robin's house when they were kids. Eduardo's take on his dad's Salvadoran pan con pavo, using a whole turkey leg and a quick, herbed slaw, captured the admiration of fans, as did his chilaquiles with wild boar. But Corazón y Miel was just too far away from its core audience, and while it had received strong support from Bell, it was not sustainable, so in 2016, the partners decided to close it. "Bell really served us, but we didn't really serve Bell," Eduardo says.

Eduardo has since opened a gastropub in Long Beach called Public Beer and Wine Shop, serving craft beers with refried beans and cheese tacos, Baja-inspired crudos, and some of the small plates that had been popular at Corazón y Miel. At this writing, he is the chef for the Blvd745 restaurant group. "It will keep me busy and allow me time to travel and do some R&D," he says, "and in a couple of years I'll open up something closer to L.A." In its three-year run, Corazón y Miel moved modern Mexican cuisine in the US forward, in the process establishing Eduardo as a principal player.

One breakout dish at a time, Eduardo Ruiz and a small group of chefs have begun to change the narrative about serious Mexican American cooking, right here in Mexican food's first American city. During his last year at Corazón y Miel, he sent his most valuable chef, another Latino, to stage in Mexico. It's not lost on him that the Mexicans and Central Americans who cook our food are rarely given opportunities for growth. Eduardo will surely open another restaurant of his own, but more importantly, he is committed to ensuring that more Latino chefs are ready for the challenge. With Angelenos like Eduardo Ruiz, Alta California cuisine is here to stay.

WILD BOAR CHILAQUILES

Eduardo Ruiz

Every state in Mexico has its own style of chilaquiles, and in the hip dining centers and new food truck lots across Mexico, chilaquiles are becoming more popular than ever. At his former restaurant Corazón y Miel, Eduardo Ruiz made a fully loaded version with boar, a nod to pre-Hispanic Mexico and L.A.'s growing fascination with wild game. You'll find wild boar at specialty meat markets and online; it typically comes cubed, although you can also find it ground. Substitute pork butt if you prefer.

For Ruiz, chilaquiles is a plato casero (homemade plate), usually garnished with whatever you have in the fridge. At Corazón y Miel he'd top it with diced jicama, heirloom cherry tomatoes, and scallions tossed in lemon juice and olive oil, and then he'd finish it with a fried egg.

Serves 6

2 pounds wild boar

½ ounce (about 1 medium) dried ancho or pasilla chile, deseeded, seeds reserved

2 ounces (7 to 8) dried guajillo chiles, deseeded, seeds reserved

Canola or other vegetable oil, for cooking

½ medium onion, thinly sliced

3 jalapeños, sliced, seeds included

5 cloves garlic, minced

¼ cup red wine or apple cider vinegar

1 teaspoon cumin powder

1 teaspoon smoked paprika

Mexican sea salt (Sal de San Felipe or Sal de Colima), to taste

1 pound fresh tortilla chips, from a tortilleria or homemade (see sidebar)

To garnish: a few tablespoons each of queso fresco (or queso cotija) and crema mexicana

Optional garnishes: diced jicama, sliced radishes, sliced scallions, diced red or white onion, chopped lettuce, sliced or diced tomato, chopped cilantro, sliced jalapeños

Set up hand meat grinder or stand mixer with meat grinder attachment. (Make sure to follow equipment directions.) It's best to place the auger/worm and body into the freezer for at least one hour before setting up the grinder; cold metal cuts meat more effectively.

Cut boar into 1½-inch cubes and put it in the freezer until really cold, at least 30 minutes. When very firm, pass wild boar cubes through the grinder, using a medium die. If you like a finer grind, pass the meat through twice. Place ground meat in a plastic or glass container, cover, and set aside in the refrigerator.

To prepare the sauce, rinse dried, deseeded chiles in cold water, place in a small pot, and cover completely with water. Bring to a boil, reduce to a steady simmer, and cook until chiles are soft, about 15 minutes. Remove chiles with slotted spoon, set aside, and reserve water.

While chiles are cooking, place a heavy-bottomed frying pan over medium heat. Add a little oil (about 2 tablespoons), heat for a moment, and sauté onion and jalapeños, stirring occasionally, until onions begin to caramelize, 8 to 10 minutes. Stir in garlic and cook for another minute or two. Set mixture aside in a bowl.

Toast 1 teaspoon of reserved chile seeds in a hot cast-iron skillet over medium heat for 1 minute, moving them around with a wooden spoon after 30 seconds to toast evenly, and set aside.

Place onion mixture, cooked chiles, vinegar, cumin, paprika, and toasted chile seeds (more or less to taste) into a blender and purée until smooth. Add about half of the reserved chile water and blend; if you like a more liquid salsa, add more of the chile water. Taste and add salt if you think it needs it. Leave salsa in blender until needed.

Heat a large frying pan or medium pot over medium heat. Swirl in more oil (about 2 tablespoons) and quickly add the ground boar. Cook 2 to 3 minutes without stirring to brown the bottom, then stir and cook until the opposite side is browned, about 2 more minutes. Add sauce from the blender and cook with the boar until sauce is heated through and flavors combine, about 5 minutes, stirring occasionally. Add chips and toss until all are evenly coated with sauce. Plate immediately.

To garnish, sprinkle a layer of crumbled queso fresco or queso cotija over chilaquiles and then spoon crema on top, spreading it all over the dish. Add any or all of the optional vegetable garnishes that you like.

HOMEMADE TORTILLA CHIPS

There's nothing like fresh, homemade tortilla chips. Plus, they're the perfect use for day-old corn tortillas. Slice your tortillas into quarters or sixths, depending on their size. Line 2 baking sheets with paper towels. Heat 2 cups canola oil in a large cast-iron skillet (or enough oil to fully cover the tortillas, depending on the size of your pan) until shimmering but not smoking. It's best to use a thermometer—the oil should be 350 degrees. Add cut tortillas in a single layer, so they are not touching, and fry until lightly browned and crisp, about 1 minute. Remove with slotted spatula to the paper towels. Continue the process until complete, making the sure the oil temperature stays steady. Toss the warm chips with sea salt to taste.

WES AVILA

After a chef competition I attended in 2012, Walter Manzke of Republique, one of the competitors, introduced me to his friend Wes Avila, who was about to open a taqueria. "Great, what kind of tacos are you doing?" I asked. Wes replied, "I'm going to make the best tacos in L.A."

I dismissed that first encounter with Wes as hot air, and I thought, "Who the fuck is this guy?" And then I went to his taco cart when he opened in front of Handsome Coffee Roasters in downtown's Arts District. Not only did Guerrilla Tacos emerge as arguably the best taco vendor in town, but Wes had also become the first Alta California chef to form his own genre. Like linebacker Lawrence Taylor, Steve Jobs, and Charlie Parker, Wes changed the rules of the game.

This seems an unlikely transformation for a Teamster turned classically trained chef. Wes was born and raised in Pico Rivera, a predominately Latino L.A. suburb, where he discovered his love of food through home-cooked meals. "Ever since I was about eleven, I was really into food, especially seafood," Wes says, and he got plenty of that while visiting relatives in Baja California. At home, there were albondigas, chiles rellenos, and chilaquiles, as well as the Americanized flavors that had found their way into Mexican American households. "We'd take those Reyna flour tortillas and fill them with fried bologna and chips cooked in pato sauce—they were like chilaquiles burritos," he says.

When Wes's mom passed away in 1995, his father, a Durango native, assumed kitchen duties for the family, imparting an education in northwest Mexican grub. "He'd do a badass menudo with like everything in it—pig parts and cow parts—and a dish he called huevos batidos," recalls Wes. "He'd scramble eggs with onions in lard until they were browned and puffed up, like a Yorkshire pudding, all poofy and spongy; sometimes when I'm feeling nostalgic, I'll throw it on the menu."

Wes's father made sure his children were well educated so they wouldn't have to do the back-breaking work he'd endured, so Wes's next move didn't go over so well. "At nineteen, I told my dad, who was a Teamster at a box company, that I wanted to get into the union. He wasn't happy about that." But for the next six years, Wes drove a forklift and did heavy lifting; it was hard, but he was doing pretty well for a kid from Pico Rivera. Still, it was a dead-end job. "I wasn't happy, and I was doing a lot of drugs and drinking. I did the kind of fucked-up work you have to do while waiting for someone to die just so you can move up."

By the age of twenty-five he'd had enough, and when his future wife decided to go for her PhD in psychology, he was inspired to go back to school as well. He enrolled at Le Cordon Bleu, because he'd always liked to cook. "The recruiter asked why I wanted to be a chef, and I said because I didn't want to do blue-collar work," says Wes. " 'But this *is* blue collar work,' he said. 'No offense, but I've done blue-collar work and this isn't shit. I'll show you blue-collar work.' " Indeed, as much he hated his old job, the work ethic it required of him helped push him to conquer the world of fine dining.

After a year and a half of school, Wes was drawn north to Carmel-by-the-Sea after reading about chef Walter Manzke, who was known for his discipline, precision, and work ethic. After a single meal, he knew he had to work there. "I did a stage, and then he brought me on full-time," says Wes. "We did thirty to forty covers a night—it was the shit, the shit. That place was a temple. I learned a lot, and Walter projected me onto a path toward fine dining." He returned to L.A. after a year, but work on the line at top-drawer restaurants doesn't pay the bills, so he took a job at the Palos Verdes Country Club, furthering his knowledge of French cuisine, in a profession where Mexicans were no more than line cooks. He wasn't exempt from the casual racism found in Eurocentric kitchens, where Mexicans were called paisas, wetbacks, and lavaplatos (ironically, those same kitchens often placed recipes by Latino cooks on their menus, un-credited.)

That changed after Wes began cooking for Gary Menes and attended the esteemed Le Centre de Formation d'Alain Ducasse, a school for the chefs who work in Alan Ducasse's restaurants. "There I learned the classics, good ingredients, and all about cooking in Europe. It helped to get past the discrimination from other cooks," he says. "After they heard I went there, they'd cut that shit out."

He continued to work at Menes's pop-ups and events for his chef mentors, but it was his Bacchanalian taquizas for family meals that revealed Wes's brilliance. "Gary always had amazing wines left over, gamays and pinots. When the crew needed something substantial, I'd make tacos and pair them with the wine."

He wasn't getting enough work, however, and he needed to make money, so in 2012, he bought a taco cart at the Mercado Olympic for $150 so he could make tacos for a party. They were a big hit, which gave him the confidence to hit the streets. "I called up Handsome Roasters in the Arts District and asked if I could park in front of their place," says Wes. And that's how Guerrilla Tacos started—an unlicensed cart bringing fine dining to the curb. His spot in front of L.A.'s premier third-wave coffee shop (where he still parks) earned critical acclaim and devotees who came for innovative tacos filled with pork jowl, pig's ears, market vegetables, and seafood purchased directly from divers. Guerrilla Tacos was just hitting its stride when a rat shut the whole thing down.

"I remember it vividly—it was August of 2013, and I'd been planning a trip to Chicago," Wes says. The police came and told him that there'd been a call and he was done street vending. The cart was unlicensed by a city that's world famous for its street food—yet has one of the most hostile policies toward street vending. "I was so stressed out that I got shingles while I was in Chicago," he says. "But I got back to L.A. on the following Monday, went to La Raza, came up with the money, and took care of all the permits in one day for my first truck. Whoever did that pushed me to get a truck because, fuck them."

From Cielito Lindo's taquitos on Olvera Street in the 1930s to the rise of the catering truck, and from King Taco's taco wagon in 1974 to Roy Choi's global food truck revolution, Guerrilla Tacos—the liberator of the taco in America—was the next logical piece in the complex and flavorful puzzle that is street food in L.A. Behind Wes's charm and affability lies a fierce insurgency against the paradigm of fine dining. Whether they're filled with foie gras, sweet potatoes, sea urchin, brisket, or his dad's huevos batidos, the point of Guerrilla's tacos is to show that the taco is worthy of the finest tables in the world, even if the table isn't present.

As it turns out, Wes was a little short-sighted in saying he was going to make the best tacos in L.A. He's actually earned an international reputation for his ingenious street-food creations. He's rejected offers to expand his menu or open a more formal modern Mexican restaurant, because the greatest triumph has been for a kid from Pico Rivera to stand among the greatest chefs in the world with a singular, humble dish in hand. Not bad for a taquero.

TUNA TOSTADA
Wes Avila, Guerrilla Tacos

There's always excitement in the air around the Guerrilla truck, a sense of culinary adventure. Will you have one of the tacos that made Wes Avila famous? Or a quesadilla or open-faced torta? Or maybe a seafood cocktail followed by a tostada? So many extraordinary options.

This recipe holds all the elements of Alta California cuisine on one crisp tostada base: the multicultural ingredients, the Baja style of plating, the locally sourced ingredients. It's a delicious, compact snack, the perfect appetizer for a summer backyard party.

Makes 5 tostadas

2 tablespoons white soy sauce or tamari
1 tablespoon furikake, plus more for garnish
1 tablespoon yuzu juice
1 tablespoon rice vinegar
1 pound ahi tuna

5 tostadas
1 avocado, sliced
$2/3$ cup Raw Tomatillo Salsa (*recipe follows*)
1 sea urchin, shucked and chopped
$1/2$ cup chopped micro chives, for garnish

HOW TO SLICE AN AVOCADO

This is an essential skill for every cook, and indeed, every Californian. Cut an avocado in half lengthwise and remove the pit by striking the pit with the blade of a knife, then turning it clockwise. It should come out easily. Hold one half of the avocado in your palm and carve out medium slices using a large metal serving spoon by turning the spoon down toward your body. Slide the spoon along the skin to pull out the slices.

Combine soy sauce, furikake, yuzu juice, and rice vinegar in a small bowl and set aside. This is the white miso.

Slice tuna into 1-inch cubes and place in a nonreactive bowl. Pour over the white miso and toss gently to combine. Spoon tuna carefully and evenly on each tostada. Top each with 3 slices avocado, and spoon about 2 tablespoons Raw Tomatillo Salsa on top (adjust according to your heat preference).

Garnish with a couple of pieces of sea urchin and cover the tostada evenly with furikake and chives.

RAW TOMATILLO SALSA

Makes 2½ cups

8 tomatillos
3 serrano chiles, stems discarded
½ cup white vinegar

4 cloves garlic, peeled
1 cup chopped cilantro
Sea salt to taste

Wash tomatillos in lukewarm water, pat dry, peel, and cut in half. Place in a food processor, add chiles, and pulse on medium-high until roughly chopped. Add vinegar, garlic, cilantro, and salt and process on high until just combined, about 45 seconds (any longer and the heat from the machine will start to cook the salsa and change the flavor). Taste and add more salt if needed. Serve immediately, or store in a covered container in the refrigerator for up to a week.

RICARDO DIAZ

In the summer of 2009, at Altamed's East L.A. Meets Napa—a healthcare fundraiser that paired Chicano restaurants from the eastside with Napa Valley wineries that had a Latino winemaker or Latino owners—it was clear that the stage was set for the dawn of L.A.'s Mexican American chef culture. Burritos, tamales, ceviches, and dishes that riffed on Mexican traditions were served with wine by Gustavo Thrace Wines, Ceja Vineyards, and Alex Sotelo Cellars. John Sedlar was there, as were other Mexican American chefs, all of whom were preparing a style of high-end Mexican cuisine that seemed to have materialized overnight—unless, of course, you'd been paying attention to what Ricardo Díaz had been doing for some time.

That year, Ricardo had launched Cook's Tortas (his first restaurant, Dorados, was also featured at the event). He was the first to blend the traditions of Mexico with the dialect of pocho gastronomy, and this is where the story of Alta California cuisine begins.

Ricardo grew up in the business as part of the family behind one of L.A.'s quintessential Mexican American chains, El 7 Mares, founded by his uncle in 1974. It brought a style of Mexican Pacific-coast seafood to L.A.'s barrios. "Back then, Latinos got their paychecks on Friday and stayed in the 'hood to avoid deportation—that was before Reagan's amnesty," says Ricardo. "They'd spend their paychecks feasting on oysters and ceviche." His family lived in East L.A. and Huntington Park before finally settling in Mexican American suburbia: Whittier. Originally from Jerez, Zacatecas (the hometown of many prominent L.A. Mexicanos), his grandfather had come to the US as part of the bracero program in the '50s and '60s, later settling in East L.A. and bringing his son, Ricardo's father.

His grandfather and father had partnered in a restaurant serving guisados, where nine-year-old Ricardo did prep in the mornings and on weekends during the summer, until Ricardo's uncle enlisted his grandfather to help him open El 7 Mares, which counted twenty-six locations at the height of its success. "From sixteen on, I did various jobs there: busboy, server, and line cook," he says. In 1989, he joined his father full-time at Gems of the Sea, an offshoot of El 7 Mares, and he was charged with importing fish to supply the rapidly expanding mariscos empire. By 2000, he was doing large-scale importing and had grown the business by 300 percent, but moving up in a family business means having to wait, and many times, tradition—not merit—dictates who gets more authority. By now he'd earned a business degree, but, having hit a dead end at Gems, he slowly drifted into the background, later extricating himself from the family business entirely to focus on cooking.

Ricardo had always felt at home in the kitchen, creating his first recipe at the age of ten. "It was fried octopus in a spicy remoulade, although I didn't find out until years later that it was a remoulade," he says. After perfecting ceviches to serve at his first restaurant, Dorado's, he tackled the torta, and it was at his new place, Cook's Tortas, that he really found his culinary voice, breaking from tradition and using quality local ingredients with Mexican American flair. "I didn't set out at first to do tortas," he says. "I wanted to make food that I actually wanted to eat, and I was thinking of a sandwich shop of some sort, but all of my recipes were Latino." He developed his own bread by experimenting for two months and eventually settling on a ciabatta-style bun for his tortas, which were layered with fillings like beef tongue, grilled vegetables, and spicy chicken.

At Cook's, Ricardo—who'd never felt bound by tradition and in fact found authenticity to be ridiculous—had created a restaurant that was as much a part of the L.A. landscape as Mozza or Animal. At Guisados in Boyle Heights, which serves tacos filled with stews (guisados) and braises, he once again showed a knack for developing a Mexican cuisine that's more East L.A. than any other style found in Mexico, if unintentionally. "I thought, why not concentrate on guisados?" he says. "There was no competition for that kind of food in Boyle Heights." The stews were based on regional dishes: cochinita pibil from the Yucatán, Pueblan mole, and northern Mexican–style succotash. Guisados was Ricardo's biggest hit to date, even though he's no longer a part of the growing chain (partner Armando de La Torre now owns the small chain).

By thirty-five, Ricardo had moved on from El 7 Mares, left Cook's to his ex-wife, and parted ways with Guisados, but his best was yet to come: Bizarra Capital (2011), Colonia Tacos Guisados (2013), and Colonia Publica (2015), a build-your-own fideos shop and craft beer bar where micheladas are made with IPAs. His fideos come with ingredients that any Mexican grandmother would approve of—queso fresco, avocado, a splash of sour cream—but also things that might make your abuela not talk to you for a week, like plantains, spinach, and cilantro chutney. At Colonia Tacos Guisados, you can get tacos of fried cauliflower, pork, and pumpkin, as well as tesmole, a southern Mexican dish. "Bizarra is a vision of Mexican food with lots of styles," says Ricardo. And it's all found in Whittier, otherwise known as the Mexican American Pasadena.

Ricardo can't help but cook with chiles, moles, and tortillas, but he's not interested in talking down to the Chicano community or pandering to stereotypes with big hats and mariachis. He cooks the way he wants, but with respect for his 'hood, having served L.A.'s barrios for decades. He's the Thomas Paine of Alta Californian cuisine. Like Paine, his approach is accessible. "The Mexican American community deserves better," he says. "They deserve good ingredients. And better beer." And that's just common sense.

FIDEOS

Ricardo Diaz, Colonia Publica

Fideos are a Mexican noodle staple served in every household, but Ricardo Diaz has turned the dish into a concept that's pure Alta California—at Colonia Publica in Whittier, he gives the same attention to fideos as other restaurants give to ramen or mole. His versions often feature a dozen or so add-ons, from such traditional Mexican ones as avocado and queso fresco to such pocho favorites as eggs and mango chutney. His aren't your grandmother's fideos (flavored by Knorr), which always blew you away with how good that could be, but they're great in their own right. This recipe is his modern classic fideos, which you can customize with whatever you fancy, including such proteins as shrimp, chorizo, and tofu.

Note that fideos are widely available in markets, but if you can't find them, vermicelli will work.

Serves 4

1 tablespoon extra-virgin olive oil
1 package (7 ounces) fideos
1 pound whole tomatoes
4 cloves garlic, minced
1 medium onion, chopped
1 teaspoon ground cumin
¼ teaspoon ground oregano
1 serrano chile (or jalapeño for mild)

Sea salt and freshly ground black pepper to taste
¼ cup chopped cilantro
2 tablespoons vinegar
7 cups chicken or vegetable stock
1 avocado, diced
Chicharrón, for garnish
1 lime, sliced

Place a large skillet over medium heat, add olive oil, and sauté the fideos, stirring constantly to avoid burning, until the pasta is lightly browned, 3 to 4 minutes. Remove the pasta from the skillet and set aside.

In the same skillet, add a little more oil and char the tomatoes on all sides. Place toasted tomatoes into the bowl of a food processor and add garlic, onion, cumin, oregano, chile, salt, pepper, cilantro, vinegar, and 2 cups of the stock and process until combined. Pour mixture into a stockpot, stir in remaining stock, add fideos, and bring to a boil. Reduce heat and simmer until the pasta is cooked, 8 to 10 minutes. Taste and salt and pepper if needed.

Serve the fideos in bowls and garnish with avocado and about 2 tablespoons of crumbled chicharrón. Add a slice of lime on the lip of the bowl for squeezing in some acid.

JOSEF CENTENO

When it comes to Mexican cuisine, what is considered authentic or regional is a riddle wrapped up in an enigma and stuffed inside a burrito. In L.A., calling something "Tex-Mex" has been a way to scapegoat it for being part of the watering down of the city's Mexican cuisine, even though L.A. has had very little true Tex-Mex cuisine. It is a regional Mexican American cuisine from, of course, Texas, and it deserves respect.

In fact, Tex-Mex cuisine has given L.A. one of its best chefs: Josef Centeno, the owner/chef of Bäco Mercat, Bar Amá, Orsa and Winston, and PYT. Born and raised in San Antonio, this tejano is one of the city's defining chefs. Because of him, saying "Tex-Mex" should no longer be a slur.

Two of Josef's grandparents fled the revolution in Mexico; others were descendants of people who'd left Ireland because of the great potato famine, settling into the land of barbecue, Selena, and rodeos. Their grandson was weaned on puffy tacos, fideos, flour tortillas, and fajitas from Taco Cabana, where his great-grandfather supplied skirt steak. "We'd go to the tortilleria, and it wasn't unheard of to eat ten flour tortillas before we got home," he says. In high school, he washed dishes at the hippest Tex-Mex spot in town. Josef then found a job a UT Austin, where he learned the ways of queso (cheese dip), first experienced vegetarian Mexican food, and became fascinated with Jonathan Waxman's modern Southwestern dishes at the '80s restaurant sensation Jams in New York. In the '90s, he headed to New York to attend the Culinary Institute of America, where he was recruited into the kitchens of the city's white-tableclothed shrines, at a time when mastering French technique and cooking in the Big Apple was every chef's aspiration.

"I staged at Jean-Georges for six months, and then at Daniel in '95, where it was cutthroat under Alex Lee, an old-guard chef," he says. "That really shaped me into a much stronger chef." He continued to build up his French credentials at La Côte Basque and Les Célébrités, where he stayed until 1999. What really commanded his attention, though, were vegetables; he was an ace with maximizing the flavors and colors of California's harvest, so he headed to the Bay Area, he says, "to get closer to the produce."

"My whole view of food had been classical and traditional—now, it was all about using minimal technique and fewer ingredients," says Josef. "Knowing the taste of English peas, and how to use herbs and acid." He landed his dream job as sous chef under David Kinch at Sent Sovi, and then became the chef de cuisine at Kinch's Manresa, a legendary restaurant in Los Gatos. At Manresa, all the walls came down, and Kinch encouraged him to cook the way he wanted.

Focus is a natural gift of this proud introvert, who once described himself on a *Chef's Night Out* episode as "being less interesting than the lake the cameraman was fixated on." Josef comes alive when talking about food, and his passion is infectious; it's an obsession that's made his original approach to cooking possible. "I was putting together an arsenal of flavors," he says, his culinary codex based on French, Basque, Japanese, and San Antonio traditions, sometimes more imagined than experienced. "When I finally went to San Sebastían, I realized that my flavors were wrong," he says. While his exposure to true Basque cooking had been limited until that trip, his Tex-Mex inclination was automatic. "One time I started to create a dish," he says, "and I realized I was actually making a pico de gallo."

After leaving Manresa, the avid surfer spent some time enjoying the waves in Santa Cruz. It was time for him to open his own place, but he didn't want to go back to New York or Texas, and he didn't think the Hollywood scene was for him. He took a job at Aubergine in Newport Beach, which kept him close to the waves, and from there went to Meson G, where he introduced L.A. to the bäco. A little later, when running the kitchen at Opus, he had an epiphany. He saw that his niche would lie between ethnic joints and expense-account restaurants, a sort of stripped-down version of fine dining; he was now ready to open his own place and easily procured the funds. And then the 2008 financial crisis touched down, causing his investors to pull out of the deal.

While skateboarding in Echo Park, the unemployed chef glided past what would eventually become Lot 1 Cafe, where he would further develop his bäco concept—and then, just as he once again dazzled critics and customers, he walked away. After some time off, he came back strong at the Lazy Ox, where he gathered his team and ideas for the iconic Bäco Mercat, which he opened in 2011. His Japanese and Italian proclivities then spawned downtown's Orsa & Winston. Ledlow (2014) is a salute to American cuisine, and most recently, PYT (2016) is the realization of his love affair with vegetables.

Still, when Josef and his girlfriend grab dinner to go, it's usually from Bar Amá, the restaurant that most represents who he is as a chef: his playful riffs on popular foods, his masterful ability to dance between the refined and the primitive, and his love for Tex-Mex, which is his muse. Bar Amá serves fajitas, dried mole eggplant, and enchiladas with wild mushrooms and leeks. There's also a super nacho hour and a gourmet take on a Taco Bell dish called the queso-rito, as well as several dishes attributed to Amá, a delicious roundup of a tejano chef's journey home.

Josef has the distinction of being L.A.'s best, most prolific, and most original chef, and his eccentric cuisines are now in vogue. "Food in L.A. in the last five years has turned upside down," says Josef, "and people are more educated because of the internet." He is a James Beard–nominated Mexican American chef, a tejano, and a marquee talent in Los Angeles, and we are very happy to blame all that on Tex-Mex.

STEAK FAJITAS
Josef Centeno, Bäco Mercat & Bar Amá

This dish goes back to Josef's childhood, reflecting the multicultural flavors of Tex-Mex cuisine—fajitas, a beloved and oft-ridiculed dish that is not much different from its Mexican relatives, the discada and the alambre. The main difference is that fajitas are more about fine cuts of steak than the bacon, hot dogs, chopped meat, and chorizos you'll see in Chihuahua, Coahuila, and Nuevo León, and the alambres of Central and Southern Mexico that are mixed with melted cheese. Discadas and alambres are served in tacos, but fajitas are a big Texas meal served on sizzling hot skillets. This is Josef's L.A. version of the dish, served on a regular plate—no pyrotechnics here.

Serves 2 to 3

¼ cup Worcestershire sauce
⅛ teaspoon chile powder
⅛ teaspoon smoked paprika
⅛ teaspoon freshly ground black pepper
⅛ teaspoon granulated garlic powder
1 tablespoon coffee grounds (preferably fresh)
1½ teaspoons brown sugar
⅛ teaspoon kosher salt

¾ pound skirt steak, trimmed
¼ cabbage (wedge)
Vegetable oil for cooking
½ white onion, julienned
2 poblano chiles, stemmed, membranes removed, seeded (seeds reserved), and julienned
6 flour tortillas

At least 2 hours before cooking, place Worcestershire, chile powder, paprika, pepper, garlic powder, coffee grounds, brown sugar, and salt in container with a lid. Stir to mix well. Add steak to the container and make sure marinade coats the meat evenly. Seal container and set aside in the refrigerator to marinate.

Prepare a grill or cast-iron skillet set to high heat and cook steak for 2 minutes on each side for medium rare. Transfer to a cutting board and let it rest for about 5 minutes. If using a barbecue grill, lay down a piece of aluminum foil so the cabbage doesn't fall through the grates. Rub cabbage wedge with oil and grill until it gets good grill marks, about 5 minutes. Move to cooler side of grill and continue cooking cabbage until it is cooked through, about another 5 minutes.

Put a skillet over high heat, pour in about 1½ tablespoons oil, and sauté the onions, chiles, and a pinch of the chile seeds, stirring frequently, for 3 to 4 minutes. Remove skillet from the heat.

Slice steak in thin strips, cutting against the grain. Toss steak in the skillet with the sautéed vegetables and give the mixture a quick stir. Arrange immediately on a plate with the grilled cabbage wedge and warmed flour tortillas. Serve with Mexican rice and beans if you like.

THOMAS ORTEGA

When speaking about his father, thirty-eight-year-old chef Tommy Ortega (complete with tattooed forearms, black-rimmed glasses, and a salt-and-pepper goatee) gets choked up and has to pause. "I get emotional when I think about my dad." After he gains his composure, he presses on, telling the story in a benumbed tone that gradually regains its vitality. Tommy's father, Ernest, was raised by the state until a friend's parents in East L.A. took him in. He didn't see many prospects for himself, and a disproportionate number of Latinos were being drafted from barrios like Boyle Heights and Lincoln Heights—so rather than wait, he volunteered to fight in Vietnam.

Mexican Americans were sent directly to the front lines, dying at twice the rate of their white counterparts, with no relief from deferments, as access to college was financially out of reach for most of them. But still, many Chicanos in the barrio viewed service as a path to acceptance. Ernest survived a tour and came back to L.A. He met Rosemary, whose own ambitions made him believe in himself, giving him a sense of belonging that the Army never did. He became an L.A. County Sheriff, while Rosemary found work as an auditor for the Pacific Stock Exchange. "Growing up, Mexican food was all I knew—tortillas made from scratch, chile colorado, and always a pot of beans," Tommy says. "Until we got older, when you had to either cook for yourself or eat a TV dinner." The hard-working couple had bought a house in Cerritos, hoping their children would succeed in that thriving town, but Tommy was too busy brawling, drinking, and getting faded to listen to his parents.

At sixteen, he got a job at a red-sauce Italian restaurant as a busboy and pizza delivery guy, working for an old Italian lady who thought it odd that he liked being in the kitchen. He earnestly inserted himself into the kitchen, making pizzas, sauces, and chicken parmigiana, and his boss encouraged him to go to culinary school. "I didn't even know what culinary school was," he says. He was nervous about the future, but he couldn't stop thinking about cooking, so he asked his dad to support him and tour the California School of Culinary Arts. For pochos, the dilemma illuminated by Abraham Quintanilla Jr.'s monologue in *Selena* manifests itself in disengagement—Tommy's father made it okay for him to unlock the key to the outside world, to become a chef.

Tommy's first real education came when he interned at Spago. "After that internship, around 1998, I ended up at Water Grill," he says. "I didn't even know what good restaurants were." The food and kitchens at Spago and the Water Grill blew him away, but there was something beyond the spectacle that rang familiar: the closeness found within a tight-knit kitchen crew. "I loved the feeling of doing a ten-hour shift and getting a beer at the end," he says. For Mexican Americans who grow up with a strong sense of family, the bonds forged during dinner rush and over late-night vices have an appeal that conjures up Sunday cookouts at your tio's with menudo, chelas, and some affectionate hazing.

His training continued at Aubergine and the Four Seasons in Newport Beach and the Dakota in San Diego. He was earning his reputation as a chef but dealing with a kitchen culture that has long valued Latinos as hard working but is dismissive of their cuisine. "Over the years, a lot of white chefs called me 'paisa,'" he says. (Meaning "cowboy," it's used among friends in the Mexican community, especially people from Sinaloa, but it's highly offensive coming from someone outside the culture.) "They were used to us being dishwashers and prep. Today, I employ about ninety-five percent Latinos. Oaxacans are monsters in the kitchen."

At this stage, Tommy really wanted his own restaurant, where he could serve the kind of food that people love to eat every day. He thought about Mexican food, of course, but he knew he'd be breaking new ground—his vision of refined Mexican cuisine then had the freshness, color, and vibrancy found in Mexico along with a Southern California sensibility, which placed him in a small group of Alta California pioneers. When he opened Ortega 120 in Redondo Beach in 2008, he decided to deploy a Mexican version of the Trojan horse to get things going—the burrito. "I threw it out as bait," he says. "I figured then I could get them to try the rest of the menu," which includes fancy nachos with a béchamel sauce, steak frites tacos—not at all strange if you've ever had tacos with french fries in Mexico City—and baby back ribs in mole. It was a struggle to find customers; non-Latino diners were unwilling to pay for medium-priced Mexican food, and unaccommodating pochos decried the innovation as inauthentic. "At one point I was in deep trouble and didn't have any money to keep it open," he says. "But then Irene Virbila did a good review in the *Los Angeles Times*, and the next day we were packed. From that weekend on, we became a destination."

Encouraged and more mature in his convictions, Tommy looked homeward to Cerritos and opened Amor y Tacos, boldly serving tater tots in mole, Doritos chilaquiles, and a Doyer dog (Dodger dog) dressed with chile colorado and crumbled chicharrón. It's the ultimate pocho taqueria, where Angelenos order tacos before their main course. In 2016 he opened Playa Amor, overlooking a pond at the Marketplace Long Beach. It marked a personal journey back to his family's roots in Baja California, showcasing local seafood, with Puerto Nuevo–style lobster at the center of the menu.

With three successful restaurants under his belt, the former scrapper from Cerritos is now a veterano of the Alta California movement. Tommy took a gamble on Mexican cuisine his way and won, in defiance of the status quo, which says that Mexican food in America should be cheap or just like your abuela made it. With each new place, Tommy raises the bar, and for his chefs, his 'hood, and his heritage, he's still in the fight.

PUERTO NUEVO LOBSTER

Thomas Ortega, Playa Amor

If you're Mexican American, there are a few destinations involving seafood that are likely to be etched into your memory, including weekends at the seafood markets in San Pedro for fried fish and oysters and trips down to Puerto Nuevo for Baja-style lobster served with beans, rice, and flour tortillas. When Thomas opened Playa Amor, one of the must-have dishes was a California version of Puerto Nuevo–style lobster—a tribute to his own memories of visiting Baja as a kid.

Serves 2

6 quarts heavily salted water (water should taste
   like the ocean)
Mixed fresh herbs: a sprig each of thyme, parsley,
   cilantro, or similar
1 bay leaf
10 black peppercorns
1 tablespoon fennel seeds

1 tablespoon coriander seeds
Two 1¼-pound Maine or spiny lobsters (preferably
   Maine, which are firmer and sweeter), or
   substitute tails (thawed if frozen)
1 cup clarified butter, unsalted
Sea salt to taste
Roasted Tomatillo Salsa (*recipe follows*)

Bring salted water to a boil in medium stockpot. Add mixed herbs, bay leaf, peppercorns, fennel seeds, and coriander seeds. Keep the court bouillon, or flavorful blanching stock, at a low boil while you prep the lobsters.

If working with live lobsters, use the tip of a knife to pierce each at the split behind the eyes, then separate the claws. (If using only tails, leave them whole.) Prepare an ice bath in a bowl big enough to fit 2 lobsters.

To blanch the lobsters, use tongs to carefully slide 1 lobster body and claws (or tails) into boiling court bouillon. After precisely 2 minutes (set a timer), remove the larger piece (lobster tail and body) and place it in the ice bath. At 4 minutes, transfer the claws to the ice bath. Repeat with the second lobster.

Once the lobsters have cooled, split the tails and bodies lengthwise down the middle with a sharp knife or kitchen scissors so they open like a book. Remove any eggs (delicious—save them if you'd like). Bring a griddle or grill to high heat, and brush the lobster tail meat with clarified butter. Then, place the tails directly on the hot griddle or grill for 2 to 3 minutes, cut side down, until meat is golden brown and caramelized. Remove and set aside. Grill the claws for another 2 to 3 minutes, flipping every so often. Crack the claws with a lobster cracker or meat mallet prior to serving.

To serve, arrange 2 lobster halves per plate with the open sides exposed and the claws alongside (provide a lobster cracker for the claws). Fill a small dish with warm clarified butter for dipping. To complete the dish, add refried beans, high-quality flour tortillas from a tortilleria, and Roasted Tomatillo Salsa.

ROASTED TOMATILLO SALSA

Makes about 5 cups

1 pound tomatillos (about 10 medium), husked
  and rinsed
1 small onion, sliced into thick rounds
10 cloves garlic, unpeeled

Two 7-ounce cans chipotle chiles in adobo
2 bunches cilantro
Sea salt to taste

Preheat the broiler to 450°. Arrange the tomatillos, onion, and garlic on a rimmed baking sheet, put under the broiler, and use tongs to occasionally flip the ingredients until all are soft and slightly charred, 10 to 15 minutes. Allow to cool.

Peel the broiled garlic and transfer with all the charred ingredients and any juices, along with the chipotles in adobo and cilantro, to a blender. Purée the salsa until you reach your desired texture—either a chunky or smooth salsa works fine.

Transfer the salsa to a nonreactive bowl and season to taste with salt. Cover the salsa and refrigerate until you're ready to serve.

ANDREW LUJAN

"Listen, being Mexican American is tough. Anglos jump all over you if you don't speak English perfectly. Mexicans jump all over you if you don't speak Spanish perfectly. We gotta be twice as perfect as anybody else." So said Abraham Quintanilla in *Selena* (1997), and it really hits the nail on the head. In 2016, *OC Weekly*

editor Gustavo Arellano wrote a piece called "In Defense of the Mexican American Chef, or No One Hates on Mexicans Like Mexicans" to castigate the bucket-of-crabs mindset in the Mexican American community that has dogged its culinary progress. As Quintanilla said, we get it from both sides, with sometimes the most vicious barbs coming from Mexican Americans, and those are the ones that cut the deepest.

It's the reality that Andrew Lujan and his sister, Christy, confronted when they opened Cacao Mexicatessen in 2009. "We knew that putting things like duck carnitas on the menu would get us some criticism, and that's pretty much what happened on Yelp—and everywhere else," says Andrew. Although Cacao was embraced by many pochos like myself, ones who've experienced the broad range of Mexico's regional cuisines, ingredients, and modernity, others were not so accepting. "The comments we got from our own people seemed harsher—they're the ones that hurt the most," says Andrew, who'd left a cushy job as a mortgage broker to open his restaurant.

The siblings grew up in Highland Park and Eagle Rock, where hipsters had their first encounters with taco trucks in the years before gentrification arrived. "Even though I was born in Mexicali, I grew up here and consider myself a pocho," he says. Traditional Mexican foods were standard during holidays, but usually whatever was in the fridge ended up in a tortilla, like bologna tacos with scrambled eggs. "The food we ate growing up was pure pocheria," he says with a laugh. "I'd love to romanticize about moles cooking for fifteen hours, but it was more about convenience. There were always salsas, refried beans, flour or corn tortillas, rice, and leftovers, but it was a fusion Mexican kitchen—my mom made meatloaf with jalapeños."

When Andrew and Christy were kids, their family opened Choo Choo's in Eagle Rock, a burger joint they ran for about seven years (with the kids helping out) without a hint of Mexico's flavors. Andrew later went into real estate, earning enough money to live the good life and help his sister attend the California Culinary Academy in San Francisco. After graduation, Christy cooked in Hawaii and L.A., until a hand injury from a kitchen accident put her career on hold. While she spoke of her frustration working in other people's kitchens, her brother contemplated his own abating enthusiasm for the real estate business—2007 wasn't exactly shaping up to be the greatest year for the industry.

After many long talks, Andrew and Christy decided to open a place that would help launch a new style of Mexican American cuisine in L.A., along with chef Ricardo Diaz, who had just opened Cook's Tortas. "There really wasn't much to go on back then. When I was googling modern Mexican cuisine in Los Angeles, restaurants like Border Grill, Lotería Grill, Chichén Itzá, La Serenata de Garibaldi, and La Casita were the only ones that came up," says Andrew. What he didn't see were modern Mexican-style tacos, and that's when the idea came for Cacao Mexicatessen. But they'd be entering uncharted aguas, placing themselves on the front lines of a fierce polemic debate over tacos, with both non-Latinos and pochos united against any taco over a dollar. The former were imposing their own cultural bias, and the latter were reactionary, inserting their self-serving ideals and an ignorance that's kept the Mexican community fragmented when it comes to the natural evolution of our restaurants, stands, and food trucks.

I remember hearing about Cacao before it opened, and I couldn't wait to try duck carnitas and the Baja-inspired dishes, like the tempura-battered stuffed chiles güeros and the Villas de Valle quesadilla with melted cheese and garden vegetables, which evoke a romantic trip to Mexico's Valle de Guadalupe wine country. Every week brings a taco special, some of which have become legends, like the chile güero taco topped with Santa Barbara sea urchin.

But as much as Cacao seemed a fit for L.A.'s food-obsessed, it was hit with bad reviews on Yelp, with people balking at what they perceived to be high prices. "If a taco costs five dollars, I'm going to fucking charge five dollars, we're not going to give it away," says Andrew. "These ingredients are expensive, and we use the best." At times they considered closing, but little by little came a growing list of positive reviews from critics and bloggers, and Andrew still needed to learn a few things about the business. "The L.A. restaurant community was such a big help," says Andrew. "I got advice from a few key people, and I started looking at the books, adding systems, and working to get butts in the seats. And today, you have Guerrilla, and Ray doing his thing at Broken Spanish, and Taco Maria—I told my sister that this is now a thing, and we're not alone."

Los Angeles is slowly learning what most Mexicans (in Mexico) and travelers already knew—Mexican food can have depth and range, from the stand, to the fonda, to the modern temples that have earned the cuisine an international reputation. And eight years later, Cacao Mexicatessen is going strong, having played an unsung but pivotal role in the story of Alta California cuisine, counting itself among the elite of L.A.'s taco royalty. In a taco city, there may be no greater honor.

SQUASH TACOS WITH PUMPKIN SEEDS & AVOCADO-TOMATILLO SALSA

Tacos de Calabacitas Cacao
Andrew Lujan, Cacao Mexicatessen

Each week, as I dig through my email inbox flooded with taco-related PR pitches and supplications, I see Cacao Mexicatessen's email about their taco of the week, and I want to jump in the car and head straight to Eagle Rock. This squash medley is a fresh Alta California take on traditional calabacitas or colache, made with local products and given crunch with pumpkin seeds. Make these tacos on a Saturday night and serve them with a glass of white wine for the ultimate Alta California experience.

Makes 12 tacos

Avocado-Tomatillo Salsa (*recipe follows*)
Roasted Pumpkin Seeds (*recipe follows*)
Squash Medley (*recipe follows*)
1 dozen 4-inch corn tortillas

1 cup feta cheese
1 cup micro cilantro, or finely chopped cilantro
   leaves

Prepare the salsa, pumpkin seeds, and squash first; the pumpkin seeds can be made a few days in advance, but the salsa is best if used on the day it's made.

When you're ready to assemble the tacos, heat a corn tortilla on a comal or griddle and place ⅓ cup Squash Medley in the center. Garnish with 1 tablespoon salsa, crumble a pinch of feta over the salsa so it stays on the taco, sprinkle about 8 pumpkin seeds on top, and finish with a pinch of micro cilantro. Repeat the steps to make the remaining tacos.

AVOCADO-TOMATILLO SALSA

5 tomatillos, washed and cut in half
1 serrano chile
½ clove garlic
15 sprigs cilantro, bottom of stems trimmed
2 tablespoons fresh lime juice

2 tablespoons kosher salt
1 cup water
½ small avocado
Sea salt to taste

Place tomatillos, chile, garlic, cilantro, lime juice, salt, and water into a food processor or blender and purée until smooth. Add avocado and purée until creamy, then add salt to taste. Store in the refrigerator until needed.

SQUASH MEDLEY

1 cup finely diced butternut squash
⅓ cup extra-virgin olive oil
Sea salt and freshly ground black pepper to taste

2 cups finely diced zucchini
1 ear white corn, shucked
½ small white onion, finely diced

Preheat the oven to 375°. Toss butternut squash in a bowl with 1 tablespoon olive oil and salt and pepper to taste and place on a baking sheet. Roast until tender, 7 to 9 minutes, and transfer to a separate bowl.

Place zucchini, corn, onion, and remaining olive oil in the bowl you used to toss the squash. Add salt and pepper to taste and toss everything to coat. Place mixture on baking sheet and roast until cooked through, 5 to 7 minutes. Add to the reserved squash, stir to combine, and taste, adding more salt if needed.

ROASTED PUMPKIN SEEDS

1 cup pumpkin seeds
2 tablespoons extra-virgin olive oil
½ tablespoon sea salt

Preheat the oven to 350°. Toss pumpkin seeds, olive oil, and salt in an oven-safe bowl, evenly coating the pumpkin seeds with salt and oil. Roast for 5 minutes. Remove, give the pumpkin seeds a good stir, and roast for 5 more minutes. Remove from the oven and set aside to cool. Store in an airtight container lined with paper, unrefrigerated, for up to three days.

BEBIDAS
DRINKS

There's so much more than the margarita to the L.A. Mexicano drinking scene, although there's nothing better than a well-made margarita on a hot summer night in Southern California. From the non-alcoholic (horchatas, aguas frescas), to the boozy (mezcales, craft beers), to the caffeinated (mocha mexicanos, rice and bean frappés), Mexican American culture has changed the way Los Angeles drinks.

PEOPLE

David Mora 154

Ulysses Romero 156

Cecilia Murrietta 160

RECIPES

Casa Vega Margarita 158

Michelada Verde 159

La Huatulco 162

Soledad's Tepache 163

DAVID MORA

Compared to San Diego and Northern California, L.A.'s craft beer scene was slow to develop, lagging behind Northern California and San Diego, finally picking up steam several years ago, especially in Downtown L.A. and on the city's fringes. But as the breweries fought for Angelenos' short attention span, one key market was overlooked: the Mexican American beer lover. The strength of the market was clear to me when I'd make my frequent trips to Boyle Heights institution Ramirez Liquors, where I'd prowl the overloaded refrigerators stocked with rare pale ales, stouts, and IPAs, flanked by hundreds of tequilas and mezcal, looking for a find.

Beyond the impressive selection of brews at Ramirez, Mexican Americans have had to leave the barrio to taste the latest craft beers and draft-only offerings. There's been no greater friend to Latino beerheads than Ricardo Diaz, who's been pouring top releases at his restaurants since 2012, and Eduardo Ruiz, who curates beers from top breweries both stateside and in Mexico for his gastropub, Public Beer and Wine Shop in Long Beach. But for the most part, pochos have lived in a craft beer desert that's populated by the played-out standards: Tecate, Pacifico, and, oddly enough, a very popular "Mexican" beer—Budweiser.

An IHS Global Insights study reports that by the end of 2019, Latino consumption of beer will have grown by thirty-one percent, while the non-Latino rate will only see seventeen-percent growth—but you don't need to tell David Mora that. "I'd see guys in my 'hood get their paychecks at the first of the month and immediately head over to Ramirez or Bill's in Atwater to buy a couple of craft beers," says David. "Why are Downtown L.A. and Silver Lake the only places where you can get a good beer? Why not Lincoln Heights?"

David grew up in Lincoln Heights. He turned twenty-one a year before he graduated from Gonzaga University with a business degree and, almost immediately after he could legally consume alcohol, began exploring L.A.'s craft beer haunts, including Father's Office, Barbara's, and Tony's Darts Away. On weekends, he'd hit the breweries down in San Diego and bring back growlers of various kinds of beer to share his passion with family and friends.

David was less than intrigued by the exciting world of accounting while pursuing his MBA at USC. "But I was surrounded by entrepreneurs, and they influenced me to save some money to satisfy my need," he says. With six units left to go in his MBA, he walked away so he could find the right space in which to quench his thirst and bring beer culture to the eastside. He found that space in Lincoln Heights, a place under a stay of gentrification and still within reach of his budget.

"I went looking for bars that were taverns or restaurants with beer and wine licenses and ones that weren't taking full advantage of their permits," he says. "I was rejected by everyone I approached until I got to the Torta Spot. The day I visited it was dingy, and there were only a few guys there—and then some women came in and did a lap dance for them." David was told that the owner, Amado Leal, was tired of the dim surroundings and was eager to sell, but he was in Mexico at the time. It was the perfect spot, the tortas were good, and "nobody was really doing craft beer and Mexican food together."

The Leals came in high on the sale price, but with some cajoling, Amado let David run the place with his son while he was away on business in Mexico. So armed with a Triple Tap and an Instagram account, he launched La Chuperia in January of 2015. "I called Stone Brewing, presented our liquor license, and got an IPA, an Allagash, and a Red," he says, glowing with the memory of how exciting it was. On his first night he made $90, which was enough to go buy another keg. After a little makeover, the seedy characters started to disappear, and the local press flipped out over the story of a torteria and craft beer bar in one of L.A.'s oldest Latino barrios.

The sales kept growing, and soon there were lines out the door. Seeing their moribund bar's revival, the Leals decided to keep the place and turned a cold shoulder toward David, who had nothing in writing with them. So he packed up his taps—by then he was running two triples and a single—and walked away.

The business was a failure for David, but his theory—that the Latino market would respond if given a better choice—proved true, and it was proven by an unknown Mexican American beer enthusiast. In the aftermath of this remarkable feat and swift ouster, he found investors and opened his own place, Cask and Hammer in La Habra, which is armed with thirty taps and boasts walls covered in graffiti art by Hembert Guardado. He's brought quality beer to yet another underserved, diverse area. "I've got my eye on these other 'hoods—Whittier, La Mirada, and Rowland Heights—for future brewpubs," David says. With a laugh, he adds, "People think we can't afford good beer because we're Mexican."

ULYSSES ROMERO

Some of the most promising coffees in the world are coming out of Mexico, especially Chiapas, Veracruz, Oaxaca, Jalisco, and even such little-known coffee regions as Colima. But in the true malinchista (self-hating Mexican) tradition that steers Mexicans away from their own products, it's been Los Angeles where third-wave Mexican coffee has most come into its own, not its home country. Unburdened by the snobbery of Mexico City's yuppies, Mexican American coffee aficionados like Ulysses Romero of Tierra Mia have been patiently seeking out the best beans in Latin America and turning them into exceptional coffee.

Ulysses attended UC Berkeley's Haas School of Business, where he earned a BS in business in 1999 before getting an MBA at Stanford. His education was financed by a profitable venture in corn and flour tortillas at his family's 100-employee-strong Romero's Food Products. "I swept floors and worked in shipping and receiving all through high school and college," says Ulysses. But rather than joining the family business (although he does serve on its board), he was determined to follow his own entrepreneurial path.

"I first got into coffee at Cal because I spent a lot of time in cafés—I liked the café culture," he says. It's hard to imagine that he was ever a coffee novice—his passion for every detail, from the bean to the cup, is as strong as a double-espresso slap to the synapses. After working in the corporate world, he took a job at Kéan Coffee and invested in a simple espresso machine, which he tested on his family. "They were the perfect market-research group," he says. "I was looking at Latinos, an underserved market for coffee."

In the early 2000s, Latinos living in neighborhoods like South Gate, Pico Rivera, and Lynwood were loyal consumers of Nescafé, 7-Eleven coffee, and, for the chipsters (Chicano hipsters) willing to drive out of their 'hoods for corporate coffee with free WiFi, Starbucks. It wasn't exactly a thriving coffee culture, but Ulysses saw an opportunity. He wasn't the first Latino barista to focus on Latin American products and customers—before Tierra Mia, there were such pioneers as Antigua Coffee House (2005) and Expresso Mi Cultura (1996, later becoming Sabor y Cultura in 2003)—but the success of his upscale chain of coffeehouses has firmly established the viability of the Latino coffee consumer.

With financial backing from college friends, he opened his first Tierra Mia in South Gate in 2008, staring down the worst financial crisis since the Great Depression with nerves that could only be rattled by a double mocha mexicano. "Some people said I was crazy," he says, "but I saw opportunities to get spaces at a good price." His crazy risk? To put chic coffeehouses in failed fast food locations: a former Taco Bell in Long Beach, a KFC in Pico Rivera, and a McDonald's in Huntington Park. The slowing economy gave these Latino suburbs a respite from the glut of fast food franchises and made way for Tierra Mia to thrive.

At first, Ulysses worked seven days a week, fourteen hours a day, serving the best coffee beans he could get, which were not (in those early days) from Latin America. It took seven months to break even, which finally allowed some breathing room to go find quality beans from Mexico and beyond. Armed with Latinos' gateway drug to specialty coffee, the frappé, he created coffee drinks with horchata, Mexican chocolate, and a delicious rice-and-bean mix to lure in Latino customers, whose only "fancy" coffee experiences to date had been Starbucks' Frappuccinos and McCafé's frappé mochas.

Once they were hooked, Ulysses steered his customers toward his mocha mexicano, cafecito cubano, and pour-over coffees. With the opening of a second location in Huntington Park in 2010 and yet another in Santa Fe Springs in 2011, he diversified his operation, adding a bakery and a coffee-roasting operation. Each of the early locations went through a similar struggle to bring in enough customers, but when Ulysses opened Pico Rivera in 2012, the word was out, and the café was mobbed from day one. At this writing, Tierra Mia has ten locations in the L.A. area—including a few outside the traditional Latino market, like in Downtown L.A.—and a pair of cafés in the Bay Area. At his biweekly cupping sessions, he runs through tastings of such varietals as bourboncillo from Finca Kassandra in Veracruz and yellow catui from Fazenda Beneficio in Presente do Sol, Minas Gerais, in Brazil. "We work with importers that are bringing in good product," says Ulysses with a sly smile, "but we're acquiring beans directly where there's no… well, no stepping on toes."

After a tasting of eight specialty coffees at the Silver Lake branch, my heart is racing as I look around and see the cool kids surrounding my table. It's late afternoon, and as the sharp sunlight chases us to another table, a young chipster snags our spot. The only Latinos in the place are him, me, and the beans in my cup. "We get a mixed crowd here," says Ulysses. "During the day it's more white people, but in the evenings, the Latino families come in." And family is what Tierra Mia is all about. "We made the decision not to have WiFi," he says. "Not because of the lack of turnover, but because there'd be no place for families to sit and enjoy coffee in the evenings. That's the kind of ambiance we want."

The coffee is outstanding, a fact that's underreported by food writers who tend to see Latino coffeehouses as separate from the Blue Bottles and Cognoscentis. "We need to work on getting the word out about our coffee," says Ulysses. Meanwhile, he keeps searching for better beans as the demand for his coffee grows. With Mexico's reluctance to serve its own beans and exploit its wealth of varietals, Tierra Mia and its fellow third-wave L.A. Latino coffeehouses have become the game changers for Latin American growers.

As I took a break during the course of writing this book to visit Mexico City and Veracruz, I grabbed a pour-over at Mexico City's trendy Buna 42 café in Roma Norte. All I could think of was that I couldn't wait to get back to L.A. so I could enjoy some real Mexican coffee.

CASA VEGA MARGARITA
Christy Vega Fowler, Casa Vega (*see profile page 38*)

Makes 1 cocktail

Lime wedges
Kosher salt
Ice
1½ ounces tequila añejo
1 ounce lime juice
¾ ounce Triple Sec

With a lime wedge, rub the rim of the cock-tail glass with lime juice and dip into a shallow dish of kosher salt. Fill glass will ice.

    In a shaker, add ice, tequila, lime juice, and Triple Sec, shake vigorously, and strain into salt-rimmed cocktail glass. Garnish with lime wedge.

MICHELADA VERDE
Ricardo Diaz, Colonia Publica (*see profile page 136*)

"I enjoy making this green version of michelada, be-cause it reminds me of the delicious aguachiles from Sinaloa," says Ricardo Diaz. At Ricardo's Colonia Pu-blica, the refreshing beer cocktail called the michelada is given the Alta California treatment, straying from the regional varieties and made with a craft beer in place of the more neutral-tasting national Mexican brands. Nothing could be better than a michelada with an aguachile, except maybe an aguachile in a glass.

Serves 4

2 serrano chiles
1 cup lime juice
¼ cup grapefruit juice
⅛ cup orange juice
1 tablespoon Worcestershire sauce
½ stick celery, chopped
1 cucumber, seeded and half peeled
1 teaspoon kosher salt, plus more for the glasses
4 lime wedges
Ice cubes
4 crisp lagers or wheat beers of your choice

Place chiles, juices, Worcestershire, celery, cucumber, and 1 teaspoon salt in a blender and blend on high until the mixture is even. Strain the mix through a medium mesh strainer.

Put kosher salt onto a small plate. Rub the rim of 4 tall glasses or beer steins with lime wedges and dip each into the salt. Fill each glass about halfway with ice and pour in 3 to 4 ounces of michelada mix, and then fill to the top with beer.

You'll have some beer left over, which you can add to the glass as you drink—that's the traditional way to drink micheladas.

CECILIA MURRIETTA

Not so long ago, I couldn't have imagined the agave revolution that would sweep Los Angeles in 2013. Suddenly the city was awash in the exotic spirits from Mexico's various agave regions (mezcal, raicilla, bacanora) as well as the non-agave spirit, sotol. Before 2013, Angelenos could only try these distillates at the homes of private collectors (myself included), or you could get some brands of rotgut mezcal in the States—like the dreaded Gusano Rojo that my grandfather used to bring back from Mexico. True, Del Maguey was around by the mid '90s, and I recall an evening at the old Tlapazola Grill on Gateway when the general manager gave me a tasting of mezcales from that ubiquitous US-based producer, but it wasn't enough to count for much.

The earliest mezcales marketed to Americans were highly smoked, apparently aimed at the cigar-and-Islay-Scotch set. As I later learned, however, that smoky characteristic is one of the liquor's least interesting qualities. After frequent visits to palenques (mezcal distilleries) and the famed mezcal bars of Mexico City, Guerrero, and Oaxaca, I began to long for the flavors of wild agave spirits accented by an array of local bacteria essences absorbed during open-air fermentation. Out of the blue, 2013 unleashed a band of mezcal producers who descended upon Los Angeles, including Cecilia Murrietta, a mezcal blogger turned spirits entrepreneur.

Born in Orange County, Cecilia moved back and forth between Mexico and Anaheim in her youth, making her both an outsider in the country of her birth as well as in her ancestral home—until she was seduced by the ritual, legends, and canons of mezcal. "We went to visit a friend of my brother's in Santiago Matatlán," she says. "His dad was a fifth-generation mezcal producer at the palenque where they make Casco Legendario." She was bitten by the agave bug, and for the next few years, she grew increasingly obsessed with mezcal, becoming a full-time hobbyist who had fallen in love with the spirit but didn't know what to do with that passion other than commandeer the social media accounts of a few producers. She may not have had a business yet, but before long she had a name—when a random person she met in 2009 called her La Niña del Mezcal, or the Little Mezcal Girl, it stuck.

In 2011, Cecilia headed to the Feria del Mezcal in Oaxaca. There was something magical in the air, with the mezcal industry positioning itself to make a big move into the lucrative American market, which already consumed seventy-five percent of Mexico's tequila and wanted more. Inspired but still without direction, she did some PR for mezcal brands, attended Douglas French's mezcalier program in New York, and created a mezcal blog. Back in Mexico City, she bolstered her brand by hosting mezcal tastings, chocolate pairings, and other agave-themed soirées, yet her shot glass was half full.

It had come time for Cecilia to acknowledge what everyone else around her already knew—she needed to bottle her own mezcal. "I researched, learned, registered my trademark, got my export license, and even did my own labels," she says. "And I did the whole thing without any lawyers. My mom and I even bottled my first production, almost a thousand bottles." Things were looking good for this upstart brand—until the first batch was held up in Tijuana and she discovered she owed $3,000 in federal alcohol tax and couldn't get it across the border until she paid up. It was money she didn't have.

She borrowed the money and enlisted the help of a customs broker, Robert Gallegos, who hooked her up with the Wine Care Group to get the first La Niña del Mezcal Espadin (a particular varietal of agave) into Los Angeles. She worked her way up to such top bars as Las Perlas and Guelaguetza, and then started meeting bartenders and cocktail bloggers who got her into some of the top showcases for artisanal spirits.

La Niña del Mezcal represents the true artisanal mezcal culture, which is safeguarded by zealots at the puritanical bars south of the border: that mezcal should be forty-five percent alcohol or higher; that respect must be given to the master mezcalero, agave, and process; and that mezcal outside the official region (the DO) is still legitimate. (They feel that the DO rules were made to protect the large producers.) In restaurants in Mexico City and New York, chef Enrique Olvera has stopped serving brands that don't follow that more radical definition of mezcal that promotes the master mezcalero and traditional methods over the commercial brands, an ideal that Cecilia has taken to heart.

The success of her brand has pissed off the establishment, in a patriarchal industry that doesn't accept outsiders (especially a pocha), but that isn't stopping Cecilia from enjoying this moment and expanding her portfolio to include several agave varietals and a bacanora. "I was depressed through most of high school," she says. "Mezcal has breathed life into me. I've grown into the person I was supposed to be. I've found the little girl—la niña—who can take over the world."

LA HUATULCO
Cecilia Murrieta, La Niña del Mezcal

This refreshing cocktail is named after the resort town of Huatulco, Oaxaca, near the Pacific Ocean, a special place for Cecilia Murrieta. Let this cocktail take you back to the beginning of mezcal's third wave, when young entrepreneurs like Cecilia began to craft artisanal mezcales for the US consumer, a trend that is just getting started. Trust me, it will dominate the Mexican spirit category in the coming years.

Makes 1 cocktail

La Niña del Mezcal Jamaica salt and edible flowers
   sea salt or margarita salt
1 lime
1½ ounces La Niña del Mezcal Espadin
½ ounce Aperol
¼ ounce Giffard Banane du Brésil liqueur
¼ ounce Giffard vanilla liqueur
1½ ounces fresh pineapple juice
½ ounce lime juice
1 ounce Coco Lopez coconut cream
1 ice cube
Crushed ice

Place the two salts on a small plate and stir to combine. Quarter the lime and rub a wedge around the rim of a tall Collins glass, then dip it in the salt mixture.

   Place mezcal, Aperol, liqueurs, juices, coconut cream, and ice cube in a cocktail shaker and shake vigorously for 30 seconds until the mixture is frothy. Pour into prepared glass without straining and top with crushed ice.

SOLEDAD'S TEPACHE
Soledad Lopez (*see profile page 61*)

There are many great tepaches out there, but count on the Oaxacans to deliver the most robust flavor to this fermented pineapple drink. Soledad Lopez uses a long fermentation to really bring out the true funky flavors. This is a perfect beverage for summer, a refreshing and layered potion that works great at a pool party or at a table laden with traditional Oaxacan food.

Makes 16 8-ounce drinks

1 whole pineapple, rind removed and
   cut into small chunks
2 pounds piloncillo (brown sugar cane)
10 cloves
1 stick cinnamon

5 black peppercorns
3 liters (12½ cups) water
Lime wedges, optional
Chile powder, optional
Kosher salt, optional

Purée pineapple in small batches in a blender and pour into a large glass jar. Stir in brown sugar and add cloves, cinnamon, and peppercorns. Pour in water and stir to combine.

Seal jar tightly with a lid and set to ferment in a cool, dry place with no direct sunlight for 10 days, gently stirring the mixture every 3 days to break up the brown sugar.

On the 11th day, taste and correct the flavors, adding more brown sugar if desired. Pour tepache through a strainer into another jar or pitcher for serving. Store in the refrigerator to cool, and serve cold over ice. If you like, rub the rims of the serving glasses with lime and dip into a chile powder–salt mixture for presentation and tradition.

AMBULANTES
TRUCKS & TAKEOUT

If there's one thing that defines L.A.'s food culture, it's the taco truck. What has become a national sensation—hand-painted food trucks serving everything from french toast to pho to lobster—is rooted in the taco truck that Angelenos of every ethnicity take as their birthright. Street food (ambulantes) takes various forms in Southern California: trucks, trailers, hand-wheeled carts, and sidewalk stands that can be quickly packed up and moved should pesky police officers come inquiring (unless they're hungry, in which case zoning laws be damned). You can eat magnificently in L.A. without ever cooking or setting foot inside a conventional restaurant, thanks to the people who cook at the city's countless ambulantes.

PEOPLE

Romulo "El Momo" Acosta 166

Raul Ortega 170

Maria Elena Lorenzo 174

Ricky Piña 180

RECIPES

Torta La Rusa 168

   Chipotle Cream Sauce 169

Red Aguachile Tostada 173

Pozole Blanco Guerrero Style ...176

Tamales de Pollo 178

Fish Tacos 182

   Ricky's Salsa Verde 184

   Ricky's Pico de Gallo 184

ROMULO "EL MOMO" ACOSTA

When I first moved to Los Angeles in 1995, I found carnitas in every Mexican restaurant, but it wasn't the carnitas I remembered from my seminal childhood road trip to Aguascalientes with my grandparents—the carnitas I ate from a brown paper bag with tortillas and pico de gallo. I remember falling asleep in the back seat and waking up to a still-warm, grease-soaked bag that was twisted and torn at the top, and I went right back to eating that carnitas.

My ideal of perfect carnitas—slow-cooked, confit-style pork, sweet and tender with a caramel tan—is among a handful of Mexican dishes that were etched into my memories in childhood. The stringy, bland, dry stuff I found in L.A. couldn't penetrate my bias, and even when a few solid vendors finally surfaced, I hardened my position further—enjoying carnitas would have to wait until my next trip to Mexico. It turns out that I just hadn't heard about Romulo Acosta, who's known as El Momo. He'd been making carnitas in L.A. since the mid-

1970s, decades before Mexican food became a hot topic in the United States and long before the city's food writers began to explore the specialists who were operating in the barrios.

El Momo was born in Salamanca, Guanajuato, and at just fourteen years old he was breaking down steers, pigs, and goats at a slaughterhouse while learning how to make carnitas at El Marranito. Two years later, he was manning the cazo (a large copper pot) for long hours by himself at his father's carniceria and carnitas shop, also making chorizos, chicharrones, and birria. "My dad had taught me everything he knew about making carnitas and butchery," says Momo. But he didn't see a chance for a stake in the business, so he headed to the US.

He'd learned to weld in Salamanca, a skill that got him a job at Faith Plating in Santa Monica, where he worked for the next sixteen years, with a side hustle making Salamanca-style carnitas on the weekends. "Around '75 or '76, a friend gave me a small cazo, and I started selling carnitas out of an apartment complex on 3rd and Alameda," he recalls.

Over the next decade, Momo crafted carnitas exclusively for the Mexican community, as the rest of L.A. had not been initiated into the true flavors of regional Mexican food—save for Barbara Hansen, who wrote a popular column in the late 1970s in the *Los Angeles Times* called "Border Line," showcasing Mexican recipes. "Cilantro and poblano peppers were really hard to find then," wrote Barbara, "and you really had to dig around and go to a tortilleria to get decent tortillas." For adventurous Angelenos, Barbara piqued interest in Mexican food, yet the public remained unaware that Carnitas El Momo was serving artisanal carnitas right in the city's center, at a sweatshop in the Fashion District.

Carnitas remained a second income for Momo until the mid '80s, when an accident at work destroyed his hand and arm, making it difficult to continue working at the factory. He picked up catering events and served tacos at the clothing factory for twenty-five years, slowly building his clientele and his reputation.

As his children grew up, they began to apprentice, honoring the system used at taco stands—you start as a cashier, dishwasher, and mobile soda jerk, move up to prep, and then learn how to cook and master the craft of a taquero. "My dad still watches me when I cook, making sure I don't mess up," says Momo's son Billy. His other son, Güicho, has earned the right cook Momo's carnitas unsupervised.

Carnitas El Momo serves carnitas from a trailer in South Central, Compton, and in front of their home in Boyle Heights, and the whole family is involved. "Even my grandchildren are learning," says Momo. Billy and his sister Adriana are in the business now, and a couple of days a week they work with their father in Boyle Heights. At the age of seventy-one, with fifty-five years logged as a carnitas artisan, Momo still gets up at 2 a.m. to begin cooking his carnitas. You'd think he'd have slowed down by now, but he has a goal: "To get another truck," he says. "It's important for the future of my family, for them to learn this trade and keep it going. Besides, I like my work, and I am thankful to God that I'm still healthy enough to work." Momo's legacy won't be preserved in the material items that are passed on when a loved one departs—in his recipes lies his patrimony. They are cultural assets that will sustain the generations of Acostas to come.

In the last few years, Carnitas El Momo has finally come into the spotlight it deserves, appearing on television, receiving tons of local and national press, and becoming a staple at food events. Back in Boyle Heights, an old-school, longtime clientele (unaware of Momo's newly acquired fame) dutifully files in every weekend for the best carnitas in the country. For me, every time I eat at Carnitas El Momo, I'm transported to the back seat of my grandfather's gold Lincoln Continental Mark VI, if just for a moment, blissfully cradling that pork-fat-stained bag of carnitas. It's everything I love about this culture, and now I don't have to get on a plane for that taste of the pueblo.

Inocencia Acosta Avendano making carnitas

TORTA LA RUSA
Super Tortas D.F.

In recent years, three Mexico City–style torta vendors have opened in L.A., and their professional torteros are making L.A. an even more amazing place to explore Mexican cuisine. Super Tortas D.F. is the best of the bunch, and its Torta La Rusa, or Russian sandwich, is a classic. The chipotle dressing, a variation on the chile-spiked Russian dressing Super Tortas uses, also makes a great base to cook shrimp and chicken.

You can use this sandwich construction to make other Mexico City–style tortas with whatever meats, cheeses, and vegetables you prefer. Note that while the recipe seems long, the sandwich-making goes quickly, so make sure to have all your ingredients prepped and within reach.

Makes 4 tortas

4 milanesas or beef top round, pounded extra thin
  (about ⅓ pound each)
Sea salt and freshly ground black pepper to taste
1 cup breadcrumbs
Vegetable oil for cooking
4 telera rolls
Butter, room temperature
Mayonnaise

12 thin slices medium-size tomato
  (about 2 tomatoes)
16 thin slices avocado
  (about 2 avocados)
2 cups pickled jalapeño strips and carrot slices
Chipotle Cream Sauce or Russian dressing
  (recipe follows)
4 slices Fud jamón de pierna or other ham
4 cups queso Oaxaca, grated

Give milanesas a good sprinkling of salt and pepper on both sides. Coat each piece with breadcrumbs, making sure to thoroughly cover the meat. (This is a street-style milanesa, so no egg.) Set a cast-iron skillet over medium heat, add oil to cover the bottom and add the milanesas. Fry until the outside is crisp and inside is tender, about 3 minutes per side. Transfer to cutting board, pat dry, slice into medium-thin strips, and set aside. They don't need to be hot when making your sandwiches, but should be above room temperature.

Slice rolls open with a bread knife and lightly brush both sides with soft butter. Heat a comal or flattop grill to medium high. Place half of each roll (what will become the bottom half of each torta) cut side down and grill until toasted, about 3 minutes, pressing lightly with a spatula. Flip over and grill the uncut side for about 1 minute. Apply a light spread of mayonnaise to the cut side of each. Top evenly with 3 tomato slices, 4 avocado slices, 6 to 8 strips of pickled jalapeños, and a pickled carrot. Spoon ½ to 1 tablespoon (depending on your heat preference) Chipotle Cream Sauce or Russian chipotle dressing over the vegetables. Set the bread bottom assembly aside.

Place the top halves of the rolls face down on the grill, and grill the ham next to them. Toast the bread for 2 minutes, then turn over and toast for 1 minute. Meanwhile, cook ham for 3 minutes on each side, and set aside when cooked.

Place the grated cheese on the grill in 4 equal small piles and cook until the edges begin to crisp, 2 to 3 minutes. Use a spackle knife (like painters use) or a metal spatula to slide under the cheese and fold it over, forming an envelope of fried cheese, taking care not to burn it. Cover each fried cheese with a top half of the rolls.

Set the bottom half of each sandwich on the grill. Place milanesas atop the vegetables, and then top with fried ham. Using a spatula, lift up the sandwich tops with fried cheese and set them atop the sandwiches. Serve immediately.

CHIPOTLE CREAM SAUCE

This variation of Super Tortas's Russian dressing also works great as a sauce for shrimp or chicken. Alternatively, you can just mix 2 cups of storebought Russian dressing with 4 chipotle peppers in adobo sauce.

½ cup chipotle peppers in adobo
¼ cup crema mexicana
½ roma tomato

2 tablespoons milk
2 tablespoons ketchup
Sea salt to taste

Place all of the ingredients in a blender and blend on high until it's a smooth purée, then place in a serving dish.

RAUL ORTEGA

L.A.'s grandest culinary celebrations, like the Los Angeles Food & Wine Festival and the *Los Angeles Times*'s Taste, have traditionally been devoid of Mexican chefs and street vendors, although that started changing around 2014, thanks to the increasing fame of such Alta California chefs as Ray Garcia, Carlos Salgado, and Wes Avila. More recently, a delightfully startling collaboration took place in East Hollywood. Chef Jessica Koslow of the hot breakfast spot Sqirl invited Raul Ortega of Mariscos Jalisco for an event called Noche Pescado, a fundraiser for the Hollenbeck Youth Center in East L.A. It was also a great excuse for her to collaborate with the award-winning food truck that has spent the last fifteen years serving the residents of Boyle Heights and beyond. Mostly, however, it was a true turning point for L.A.'s food culture.

The bespectacled Raul, who looks like a cross between a school principal and a marinero (sailor), didn't come to the attention of Angelenos until 2008. He was born in San Juan de Los Lagos, Jalisco, a religious center that does a good business in bliss chains, rosaries, and some amazing street food. It's the kind of enterprise that evolves when your hometown has its very own miracle-working Virgin of the Immaculate Conception. From a very young age, Raul helped run his father's hotel, El Hotel Coahuila, which served some of the one million–plus pilgrims who show up every year between late January and early February.

"I had an issue with my dad when I was eighteen," Raul says. "I worked for his fabric business and ran his hotel—I did everything, even mopping the floor, but I wasn't getting paid." Fed up, he headed to L.A. to join his uncle at Los Pericos, a Pomona-based manufacturer of tostadas, taco shells, and chips. "But it was the same thing there—I wasn't given the opportunity to grow," he says. He knew he had to do his own thing, but before he could get there, he had to survive on pure hustle.

At the age of twenty, Raul worked at a recycling center while learning English at school. He then worked briefly in King Taco's commissary and did maintenance work. "On the side, I bought cars at auctions and fixed them up and sold them." (He still does much of the mechanic work for his trucks.) While working at L.A. Envelopes in 1999, he saved up enough to get a small catering truck and began selling mariscos at the Alameda Swap Meet and El Faro Plaza. "I sold ceviches, oysters, and cocktails until the police kicked me out," he says.

By then, however, he'd built a reputation for seafood, and he also sold tacos de cabeza out of his Boyle Heights house, right across Olympic Boulevard from where he now parks his truck. So when an opportunity opened up, he already had a clientele. That opportunity took the form of Martín Ramirez, another San Juan de Los Lagos native; the two met when Martín was cooking at the Mariscos 4 Vientos truck, also across the street. One Wednesday, Martín got fired, and the friends kicked into gear. "We rented a truck that day," says Raul. "On Thursday we prepped, and by Friday we were out selling."

Martín's father, Antonio, is credited as the originator of the shrimp taco so popular both in San Juan de Los Lagos and now in Boyle Heights. (The cooks at about a dozen Boyle Heights trucks, stands, and carts either hail from San Juan or have added the shrimp tacos to their menus.) Mariscos Jalisco's signature taco is now such a local attraction that at one restaurant just south of Boyle Heights, the menu reads, "East L.A.–style shrimp tacos." Martín contributed the shrimp taco recipe to the Mariscos Jalisco enterprise, which has made them national stars in the food-truck firmament.

"For the first seven months we really struggled," says Raul, "but then Lent came, followed by a good summer, and then we were okay." (Because it's seafood, the shrimp taco is a Lenten dish.) The recipe is more guarded than the Vatican Papers—at food festivals, Raul is known for requesting a private cooking area to conceal his recipe. They stuff a mixture of shrimp and secret ingredients into a corn tortilla, then deep-fry it and serve it with a mild and lightly fermented tomato salsa, some cabbage, and a couple of thin slices of avocado. Also on offer are tostadas covered in ceviche or aguachile (spicy shrimp), as well as tangy seafood cocktails, all served to a steady line of both Boyle Heights locals and fans from across L.A. and beyond.

Raul moves between the truck and his adjacent indoor seating area, switching easily between the roles of host and manager, chatting with customers and making sure the food is coming out the way he likes. His truck has captured the imagination of the city, garnering him the local and national press, television appearances, and awards (including the Vendy cup) that he deserves. In many best-restaurant lists, Mariscos Jalisco is one of only a handful of traditional vendors who are included alongside L.A.'s biggest chefs. But it was Jessica Koslow who took it a step further by asking him to collaborate.

It's a validation that should reverberate through the food community and beyond—that traditional Mexican food from trucks like Raul's should be placed on the highest possible pedestal.

RED AGUACHILE TOSTADA

Raul Ortega, Mariscos Jalisco

If you thought you'd be scoring the recipe for Mariscos Jalisco's award-winning shrimp taco, you'll be disappointed—even Wikileaks can't get ahold of it. But Raul was happy to share his aguachile tostada, a tasty, spicy snack that's perfect for a warm L.A. evening, especially when paired with a cold beer or michelada.

Serves 6 to 8

2 pounds fresh medium shrimp, peeled, deveined, and halved lengthwise

1 cup lime juice, divided

2 habanero chiles, stems removed (more if you like it hot)

3 jalapeño chiles, stems removed

2 serrano chiles, stems removed

2 chipotle chiles in adobo

1 large cucumber, peeled, deseeded, and sliced into bite-size chunks (about 1½ cups)

2 red onions, halved and sliced thin with a mandoline (about 2½ cups)

½ cup ketchup

½ cup V-8 juice

2 teaspoons freshly ground black pepper

Sea salt to taste

¼ cup Huichol salsa

1 package tostadas

5 to 6 avocados, pits removed and halved

Put shrimp in a nonreactive bowl and pour over ¾ cup lime juice. Toss shrimp to make sure they're well coated. Cover with a lid or plastic wrap and set aside in the refrigerator for 2 hours. The acid from the lime will cook the shrimp.

Place habaneros, jalapeños, serranos, and chipotles in a blender with remaining ¼ cup lime juice and blend until combined. Set salsa aside.

When shrimp has been "cooked," remove from refrigerator and stir in cucumber, onion, ketchup, V-8, pepper, and reserved salsa. Taste and add salt as needed. Cover bowl and return to the refrigerator for 1 hour.

Remove from the refrigerator, taste, and add salt and/or pepper if needed. Stir in salsa Huichol, which will help the dish achieve the vibrant color it has at Mariscos Jalisco. (This won't make it much spicier, but if you're satisfied with the flavor and color, you can leave out the Huichol.) If it's too spicy for you, add a little more ketchup to add sweetness and lower the heat.

Arrange shrimp evenly on a tostada, cut side down, without overlapping, and spoon over about 3 tablespoons of vegetables. Drizzle with aguachile liquid from the bowl. Take a halved avocado, scoop out 4 slices with a large metal serving spoon, and arrange them evenly on top of the tostada. Repeat for the remaining tostadas and serve immediately.

MARIA ELENA LORENZO

It's no surprise to the ultra-food-obsessed folks in L.A.—the ones who will drive to the San Gabriel Valley for Chengdu cuisine and know every good ramen spot in Torrance—that you have to prowl the streets of South

L.A., Watts, and Compton to find some of the best regional Mexican cuisine in town. These historically African American neighborhoods have seen an influx of Mexican and Central American immigrants in recent decades, and it's all reflected in the local food. Since the L.A. riots, which triggered a migration of African Americans to the Inland Empire and the south, there's been a steady immigration of Latinos, who now make up seventy percent of the population of Watts.

These shifting demographics have transformed the main thoroughfares and smaller avenues on either side of the 110 Freeway, where a street-vendor mecca has flourished. One of those vendors is Maria Elena Lorenzo from El Llano de la Barra, Guerrero, who began selling tamales and regional Mexican dishes in the wake of the riots.

Like most girls who lived in La Costa Chica, Elena learned to cook and make tortillas at a very young age, and then went to work at her mom's fonda, which served Costa Chica dishes. "I would go to the molino at 7 a.m. to grind our nixtamal," she says. "And after school, I cooked lots of stews, tamales, and recados—it was a lot of work!"

At seventeen, she got a job at the convention center in Acapulco, cooking Mexican and international food for the employees' café. She met her husband, Juan Irra, there, after he'd been lured over by a chef friend to try Elena's white pozole. By her mid-twenties, this shy Afro-Mexican woman was already a veteran cook, yet she was willing to transition to being a full-time mother while Juan supported the family.

In 1992, when the local economy struggled, Juan and Elena moved to L.A. with their four daughters, Teresa, Judepth, Nayeli, and Maria, all of whom have become outstanding cooks. (They later had two more children in the US, Heidi and Ulises.)

The smoke and debris from the L.A. riots had cleared by the time Elena and her family arrived in Watts, but many buildings and businesses never returned. South L.A. was already forty-five percent Latino, which made the transition easier. Elena started by selling tamales to markets and in front of her house. Her tamales weren't Guerrero style, because inexpensive corn-husk tamales were more suited to the local clientele, as is still the case today; neighborhood patrons demand a filling meal at an affordable price.

By 2006 Elena and Juan had saved up enough for a trailer, which they park just around the corner from their home, and at last, she was able to expand the menu for Tamales Elena. "We had to have carne asada burritos, because both Mexicans and African Americans in the community love them," she says, "but we also added Guerreran menudo on the weekends and beef birria." Their tacos also included some offal cuts like steamed beef tongue, lips, and brains, foods that only a handful of their Mexican customers would appreciate.

I was one of those customers, driving forty-five minutes on Sunday mornings just for a sublime bowl of menudo. Her trailer is one of the only places in L.A. where you can get a regional-style meal cooked with all fresh ingredients, and I was surprised that I hadn't seen cooking like this even in L.A.'s best Mexican restaurants. Then came an invite to Elena's daughter Maria's birthday party. "We're going to make pozole, and we want you to try it," her daughter Teresa said. I went straight to the back of the house to get a preview and found a huge pot filled with an entire hog's head simmering over a charcoal fire, something that you rarely see these days, even in Mexico. The best pozole comes from Guerrero, and this was even better than what I'd had in Acapulco: a rich, milky stock filled with pork. Laid on the table were the accompanying tostadas, avocado, onions, chiles, oregano, chicharrones, and limes. It was the best Mexican cooking I'd ever experienced in L.A., and it was served out of a trailer in Watts.

The whole family gets involved in preparing tamales every evening, a task filled with chismes (gossip) and playful teasing that can go on for hours. "Unless they want to go out—then they can do it quick," says Teresa about her sisters. Elena is also such a good culinary teacher that another of her daughters, Judepth, was recruited for John Sedlar's Rivera. Judepth received formal training while at Rivera, but the most important lessons came from Elena herself—and her lessons were also passed along. "The moles I make, and the pozole and stews, come from my mother and grandmother," says Elena. "They showed me their secrets and every pass of the preparation, and most importantly, that everything has its time to cook."

Visiting Tamales Elena on a day that they're serving one of their regional plates, or placing a special order for their delicious banana-leaf tamales, is like taking a trip to one of the pueblos magicos (magical small towns) in Mexico and stumbling across a fonda full of colorful regional plates. Watts can also be an enchanted place, if you know where to look.

POZOLE BLANCO GUERRERO STYLE
Maria Elena Lorenzo, Tamales Elena

Most restaurants in L.A. (and the US) serve a generic pozole made with canned hominy, but Elena's Guerrero-style version is the real deal. What makes it special is using proper hominy, the ancient corn that gives this stewy soup such a fantastic flavor. You'll need to go to a Mexican market like Vallarta or Northgate (some small neighborhood markets have it, too) to get maiz para pozole precocida, or precooked hominy, and plan on having a (big!) simmering pot for at least six hours. If you can't find it, you can use canned cooked hominy—just reduce the initial cooking time from three hours to thirty minutes.

Serves 15 to 20

8 pounds precooked hominy
1 head garlic, peeled
1 large onion, peeled
Sea salt to taste
1 hog's head, cut into small pieces
1 pound pork leg, skin on

Accompaniments
1 large onion, finely chopped
Mexican oregano to taste
10 to 15 serrano chiles, or 10 jalapeño peppers, finely chopped
Chile flakes to taste, optional
½ pound chicharrones, broken into small pieces
10 to 15 limes, cut into wedges
10 radishes, thinly sliced
7 avocados, halved
12 tostadas

In a very large stockpot, place hominy, garlic, and onion and add enough water to cover at 4 to 5 inches above the hominy. Bring to a boil over high heat. Reduce heat, cover, and simmer, stirring occasionally, until hominy opens up and flowers, about 3 to 3½ hours, adding more hot water as needed so the hominy is always covered with 4 to 5 inches of water. Add salt to taste, checking the stock for salt levels.

Add all of the pork parts and simmer, uncovered, for another hour, skimming off fat as needed. Cover and cook for another 40 minutes to an hour until the hominy is al dente, or soft, depending on your preference, and the pork is tender and thoroughly cooked (only the pig's ears will be too tough to eat). This may take another hour or even two.

Remove the hog's head from the pozole, cut it into smaller pieces (separating the tongue), and place them in a serving dish. Lay out all the accompaniments in serving dishes.

To serve, ladle pozole stock and hominy into a soup bowl with 2 to 3 pieces of hog's head. Dress with a tablespoon of onion, a pinch of oregano and serrano chiles and/or chile flakes, a spoonful of chicharrones, a

squeeze of lime, and sliced radishes. If you like, take half of an avocado and slice a couple of pieces with your spoon, adding more as you go. Break off small pieces of a tostada to scoop up the pork and hominy.

All of these condiments are flexible, and everyone is expected to add their own preferences, so add or subtract whatever you like—with pozole, the customer is always right.

TAMALES DE POLLO

Maria Elena Lorenzo, Tamales Elena

The tamal was first introduced after the innovation of nixtamalization, the process of transforming corn by cooking it in slaked lime to produce a useful and nutritious substance for making tortillas, hominy, and tamales. It was the original modernist technique. Mexico's thirty-two regions and countless micro-regions all have their own styles of tamales, each with its own wrappers, stews, and principal ingredients. For decades, Elena has been making banana-leaf tamales, the tender and tasty packages sold in the mornings with atole (a masa drink) in the Costa Chica. Her tamales are different from the ones you'll come across in most tamal shops in East L.A.—they're flavored with costeño chiles, an essential Guerrero flavor.

To make tamales, you'll need a vaporera (tamal steamer), which you can find fairly inexpensively at a Mexican market, at Target, or online.

Makes 25 tamales

1 to 2 packs banana leaves
5 costeño chiles
6 guajillo chiles
½ large onion, cut into small chunks
3 cloves garlic
1½ teaspoons dried oregano
1 pinch ground cloves
1 pinch freshly ground black pepper
1 pinch cumin
1½ teaspoons vinegar

1 pound tomatoes (any kind), halved
3 to 3½ cups chicken stock
   (*see recipe page 74, or storebought*)
½ cup cooking oil, plus more for cooking
Sea salt to taste
2 pounds boneless chicken leg/thigh meat,
   cut into thin strips
2½ pounds prepared masa for tortillas
¼ cup pork lard

First, prepare the banana leaves by cutting into pieces about 1 square foot. Pass leaves over an open flame until they are soft and flexible enough to fold easily, taking care not to burn them. Set aside.

Lightly toast chiles on a comal or griddle over medium heat, about 30 seconds per side, taking care not to burn them, which will impart a bitter taste. Cool them and remove and discard stems, seeds, and membranes. Put chiles into a food processor or sturdy blender and add all but one piece of onion, the garlic, oregano, cloves, pepper, cumin, vinegar, and tomatoes. Blend to combine and add enough chicken stock (about 1 cup) to create a sauce consistency. Strain into a bowl and set aside.

In a large skillet over medium-high heat, swirl in some oil and char the reserved piece of onion to flavor the oil. Add sauce and 1 cup chicken stock. Cook, stirring, until it reaches a boil. Taste and add salt as desired. The sauce should be liquid; if it's too thick, stir in a little more chicken stock. Remove sauce from heat and let cool to room temperature. Stir in chicken and let it sit in the sauce for 1 to 2 hours in the refrigerator. You want to get lots of flavor but don't want to cook the chicken at this point—that will take place in the steamer.

In a large mixing bowl, mix masa, ½ cup oil, lard, and ½ cup chicken stock. Work the masa with your hands until well combined. (It helps to moisten your hands with lukewarm water.) Add more chicken stock in small batches as you knead, until the masa is soft and easy to work with. To test it, use Elena's mother's method: Drop a small piece in a glass of lukewarm water, and if it floats, it's ready.

Add water to the vaporera up to just below the grate, and line the grate with banana leaves, leaving a golf-ball-size hole in the center so steam can pass through.

To fill the tamales, place a banana leaf on a flat surface and spread about a half-cup of masa over the leaf. Place a tablespoon of the chicken stew in the center of the masa, fold the leaf into a rectangle, and fold over the ends. You can use a second leaf to secure the package. Cut a thin piece of twine from the banana leaf to tie the tamal shut. You can also hold the tamal inside the leaf by wrapping it in a piece of foil. Set the tamales upright in the steamer in a circle around the perimeter, working inward, building layers until you reach the center, steering clear of the hole. You can stack tamales on top of each other if you need to and have room.

Cover tamales with a layer of banana leaves and seal the lid tightly by applying masa to the lip of the pot, using it as an adhesive to keep the lid airtight. Steam over high heat for 1½ hours. Remove the tamales and serve immediately, or store in a cooler to keep them warm until it's time to serve.

RICKY PIÑA

Los Angeles is a taco town. When visiting the city, one of the founding fathers of modern Mexican cuisine, Guillermo Gonzalez, said, "You guys have more varieties of tacos than we have in Mexico, and no rules—

it's amazing." The city's taco culture began on Olvera Street in 1934; forty years later, King Taco ushered in the age of food trucks; and in 2008, Roy Choi's Kogi pimped out the food truck and started a revolution. But Ricky Piña of Ricky's Fish Tacos was the first to seduce a crossover audience with a Mexican tradition: the fish taco.

In Mexico, most tacos are made by specialists, with a cryptic classification system whose regional permutations would confound Pliny the Elder. There were a few hidden taco experts around L.A., but for the most part, the city's Mexican American loncheras (catering trucks sometimes unfairly called "roach coaches") and taquerias served a variety of meats all cooked on a griddle, rejecting the specialization that led formally trained taqueros to master a particular variety: carne asada, al pastor, guisados, fish tacos, or others. Each style of taco is made with specific equipment to facilitate the cooking method best suited to the ingredients. L.A.'s non-Latinos mostly settled for cheap, adulterated tacos that were indistinguishable from one another. When Ricky brought his Ensenada-style fish tacos to Silver Lake and set up under a bright umbrella, he introduced taco specialization to all Angelenos.

Ricky was born in El Maneadero in Baja and grew up in Ensenada, the fish taco capital of the world. His family moved around a lot as his father unsuccessfully tried to make a living as a rancher, but there was one place they were able to have some stability: Rancho Bonito. "That's where I fell in love with my mom's cooking, seeing her cook over a wood fire and make tortillas," says Ricky. "Even our horse would stick his head in the kitchen for a tortilla."

By the age of sixteen, his parents had moved north of the border to find work, leaving Ricky as the house cook for three of five older siblings, making fish soup, siete mares with local olives, carne asada, and pasta. "I read American cookbooks from the '80s to get more ideas," says Ricky, who had studied English and English literature in school. He also got certified to be a clinical lab technician, a skill that brought him to Reseda in 1988 for a job at SmithKline Beecham (now GlaxoSmithKline).

Ultimately, it was a well-timed vacation in Cabo that would set him on his culinary path. His vacation was extended three years when Ricky was recruited as a tour guide, thanks to his good looks and warm personality—a trait that would later endear him to L.A. food lovers. When it was time to get out of Cabo, he returned to Ensenada and opened an ice cream shop. Unfortunately, this was right before an El Niño hit, bringing cold weather that kept sales low, driving him out of business and back to L.A., where he became a florist.

Frequent trips to visit family in Ensenada ensured that Ricky got his fish taco fix, but it took a force majeure to drive him over the edge and inspire him to choose his ultimate career. While managing three floral shops in L.A., his car broke down. "I was without a car for six months," he says. "I'd never eaten fish tacos outside of Ensenada, but I tried some places in my neighborhood and didn't like them. So the next time I went home I got my mom's recipe."

He brought home ingredients from Ensenada and made fish tacos for friends, who all encouraged him to open a stand. He'd always been an entrepreneur at heart, and finally, in October of 2008, he took a traditional concave comal, attached it to an old desk, added wheels, and fashioned a taco cart. After doing some test runs, he started setting up on Sunset and Hyperion on weekends. Some of his customers set him up with a Twitter account, which was catching on in the food world thanks to the Kogi Truck, and bloggers started spreading the word, too. There was a tremendous buzz in the food community about this cool, engaging street vendor from Ensenada, who spoke good English and made real fish tacos just like you can get in Baja.

And although Ricky had become a mainstream hit, he remained a rigid traditionalist—the kind of taco master who should have been embraced by Mexican Americans, but not at $2.50 a taco. I once saw a woman jump off a bus right in front of his stand, one hand still on the accordion-style door, and ask, "How much for a taco?" When he told her, she uttered an insult, snapped a dismissive backhand gesture, and jumped back on the bus. But in Silver Lake, hipsters, bloggers, and taco lovers flocked to Ricky's Fish Tacos, turning him into a star. After Valentine's Day in 2010, his boss at the flower shop said, "Ricky, you're only working here three days a week—why don't you go and make your fish tacos?" So he moved to Virgil, made fish tacos full-time, and in 2013 saved up enough to buy a food truck, finally legitimizing his operation (which had been illegal, as are most all street carts in L.A.).

Ricky's Fish Tacos opened up the taco scene and became part of a handful of stands that have shaped a new narrative about street food and tacos in L.A. He helped inspire other taqueros to "make tacos great again," as Wes Avila campaigned in 2016. "I'm a perfectionist," says Ricky with a smile. "Even when I was illegal, I had to be the best."

FISH TACOS
Ricky Piña, Ricky's Fish Tacos

"In my family, we made fish tacos whenever friends or relatives came to visit," says Ricky Piña, so when he moved to L.A. from Baja, it was a natural fit for him to start his own stand. Invite your friends, be sure to have plenty of Mexican beer on hand, and enjoy this Piña family tradition from the fish taco capital of the world, Ensenada.

NOTE: Don't use handmade or heirloom corn tortillas for Baja-style fish tacos, because the corn flavor will overpower the balance of flavors. Use white corn tortillas, warmed on a comal or griddle, and then allow them to cool to just above room temperature. In Baja, the tortilla is merely a holder for the fried fish and chilled condiments.

Makes 12 tacos

3 pounds cod, swai, or other firm white fish fillets
1 cup plus 1 teaspoon sea salt
5 cloves
2 tablespoons garlic powder
1 cup all-purpose flour, or a Mexican brand of flour like El Rosal from Baja if you can get your hands on it
2 tablespoons dried Mexican oregano
1½ teaspoons baking powder (or beer)
½ cup yellow mustard
½ cup mayonnaise
1 pound lard, such as Farmer John's pork lard

To serve:
Ricky's Salsa Verde (*recipe follows*)
Ricky's Pico de Gallo (*recipe follows*)
1 cup crema mexicana or mayonnaise
2 cups thinly shredded green cabbage
6 limes, cut into wedges for serving
1 dozen white corn tortillas

Cut fish into rectangular strips about 5 inches long by 1 inch thick. To make the brine, put 1 quart water in a large container or nonreactive bowl and stir in 1 cup salt, cloves, and garlic powder. Add fish to the brine (there should be enough to cover) and refrigerate for about 2 hours.

When it's almost time to fry the fish, combine flour, 1 teaspoon salt, oregano, and baking powder in a large mixing bowl. Fold in mustard and mayonnaise. You should have a smooth, homogenous batter about the consistency of a light pancake batter so that it evenly coats the fish fillets. Add water if the batter is too thick.

Lay your condiments out before cooking the fish: salsa verde, pico de gallo, crema, shredded cabbage, lime wedges, and corn tortillas for your guests to assemble their own tacos, Baja style. If you want to really spice things up, make a variety of salsas and maybe some shredded cabbage pickled in lime for contrast.

Preheat the oven to 250° and line a baking sheet with paper towels. Remove fish from the brine and pat dry with paper towels. Heat a large Dutch oven or other heavy-bottomed pot over medium-high heat and add enough lard so fat melts to a height of roughly 2 inches. When the fat reaches 350° (check with a thermometer), use tongs to dip 2 or 3 fish fillets, one by one, into the batter so all sides are evenly coated. Lightly shake off excess batter. Place fillets carefully in the hot oil for 1 minute, then pierce the batter with the tongs and flip the fillets. Cook fish for 1 minute on the other side, then pierce the batter once more with the tongs and cook for another 1 to 2 minutes, depending on the thickness of the fish. Transfer the fried fillets to the paper-towel-lined baking sheet to remove the excess oil. Put the baking sheet in the oven to keep fish warm while you fry the remaining pieces. Make sure the oil is back to 350° before adding another batch of fish.

To serve, put a hot fish fillet into a room-temperature tortilla. Let everyone add his or her own condiments and finish with a squeeze of lime.

RICKY'S SALSA VERDE

2 jalapeños, stemmed
6 medium tomatillos, husked and rinsed
1 large onion, cut into chunks
1 sprig cilantro
Sea salt

Heat a large cast-iron skillet or ceramic pan over high heat. When hot, add jalapeños, tomatillos, and onion and cook until blistered, turning often to evenly char the vegetables.

Transfer the vegetables to a blender, add cilantro and 1 cup water, and blend until chunky. If the salsa is too thick for your liking, add a little more water. Season to taste with salt.

RICKY'S PICO DE GALLO

8 roma tomatoes, seeded, diced, and drained
1 medium onion, diced
1 to 2 jalapeño chiles, to taste, stemmed, seeded, and diced
2 sprigs cilantro, chopped
Juice of 3 key limes
Sea salt

Gently fold tomatoes, onion, chiles, and cilantro together in a large nonreactive bowl (stainless steel or plastic). Squeeze lime juice over the salsa, season with salt to taste, and stir gently until combined.

CENTRO DE ABASTOS

MARKETPLACES

A taqueria is nothing without a good tortilla. A ceviche can always use a splash of a great hot sauce. And a home cook can't tackle a pozole or mole without a visit to a well-stocked Mexican market. This chapter is but an introduction to some of the products and markets found in Los Angeles; see the Neighborhood Resources chapter for more detailed recommendations.

PEOPLE

Hualterio Merino 186
Francisco Ramirez 188
Ricardo Cervantes. 190

RECIPE

Isthmus-Style Cornbread 192

PLACES

Los Cinco Puntos 193
Northgate Gonzalez Markets. . . .193

HUALTERIO MERINO

In terms of passions, brand loyalty for Mexican hot sauces ranks a close third behind La Virgen de Talpa and soccer clubs. This is why the more expensive, higher-quality, American-made hot sauces, fashioned specifically for heat seekers and collectors, have had no place on the plastic tables of the Mexican seafood cocktailer. It's also had to do with taste—those lacto-fermented hot sauces, made with Fresno chiles and fancy techniques, can overwhelm a campechana (mixed seafood cocktail), while a commercial bottle like Yucateco blends into a coctél de mariscos the way Heinz ketchup marries with a burger. All that changed, however, when Hualterio Merino came along and cracked the hot sauce code with Salsa Sinaloa, which has practically become an accessory at L.A.'s loncheras (Mexican food trucks).

Hualterio has been working since the age of seven, when he washed cars in El Carrizo, a small northern Sinaloan town. At age nine, he became an entrepreneur, using a street vendor's tricycle to sell bread made by ranchers to nearby towns. By the time puberty hit, he'd added fruit and cheese to his inventory, precociously mastering business from a bicycle, then expanding to sell fresh shrimp at a roadside spot where drivers were forced to slow to a crawl near speed bumps. His salesman chops landed him a job selling pan Bimbo (Mexico's Wonder Bread) before setting out to make his fortune in the US.

Naturally, he got a job in shipping and receiving at a tire company, but in 2007, an unforeseen venture presented itself when he was offered the job of head cook in the Van Nuys courthouse cafeteria. Back in El Carrizo—in between his other gigs—he'd worked at Lico's Restaurante, a truck stop that served typical Mexican food. "At the courthouse, I thought the food was too simple: eggs, potatoes, bacon, and sausage," Hualterio says. "So I added my own salsa, which became a hit with the judges, police officers, and secretaries."

Encouraged, he added menudo, which became a big seller, then such daily specials as flautas, "and then people started making requests that weren't on the menu, like huevos rancheros and huevos a la Mexicana," he says. In 2012, a new boss brought in his own chef, leaving Hualterio out of work. He kept thinking about how people had responded to his salsa, so he set up a test kitchen in his garage to make a salsa that would defy all odds and become a fixture in L.A.'s Mexican seafood landscape.

"I went door to door—Mariscos Jalisco was one of my first customers—with my own handmade labels," he says. "I was honest, though, letting them know I'd made it in my garage." He made cold calls to food trucks, unlicensed stands, Mexican butcher shops, stores, and restaurants, dropping off samples and doing COD orders. Slowly but surely, Salsa Sinaloa bottles started to show up around town. But it wasn't an easy sell.

Cooks like Raul Ortega of Mariscos Jalisco valued the quality—Hualterio uses only fresh, category-one chile peppers instead of the chile powders used by cheaper brands, and he eschews artificial colors and additives. "The problem wasn't the people, who could taste the difference—it was the stores," says Hualterio. "My salsa costs $1.90 wholesale, and Tapatio is only fifty cents, so they'd tell me to go to hell!" Undeterred, he sold Salsa Sinaloa from his truck, and through the popularity of his Instagram account, people started asking retailers to carry his hot sauce. Then he picked up a distributor that put him in local markets.

Hualterio now produces seven salsas, a michelada mix, bouillon powder, and cookies, and the list keeps growing. "I keep getting ideas from my customers—they're constantly asking for new products," he says proudly. On his Instagram account, he playfully advertises his clients' restaurants with a "highly recommended" or his tongue-in-cheek catchphrase, "Esta maldita dieta me esta dejando en los puros huesos." ("This terrible diet is sticking to my hips.")

His success comes from combining traditional flavors with customer service, and it doesn't hurt that his product is healthy and eco-conscious. "My sauce changes with different batches of chiles and different seasons, because I use natural products," says Hualterio. And, while his initial goal wasn't environmentalism, the fact that he uses only glass bottles is admirable.

It's no secret that one of Mexico's most popular hot sauces, Tapatio, isn't made in Mexico at all—it comes from Vernon, an exclusively industrial city just south of downtown L.A. And now that Hualterio has become a national hot sauce player, leaving his garage for a large production facility in Ontario, it's worthy of note that L.A. has become an international hot sauce capital.

If you eat Mexican seafood in L.A., you'll see the usual Tapatio, Cholula, Búfalo, Yucateco, Huichol, and/or Valentina sauces on the table, but now you're likely to see Salsa Sinaloa, too. It has broken through the immovable Mexican market with a better product that has captured the taste buds of spice-loving Angelenos.

FRANCISCO RAMIREZ

When Mexico's biggest chefs joined the campaign to ban GMO corn in Mexico and protect the fifty-nine varieties of corn (all descended from their oldest ancestor, teocintle) that were born in the Valle de Tehuacán, Puebla, the fight spilled north of the border in 2015. After more than eighty of Mexico's most popular chefs signed a declaration against trans-genic corn, L.A. chef Carlos Salgado organized a petition in America, where heirloom Mexican corn was gaining traction with Alta California chefs.

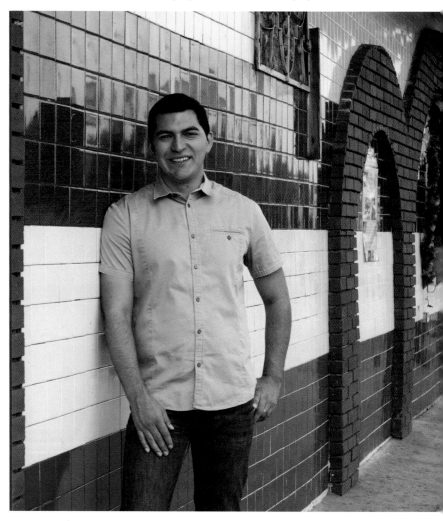

By that time, a handful of Alta California chefs were using heirloom corn from Jorge Gaviria's New York–based company, Masienda—namely, Ray Garcia, Carlos Salgado (who had started his own tortilleria), and Eduardo Ruiz. In the same year, Francisco Ramirez, who was running his family's Boyle Heights institution, La Princesita Tortilleria, reached out to Jorge Gaviria to see what the fuss was all about. "I contacted him myself, because I'd seen a few New York restaurants like Cosme and Empellón posting pictures on Instagram of dishes made with his corn," says Francisco.

His father, Francisco Ramirez, Sr., purchased the original La Princesita in 1972, taking over a space that had been occupied by another tortilleria in one of L.A.'s masa nuclei. There is no greater concentration of tortillerias than in the eastside barrios of East L.A.—Boyle Heights, Lincoln Heights, and El Sereno—where Mexican women, restaurant chefs, and street vendors stock up on fresh masa and tortillas recien hecha (recently made).

In 1985, before they began to open branches on the eastside, La Princesita added a retail component, and their flour tortillas came shortly after. Francisco helped out as a kid during Christmas break, bagging masa and counting tortillas. It was a family affair during the high tamal season, which stretches from La Posadas on December 16th to Día de la Candelaria on February 2nd. The tortilleria's success was enough to pay for Francisco's bachelor's degree in accounting and finance, but he wasn't sure he wanted to go into the tortilla business. His father's failing health and old age, however, made him realize that his family needed him, so he got more involved and took the business in new directions.

"La Princesita was doing well, but the product was priced a little higher than its competitors, which worked for families looking for a quality product, but the restaurants weren't interested," says Francisco. "They didn't want to pay the higher price, so by 2010 we had completely stopped selling to restaurants." A big problem with L.A.'s Mexican cuisine from the 1980s on was that pocho restaurants and street vendors had made a deal with the devil: Maseca, a commercial masa maker that both lowered the tone of Mexican cuisine and drove traditional tortillerias out of business on both sides of the border.

While L.A.'s Mexican restaurants were neglecting their ancestral product, many of La Princesita's vendors that had been there since the beginning were beginning to fade away. "I was trying to understand both who we were selling to and what ingredients we were using," says Francisco. "Many of our ingredients vendors had gone out of business, which really affected the quality of our flour tortillas." This led him to find natural additives for their flour tortilla production, and later, to add heirloom Mexican corn tortillas for select customers and chefs coming to town for events. Heirloom corn, Mexican American chef culture, and an old-school mom-and-pop shop all intersected in the war on transgenic corn, right on the heels of a national discussion about genetically modified foods and food safety. With all the talk of gentrification and gentefication (businesses opened by upwardly mobile Mexicans returning to the barrio) in Boyle Heights, La Princesita has put the raza in the masa, growing their business while maintaining close ties with a neighborhood on edge.

"I feel good about making quality tortillas, because I believe in a healthy lifestyle, and I care about my community, and the only way I can do that is by making tortillas as natural as I can," says Francisco, who stays in shape by running with the Boyle Heights Bridge Runners every Wednesday.

Today, the who's who of L.A.'s Mexican food scene all use La Princesita's tortillas: Guerrilla Tacos, Mexicali Taco Co., Loqui, Broken Spanish, 4 Vientos, Chichen Itza, Salazar, and many more. At the 2016 Tacolandia by *LA Weekly*, La Princesita pressed 60,000 tortillas using Masienda corn to supply the 120-plus vendors, an effort aimed at enlisting participating Mexican restaurants and taquerias to use better tortillas.

"We're doing something important here, and we're working with Mexican farmers to preserve corn varieties," says Francisco. And in the tortilla center of the country, there is perhaps no greater civic duty to the City of Angels than to produce a well-made tortilla.

RICARDO CERVANTES

Santa Monica, a city where three out of every four people are white, is the last place you'd expect to find people sipping cinnamon-spiked café de olla and snacking on cute piggy-shape molasses cookies. True, Santa Monica has always loved Mexican flavors, especially if they involve chips, salsa, margaritas, and melted cheese. But the fact that La Monarca Bakery—a traditional Mexican bakery created by Monterrey-born Ricardo Cervantes and his business partner, Alfredo Livas—blends so seamlessly into the fabric of life west of the 405 says a lot about Mexican food in Los Angeles. "We always had a general audience in mind," says Ricardo. "The idea was to be the In-N-Out of bakeries." To reach that goal, however, they knew they'd first have to prove themselves with the Mexican American community.

Ricardo, whose boyish, telenovela-star looks contrast with his fiery Monterrey accent (everyone from Monterrey sounds like they're screaming), seems an unlikely panadero (baker), but he grew up interested in food, and, as all regios did, he lived for the grill. "We'd always get together at someone's house and grill carne asada with salsas tatemadas" (fire-roasted salsas). Back then, it was just a tradition and a hobby that glowed steadily like the first embers of a barbecue pit as he went to study at Tecnologico de Monterrey, one of the top colleges in Latin America. He graduated with a degree in finance and accounting before going to work for Grupo Sitsa, a distributor of heavy machinery for agriculture, construction, and mining—work that kept him away from his growing interest in consumer businesses. Finally, in 2001, he headed to Stanford to get an MBA, and also landed an internship at Saatchi and Saatchi to work in Hispanic marketing.

During this time, Ricardo had his first exposure to L.A.'s Mexican and Latino communities. "I'd spent a lot of time in Texas, and I saw it didn't have a very diverse Mexican population," he says. "I'd heard about the huge and diverse Mexican population in L.A., but to see it was eye opening." He felt at home in L.A., and his time there inspired him to get together with his future business partner, Alfredo Livas, to plan a consumer-based business targeting L.A.'s Mexican audience. They saw gold in cakes, pan dulce, and café de olla.

In terms of customer service, tidiness, and quality, Mexican and other Latin American bakeries in Los Angeles had always fallen far below their counterparts in the Spanish-speaking Americas. Ricardo felt that the city's bakeries were doing the best they could with what they had, but they weren't measuring up.

Perhaps it would have been easier for them to open in a community that didn't already have Mexican bakeries, given their professional branding and upscale focus, yet they settled on one of L.A.'s most Mexican of cities: Huntington Park, which is encircled by panaderias armed to the teeth with inexpensive conchas, teleras, and polvorones. "To us, many players meant the market was big, and it was a chance to measure ourselves," says Ricardo. So in 2006, two Stanford grads turned Mexican bakers opened the first La Monarca Bakery.

"We were more expensive than all the other bakeries," he says. "We didn't use preservatives or food coloring, and we'd decided to cook from scratch—no one else was using different flours and butters." The pair had spent lots of time reading baking books, like the Culinary Institute of America's *Mastering the Art and Craft of Baking and Pastry,* and researching, developing, and testing their own recipes. "We relied on our taste memories from childhood," says Ricardo—and to spur those memories, they took a sweet journey to visit Mexico City's grandest bakeries, as well as small-town operations in Michoacán and Nuevo León.

It wasn't easy, however, for a couple of Stanford-educated entrepreneurs, likely taken for fresas (slang for upper-class Mexicans), to win the hearts and minds of Huntington Park, a barrio born of recent arrivals from Mexico and upwardly mobile families from East L.A., people who turned up their noses at La Monarca's prices. But they were undeterred. "We gave away the product if people thought it was too expensive—they'd realize it was something different and come back," says Ricardo.

Today, the original La Monarca still stands (albeit with fewer competitors), and they've added eight branches, with four more in development at this writing. Some are in the Mexican American Edens—Boyle Heights and Whittier—but they're also in South Pasadena, Santa Monica, and within walking distance from my pad in Hollywood. As is the highly diverse land of Hollywood, La Monarca's clientele is quite mixed. "Mexico's cuisine has exploded in the US, and especially in L.A., in the last fifteen years," says Ricardo. "Mostly it's been on the savory side—but now sweets are coming up." Just as they'd planned.

La Monarca is just another coffee shop here in Hollywood, sharing an intersection with a Roscoe's Chicken and Waffles and a Sugarfish, just north of a cluster of Oaxacan and Central American businesses and west of Thai Town. It's where sipping a cold-brewed café de olla to go with a vegetarian chorizo torta is as normal as leaving a Dodgers game after the seventh-inning stretch, in a city where eating Mexican food defines us as much as Vin Scully.

ISTHMUS-STYLE CORNBREAD
Ricardo Cervantes & Alfredo Livas, La Monarca Bakery

Mexico is the epicenter of corn, with more than fifty-nine known species and thousands of varieties. Throughout the centuries, corn has been more than just a staple food of the Mexican population—Octavio Paz, the Nobel Prize–winning poet, once said, "The invention of corn by the Mexicans is only comparable to the invention of fire by mankind." Corn dates back to at least 4250 BC, and the oldest preserved cob was found in Oaxaca. Cornbread, especially this Isthmus-style version, is truly representative of Mexico's gastronomy.

La Monarca, a family bakery with many locations throughout L.A., makes a traditional pan de elote (cornbread) using fresh sweet corn instead of cornmeal, which is more customary in the United States. This fresh-corn version has more of a spoonbread-like texture. In Oaxaca, cornbread is typically fried, but La Monarca bakes theirs, in adherence to their philosophy of creating full-flavored traditional recipes without frying.

Makes 12 generous slices

6 ears fresh sweet corn, kernels only
6 eggs
1 can condensed milk
6 tablespoons unsalted butter, melted and cooled
1 tablespoon vanilla extract
$1\frac{1}{4}$ cups all-purpose flour
1 teaspoon baking powder

Preheat the oven to 340°. Butter two 8-inch-round baking pans. Place corn kernels and eggs in a food processor and process to grind together. Add condensed milk, butter, and vanilla and process until smooth.

In a separate bowl, stir together flour and baking powder. Fold milk-butter mixture into flour until just combined.

Divide batter evenly between pans and bake, rotating halfway through, until a toothpick comes out clean, about 1 hour and 10 minutes. (It should take about 30 minutes in a convection oven.) Allow to cool slightly, then cut into thick wedges (6 per pan), and serve warm.

LOS CINCO PUNTOS

The life of every barrio in Los Angeles revolves around its mercados, carnicerias (butcher shops), abarrotes (convenience stores), panaderias (bakeries), and tiendas (stores) where cooks can find the ingredients for their menudo, tamales, and the essential sauces that form the backbone of their family recipes. The Sotelo family was already in the grocery business in the 1950s before opening Los Cinco Puntos in 1967. It's become a Boyle Heights institution, located at the five-point intersection of Cesar Chavez, Indiana, and Lorena. There's always a line for the market's famous carnitas, thick corn tortillas, tamales, and even the whole roasted lamb skulls used for making tacos. Plus, all the salsas, guacamoles, and cactus paddle salads you'll ever need are made on the premises. Some customers take hours to get out the door, opting to stay awhile to enjoy a carnitas taco or two after shopping. Others order from Los Cinco Puntos's full menu at their small stand on the left side of the market, taking the food to dine at a sidewalk table. Visiting a market like Los Cinco Puntos is not just a matter of convenience for many in L.A.'s Mexican community—it's nostalgia for weekends shopping with your grandparents, a family outing scented with chiles, steaming masa, and boldly flavored meats.

NORTHGATE GONZALEZ MARKETS

One of the biggest culinary advantages Los Angeles has over the rest of the country are its many Latino-owned regional supermarket chains: Vallarta, El Super, Superior, some others that cater to Central American communities, and Northgate Gonzalez. The Northgate Gonzalez chain began in 1980 in Anaheim, when Miguel Gonzalez Jimenez and his son, Miguel Gonzalez Reynoso, took over the struggling Northgate market, adding their family name to the 2,500-square-foot business. Today there are some forty Northgate Gonzalez supermarkets in practically every Mexican enclave, where you can find tortillas, masa, corn for pozole, baked goods, prepared foods, and supermarket shelves full of Mexican and Latin American products. Even quelites, foraged greens you normally have to buy off ambulant vendors, are found in the produce section. The chile selection is off the charts, and the meat department features housemade chorizos, head-to-tail cuts, and marinated meats for carne asada and al pastor. Restless in its mission to serve the Mexican American community, Northgate Gonzalez is also the go-to place for many of L.A.'s best chefs when they're looking for Mexican and Latin American ingredients.

NEIGHBORHOOD RESOURCES

A comprehensive guide to the restaurants, cafés, trucks, markets, tortillerias, bars, stands, coffeehouses, mercados, bakeries, and carnicerias could (should?) fill a book of its own. So the collection of recommendations here is but a taste of what's available in the greater Los Angeles area, but the roster does include most of my personal favorites.

Central L.A.....................196

Eastside........................201

Northeast & the Verdugos 205

San Gabriel & Pomona Valleys ..209

San Fernando Valley...........212

Westside.......................215

South Bay......................219

Harbor.........................222

South L.A. 224

Southeast......................227

CENTRAL L.A.

From the humble beginnings of El Pueblo de Nuestra Señora la Reina de los Ángeles del Río de Porciúncula, or Los Angeles, to its urban renewal and its modern-day loft culture, the city's center is home to the past, present, and future of L.A.'s Mexican cuisine. And just west of downtown, in Mid-City, Koreatown, and Hollywood, you'll find the most important center of traditional Oaxacan cuisine in the United States and the largest Oaxacan restaurant scene outside of Oaxaca. Alongside the packaged snacks and drinks in convenience stores, you'll see grasshoppers and tlayudas, and you might hear Zapotec at bus stops. America's taco obsession began here on Olvera Street, and Mexican American chefs now operate top destination restaurants in the city's revitalized downtown and flourishing Arts District. Here is where revolutionary pocho chefs are carving their initials into America's culinary landscape.

Homegirl Café is the restaurant component of Homeboy Industries, a pioneering nonprofit that combats gangs by creating jobs.

POCHO CUISINE

Cielito Lindo
E-23 Olvera St., Downtown
(213) 687-4391, cielitolindo.org
Recommended: Beef taquitos with avocado sauce

El Cholo, the Original
1121 S. Western Ave., Harvard Heights
(323) 734-2773, elcholo.com
Recommended: Sweet green-corn tamales,
Sonora-style enchiladas, guacamole, margaritas

El Compadre
7408 W. Sunset Blvd., Hollywood
(323) 874-7924, elcompadrerestaurant.com
Recommended: Camarones a la diabla, margaritas,
fajitas

Homegirl Café
130 W. Bruno St., Chinatown
(213) 617-0380, homeboyindustries.org
Recommended: M'jas con papas, Jorja's tacos,
Conuelo's sandwich

Homestate
4624 Hollywood Blvd., East Hollywood
(323) 906-1122, myhomestate.com
Recommended: Breakfast tacos, migas, queso,
Frito pie

La Golondrina Café
17 Olvera St., Downtown
(213) 628-4349
Recommended: Margaritas, chile relleno de jaiba,
carne asada a la tampiqueña

Yuca's Hut
2056 Hillhurst Ave., Los Feliz
(323) 662-1214, yucasla.com
Recommended: Cochinita pibil tacos and burritos

Yuca's on Hollywood
4666 Hollywood Blvd., Los Feliz
(323) 661-0523, yucasla.com
Recommended: Cochinita pibil, tamales,
breakfast burritos

REGIONAL MEXICAN

Antequera de Oaxaca
5200 Melrose Ave., Larchmont
(323) 466-1101
Recommended: Empanadas de mole amarillo,
tlayudas, salsa de queso

Expresión Oaxaqueña
3301 W. Pico Blvd., Arlington Heights
(323) 766-0575, expresionrestaurant.com
Recommended: Torta sexy, taco de la abuela,
coloradito de pollo

Gish Bac
4163 W. Washington Blvd., Arlington Heights
(323) 737-5050, gishbac.com
Recommended: Goat barbacoa, enfrijoladas,
mole negro, tlayudas

Guelaguetza
3014 W. Olympic Blvd., Harvard Heights
(213) 427-0608, ilovemole.com
Recommended: Chapulines a la Mexicana,
festival de moles, estofado, tlayuda choriqueso

La Flor de Yucatán Catering and Bakery
1800 S. Hoover St., Pico-Union
(213) 748-6090, laflordeyucatan.net
Recommended: Cochinita pibil, frijol on puerco,
relleno negro, kibbehs, tamales

Las 7 Regiones de Oaxaca
2648 W. Pico Blvd., Pico-Union
(213) 385-7458
Recommended: Mole negro, mole verde,
tamal oaxaqueño, entomatada

Lotería Grill
Original Farmers Market, 6333 W. 3rd St., Fairfax
(323) 930-2211, loteriagrill.com
6627 Hollywood Blvd., Hollywood
(323) 465-2500, loteriagrill.com
Recommended: Chicharrón de queso,
taco sampler, chilaquiles, huevos divorciados

Mexicali Taco Co.
702 N. Figueroa St., Chinatown
(213) 613-0416, mexicalitaco.com
Recommended: Tacos de carne asada, vampiros,
cachetadas

Tlayuda L.A.
5450 Santa Monica Blvd., East Hollywood
(213) 261-4667, tlayudala.com
Recommended: Tlayudas, mole sauce tacos,
memelitas

ALTA CALIFORNIA

Bar Amá
118 W. 4th St., Downtown
(213) 687-8002, bar-ama.com

Recommended: Puffy taco, queso, fajitas,
Ama's steak ranchero

Broken Spanish
1050 S. Flower St., Downtown
(213) 749-1460, brokenspanish.com
Recommended: Lamb neck tamal, camote,
chochoyotes, chicharrón

B.S. Taqueria
514 W. 7th St., Downtown
(213) 622-3744, bstaqueria.com
Recommended: Campechana verde, tacos, duritos

Guerrilla Tacos
Food truck, various locations
guerrillatacos.com
Recommended: Tacos, seafood tostadas,
white truffle quesadilla

MEXICAN STEAKHOUSE

Salazar
2490 N. Fletcher Dr., Frogtown/Atwater
salazarla.com
Recommended: Carne asada tacos, flat-iron steak
with sides for tacos, pork chop

BARES Y ANTROS

Club Mayan
1038 S. Hill St., Downtown
(213) 746-4287, clubmayan.com
Recommended: Dancing

The Conga Room
800 W. Olympic Blvd., Downtown
(213) 745-0162, congaroom.com
Recommended: Salsa dancing

El Carmen
8138 W. 3rd St., Beverly Grove
(323) 852-1552, elcarmenla.com
Recommended: Tequila from one of the biggest
selections in L.A.

La Cita
336 S. Hill St., Downtown
(213) 687-7111, lacitabar.com
Recommended: Live music, Bloody Marys, and
beer in a Tijuana-style dive bar

Las Perlas
107 E. 6th St., Downtown
(213) 988-8355, 213nightlife.com/lasperlas
Recommended: Mezcal, tequila

Lotería Grill
6627 Hollywood Blvd., Hollywood
(323) 465-2500, loteriagrill.com
Recommended: Chicharrón de queso, tequila,
micheladas, tacos

Mas Malo
515 W. 7th St., Downtown
(213) 985-4332, masmalorestaurant.com
Recommended: Tequila, mezcal

The Mexican Village
3668 Beverly Blvd., Koreatown
(213) 385-0479, themexicanvillage.com
Recommended: Salsa dancing

CAFEÍNA Y PAN DULCE

Panaderia Celaya Bakery
1630 W. Sunset Blvd., Echo Park
(213) 250-2472, celayabakery.com
Recommended: Pan dulce

Panaderia Santo Domingo
3418 W. 8th St., Koreatown
(213) 427-9793
Recommended: Pan dulce oaxaqueño

Tlacolula Panaderia y Carniceria
5167 Venice Blvd., Mid-City
(323) 692-7494
Recommended: Pan dulce, chilaquiles

AMBULANTES

El Chato Taco Truck
5300 W. Olympic Blvd., Mid-Wilshire
(323) 202-6936
Recommended: Mexican American tacos

Leo's Taco Truck
1515 S. La Brea Ave., Mid-City
(323) 346-2001, leostacostruck.com
Recommended: Al pastor, alambres, gringas

Ricky's Fish Tacos
1400 N. Virgil Ave., East Hollywood
(323) 395-6233, Twitter: @RickysFishTacos
Recommended: Fish tacos, shrimp tacos

Quesadillas Oaxaqueñas
1246 Echo Park Ave., Echo Park
Recommended: Blue corn quesadillas

Tacos Tamix
2402 W. Pico Blvd., Pico-Union
Recommended: Al pastor, alambres, mulitas

Taco Zone Truck
1342 N. Alvarado St., Echo Park
Recommended: Mexican American tacos

MERCADOS

Carniceria La Oaxaqueña
3701 W. Pico Blvd., Arlington Heights
(323) 373-9803, laoaxaquenamarket.com
Recommended: Oaxacan food products, meats,
tlayudas, cheeses

Chiles Secos
Grand Central Market, 317 S. Broadway,
Downtown
Recommended: Moles, chiles, seeds

El Valle Oaxaqueño
1601 S. Vermont Ave., Ste. 106, Pico-Union
(323) 734-0042, elvalleoaxaqueno.com
Recommended: Oaxacan and Mexican produce,
imported foods, meats, and dry goods

Mercado Benito Juarez
3270 W. 8th St., Koreatown
(213) 351-0638, oaxacaenlosangeles.com
Recommended: Oaxacan and Mexican produce,
imported foods, meats, and dry goods

Mercado Olympic (aka Piñata District)
E. Olympic Blvd. northwest of S. Central Ave.,
Fashion District
Recommended: Street food, produce, candies,
piñatas, chiles, herbs, spices, seeds

Villalobos Meat Market
5244 Santa Monica Blvd., East Hollywood
(323) 665-1923
Recommended: Produce, meats, cheeses

TORTILLERIA

Acapulco Tortilleria
1309 S. Vermont Ave., Pico-Union
(213) 480-8431
Recommended: Tortillas, masa

EASTSIDE

The eastside is where everyone goes to get tortillas north of the 10 Freeway, and where an original style of Mexican American food, old-school Chicano cuisine, and pocho burrito culture are as essential to the region's identity as cruising Whittier Boulevard. Some of the nation's best regional street food and restaurants are found here, representing Jalisco, Zacatecas, Puebla, and a few outlying states. Young pocho chefs have also opened places worth a trip, whether it's a new style of Mexican American eatery or a burger joint inside a liquor store. A shopping trip to El Mercado de Los Angeles (or El Mercadito) is a must, as is standing in line for tamales at Los Cinco Puntos on Christmas Eve morning. Nighttime is for tacos de fritanga (fried) and steamed beef head tacos at taquerias and from trucks. Welcome to Chicano Shangri-la.

Parade day in East L.A.

POCHO CUISINE

Al and Bea's
2025 E. 1st St., Boyle Heights
(323) 267-8810
Recommended: Bean and cheese (green sauce),
Al and Bea's Special, guacamole fries

Ciro's Restaurant
705 N. Evergreen Ave., Boyle Heights
(323) 269-5104
Recommended: Flautas, steak picado

Guisados
2100 E. Cesar Chavez Ave., Boyle Heights
(323) 264-7201
Recommended: Chiles toreados taco,
bistec en salsa roja taco, Armando Palmero

La Azteca Tortilleria
4538 E. Cesar Chavez Ave., East L.A.
(323) 262-5977
Recommended: Chile relleno burrito,
flour tortillas to go

Lupe's No. 2
4642 E. 3rd St., East L.A.
(323) 266-6881, lupesno2.com
Recommended: Bean and cheese (red sauce),
chile relleno burrito

Manny's El Tepeyac
812 N. Evergreen Ave., Boyle Heights
(323) 268-1960, eltepeyaccafe.com
Recommended: Original Hollenbeck burrito,
Original Okie, chile verde, huevos rancheros

REGIONAL MEXICAN

Birrieria Nochistlán
3201 E. 4th St., Boyle Heights
(323) 268-0319
Recommended: Goat birria

La Serenata de Garibaldi
1842 E. 1st St., Boyle Heights
(323) 265-2887, laserenataonline.com
Recommended: Asada tampiqueña,
shrimp in chipotle, Campeche-style fish

Las Molenderas
2635 Whittier Blvd., Boyle Heights
(323) 269-2812
Recommended: Mole!

Raspados Nayarit
3426 N. Broadway, Lincoln Heights
(323) 222-5006
Recommended: Raspados, Tacos tuxpeños, tuba,
tejuino

ALTA CALIFORNIA

Puertos del Pacifico
1240 S. Soto St., Boyle Heights
(323) 262-0203, puertosdelpacifico.net
Recommended: Octopus zarandeado, aguachile,
Costa Azul shrimp

BARES Y ANTROS

Cities Restaurant
4512 E. Cesar Chavez Ave., East L.A.
(323) 526-4555, citiesflavor.com
Recommended: Escargot en croute, tuna tiradito

Eastside Luv Wine Bar y Queso
1835 E. 1st St., Boyle Heights
(323) 262-7442, eastsideluv.com
Recommended: Micheladas

La Chuperia
1145 N. Mission Rd., Lincoln Heights
(626) 354-0267
Recommended: Craft beer, tortas

Las Palomas
1837 E. 1st St., Boyle Heights
(323) 264-5900
Recommended: Micheladas

BEBIDAS

East L.A. Wholesale Beverage
3666 Whittier Blvd., East L.A.
(323) 262-5124

Ramirez Beverage Center
2765 E. Olympic Blvd., Boyle Heights
(323) 266-2337, ramirezliquor.com

Ramirez Liquor
736 S. Soto St., Boyle Heights
(323) 261-2915, ramirezliquor.com

CAFEÍNA Y PAN DULCE

La Monarca Bakery
5700 E. Whittier Blvd., Commerce
(323) 869-8800, lamonarcabakery.com
Recommended: Molletes, café de la olla
(cold brew), organic Oaxacan dark roast

Primera Taza Coffee House
1850½ E. 1st St., Boyle Heights
(323) 780-3923, primeratazacoffee.com
Recommended: Americano, lonches,
mascarpone cheesecake

AMBULANTES

Carnitas El Momo
2411 Fairmount, Boyle Heights
(323) 627-8540
Recommended: Carnitas, birria, montalayo

Cemitas Los Poblanos Truck
3500 Whittier Blvd., Boyle Heights
(323) 268-2209
Recommended: Cemita poblana

Mariscos Jalisco
3040 E. Olympic Blvd., Boyle Heights
(323) 528-6701
Recommended: Shrimp tacos, ceviche, aguachile

Tacos Cuernavaca
5511 E. Whittier Blvd. at Eastmont Ave., East L.A.
(323) 671-8442
Recommended: Cecina taco, picaditas, alambres

Tacos Quetzalcoatl
4827 E. Olympic Blvd., East L.A.
Recommended: Omega-2 taco, taco de carne
enchilada, omega-2 quesadilla

MERCADOS

El Mercado de Los Angeles
3425 E. 1st St., Boyle Heights
(323) 262-4507
Recommended: Mole paste, chiles, spices,
kitchenware

Los Cinco Puntos
3300 E. Cesar Chavez Ave., Boyle Heights
(323) 261-4084, los5puntos.com
Recommended: Tortillas, carnitas, tamales

Mini-Mercadito @ El Mercado de Los Angeles
3425 E. 1st St., Boyle Heights
(323) 262-0303
Recommended: Moles, chiles, sweets, nuts, seeds,
spices

Northgate Gonzalez Market
425 S. Soto St., Boyle Heights
(323) 262-0595, northgatemarkets.com
Full-service Mexican and Latin American market

Vallarta Supermarkets
3425 Whittier Blvd., Boyle Heights
(323) 980-4400, vallartasupermarkets.com
Full-service Mexican and Latin American market

TORTILLERIAS

Acapulco Mexicatessen
929 S. Kern Ave., East L.A.
(323) 266-0267

La Gloria Foods Corporation
3455 E. 1st St., Boyle Heights
(323) 262-0410

La Imperial Tortilleria
3717 E. 1st St., East L.A.
(323) 261-4151

La Princesita #1
3432 E. Cesar Chavez Blvd., East L.A.
(323) 267-0673, laprincesitaylablanquita.com

La Princesita #3
2514 E. Cesar Chavez Ave., Boyle Heights
(323) 265-0020, laprincesitaylablanquita.com

Tortilleria San Marcos
1927 E. 1st St., Boyle Heights
(323) 263-0208

NORTHEAST & THE VERDUGOS

From the late 1990s to around 2005, during the hipster revival fueled by Pulitzer Prize–winning food writer Jonathan Gold and the food bloggers and snarky food chat-board jockeys he inspired, Highland Park in L.A.'s northeast region became the home of the taco crawl. While traditional vendors had yet to reveal themselves to outsiders, adventurous Angelenos came here for Mexican American tacos—meats cooked on a flattop and tossed onto a pair of tattered, industrial tortillas covered with way too much onion and cilantro and a splash of salsa.

Today, at the trucks and tables in the northeast's "parks" (Highland, Glassell, and Cypress) and the Verdugo communities of Eagle Rock, Atwater, Pasadena, and Altadena, pochos grab burritos and white and Asian customers dress their own tacos like pros under the pale glare of a trim of white lightbulbs. Some of the city's best-known Mexican American food is found in these parts, from old-school classics to such modern magnets as Cacao Mexicatessen in Eagle Rock and Salazar in Atwater.

Highland Park's classic El Arco Iris

POCHO CUISINE

El Arco Iris
5684 York Blvd., Highland Park
(323) 254-3402, elarcoiris.net
Recommended: Chile verde, Gus's special, bean and chile colorado burrito, enchilada combination plate

El Atacor
3520 N. Figueroa St., Cypress Park
(323) 342-0180, taqueriaelatacorrestaurants.com
Recommended: Carne asada nachos, tacos de papa, enchiladas rojas

El Huarache Azteca
5225 York Blvd., Highland Park
(323) 478-9572
Recommended: Super huarache de asada, huevos divorciados, mole rojo

El Taquito Mexicano
490 N. Lake Ave., Pasadena
(626) 356-9411
Recommended: Chicharrón taco

La Cabañita
3447 N. Verdugo Rd., Montrose
(818) 957-2711, cabanitarestaurant.com
Recommended: Moles, huevos divorciados, enchiladas verdes, margaritas

Lupita's
2634 Idell St., Cypress Park
(323) 223-7835
Recommended: Chilaquiles, menudo, chile rojo

My Taco
6300 York Blvd., Highland Park
(323) 256-2698, my-taco.com
Recommended: Tacos de barbacoa, carne asada fries, potato tacos

Tacos Poncitlan
2291 N. Lincoln Ave., Altadena
(626) 398-0439
Recommended: Birria, camarones burrito, al pastor, chile verde, adobado

Tacos Villa Corona
3185 Glendale Blvd., Atwater Village
(323) 661-3458, locu.com
Recommended: Breakfast burritos

REGIONAL MEXICAN

Metro Balderas
5305 N. Figueroa St., Highland Park
(323) 478-8383
Recommended: Carnitas, huaraches, pambazos

ALTA CALIFORNIA

Cacao Mexicatessen
1576 Colorado Blvd., Eagle Rock
(323) 478-2791, cacaodeli.com
Recommended: Sea urchin chile güero taco, carnitas de pato taco, Mexican craft beer, Mexican wine, mission fig mole poblano

Maestro

110 E. Union St., Pasadena

(626) 787-1512, maestropasadena.com

Recommended: Lamb barbacoa tacos, chicken tinga enchiladas, ceviche, duck carnitas with salsa chapulines, mezcal cocktails

BARES Y ANTROS

La Cuevita Bar

5922 N. Figueroa St., Highland Park

(323) 255-6871, lacuevitabar.com

Recommended: Mezcal and tequila cocktails

Los Candiles Night Club

2100 Cypress Ave., Glassell Park

(323) 222-3432, loscandilesnightclub.com

Recommended: Live music, drag show, drinking

The Hermosillo

5125 York Blvd., Highland Park

(323) 739-6459, thehermosillo.com

Recommended: Pork belly tacos, craft beer

Urbano Mexican Kitchen

147 W. California Blvd., Pasadena

(626) 578-1160, urbanomexicankitchen.com

Recommended: Carne asada fries, Mexican craft beer, tacos urbano

CAFEÍNA Y PAN DULCE

Café de Leche

5000 York Blvd., Highland Park

(323) 551-6828, cafedeleche.net

Recommended: Horchata con expresso, Mexi mocha, housemade cold brew

La Monarca Bakery

5833 N. Figueroa St., Highland Park

(323) 258-5470, lamonarcabakery.com

Recommended: Pan dulce, molletes, cakes, iced café de olla, organic Oaxacan dark roast

La Perla Bakery

6645 N. Figueroa St., Highland Park

(323) 255-1688

Recommended: Pan dulce

Tierra Mia Coffee

5528 Monte Vista St., Highland Park

(323) 344-3844, tierramiacoffee.com

Recommended: Horchata latte, mocha mexicano, chocolate mexicano de Guadalajara

AMBULANTES

El Mar Azul Truck

4700 N. Figueroa St., Highland Park

(323) 327-7744

Recommended: Seafood tostadas, seafood cocktails

El Taquito Truck

Nishikawa parking lot, 510 S. Fair Oaks Ave., Pasadena, (626) 577-3918

Recommended: Mexican American–style tacos

Elotes (Corn Man)

2338 Workman St., Lincoln Heights

(323) 343-0825

Recommended: Elotes

La Estrella Taco Truck
York Blvd. west of Ave. 54, Highland Park
Recommended: Mexican American–style tacos

Tacos El Pelon
York Blvd. and Ave. 52, Highland Park
Recommended: Mexican American–style tacos, mulitas

Tacos El Pique
York Blvd. and Ave. 53, Highland Park
Recommended: Mexican American–style tacos

MERCADOS

El Super
5610 York Blvd., Highland Park
(323) 916-8218, elsupermarkets.com
Full-service Mexican and Latin American market

Guerrero Produce Market
5535 York Blvd., Highland Park
(323) 258-2251
Recommended: Produce, meats, sundries

Superior
133 W. Ave. 45, Highland Park
(323) 223-3878, superiorgrocers.com
Full-service Mexican and Latin American market

TORTILLERIA

Tortilleria La California
2241 Cypress Ave., Glassell Park
(323) 221-8940
Recommended: Corn tortillas

Highland Park's Tuesday farmers' market is a good resource for ingredients and tacos.

SAN GABRIEL & POMONA VALLEYS

Driving to the San Gabriel Valley is routine for Angelenos in search of regional Chinese cuisines and other Asian specialties, but it's also notable as the home of Babita, one of the only places in L.A. for Mexican fine dining that predated the current boom. And even with the huge Chinese communities, the 626 still counts Latinos as the largest group in its forty-seven towns and neighborhoods. In recent years, the SGV has become home to the best northern burrito joint in the entire country, Burritos La Palma. It's also where the father of Alta California cuisine, Ricardo Diaz, has built a Mexican American fiefdom in the Chicano hamlet of Whittier. Elsewhere are hidden gems amid the usual gloppy cheese parlors of pocho excess, adding to the excitement of discovery that makes the SGV both an Asian *and* Mexican food haven.

Babita Mexicuisine's facade belies its gourmet menu.

POCHO CUISINE

Chano's Drive-in
1030 E. Las Tunas Dr., San Gabriel
(626) 451-0663
Recommended: Chano's burrito, Chano's fries,
pastrami nachos

Cook's Tortas
1944 S. Atlantic Blvd., Monterey Park
 (323) 278-3536, cookstortas.com
Recommended: Lengua torta, bacalao torta

Spanglish Kitchen
526 N. Atlantic Blvd., Alhambra
(626) 589-0482
Recommended: Tacos, breakfast burrito

REGIONAL MEXICAN

Babita's
1823 S. San Gabriel Blvd., San Gabriel
(626) 288-7265, babita-mexicuisine.com
Recommended: Shrimp Tompolobampo, güeritos
rellenos, mixiote lamb shank, crab chile relleno

Birrieria Calvillo Aguascalientes
12056 E. Valley Blvd., El Monte
(626) 443-1942
Recommended: Birria de chivo

Burritos La Palma
5120 N. Peck Rd., El Monte
(626) 350-8286
Recommended: Burrito de birria, bean and cheese
burrito, burrito especial

Playas de Nayarit
9817 Garvey Ave., El Monte
(626) 579-2927
Recommended: Aguachile, ceviche de camaron,
pata de mula

Tacos Baja
16032 Whittier Blvd., Whittier
(562) 945-8121, tacosbaja.com
Recommended: Fish tacos, shrimp tacos, cocteles

ALTA CALIFORNIA

Bizarra Capital
12706 Philadelphia St., Whittier
(562) 945-2426
Recommended: Shrimp taco, enmoladas de pollo,
ceviche de aguachile, costa azul

Colonia Publica
6715 Greenleaf Ave., Whittier
(562) 693-2621
Recommended: Fideo, Mexi-dogs,
taco de choriqueso, micheladas

Colonia Tacos Guisados
11114 Whittier Blvd., Whittier
(562) 699-2424
Recommended: Tesmole taco, cauliflower taco,
lengua taco

MERCADO

Northgate Gonzalez Market
3828 N. Peck Rd., El Monte
(626) 442-8200, northgatemarkets.com
Full-service Mexican and Latin American
supermarket

TORTILLERIAS

La Blanquita Tortilleria
11859 E. Valley Blvd., El Monte
(626) 575-8606, laprincesitaylablanquita.com
Recommended: Corn tortillas, masa, flour tortillas

La Chapalita Tortilleria
9643 E. Remer St., South El Monte
(626) 443-8556, lachapalita.com
Recommended: Corn tortillas, masa

Ramirez Meat Market
4005 La Rica Ave., Baldwin Park
(626) 338-0189, ramirezmeatmarket.weebly.com
Recommended: Corn tortillas, meats

SAN FERNANDO VALLEY

The vast flattened asphalt sprawl of strip malls; the relentless, overheated boulevards that tax your car's AC; the apartment complexes occupied by aspiring actors and musicians—this is the San Fernando Valley, the birthplace of Chicano rock 'n roll, Ritchie Valens, and the Mexican American Kevin Bacon, Danny Trejo. The oft-maligned Valley has long been and still is an underrated destination for Mexican food. Even most food writers are unaware of the excellent Michoacán-style restaurants, trucks, and extra-thick corn tortillas found in and around Pacoima (East L.A. also has these thick tortillas). Some of the earliest Mexican American food to be served off Olvera Street appeared in the Valley, and there's no better place in L.A. to hear touring banda and norteña acts. Lately, the Valley has picked up some unique regional restaurants, making locals happy and inspiring outsiders to make the trek over the hill.

Danny Trejo, the patron saint of Pacoima

POCHO CUISINE

Casa Vega
13301 Ventura Blvd., Sherman Oaks
(818) 788-4868, casavega.com
Recommended: Molcajetes, margaritas, steak picado, chile colorado

Fiesta Taco
1110 N. Hollywood Way, Burbank
(818) 558-6645
Recommended: Burrito chile colorado, mucho macho enchiladas, burrito Massiel

Henry's Tacos
4389 Tujunga Ave., Studio City
(818) 769-0343
Recommended: Tacos, tostadas, taco burger

Presidente Restaurants
Various locations, presidenterestaurant.com
Recommended: Tostada de pollo, beef fajitas, chimichangas

REGIONAL MEXICAN

Birrieria Apatzingan
10040 Laurel Canyon Blvd., Pacoima
(818) 890-6265
Recommended: Birria, enchiladas Apatzingan style, chavindecas

Cemitas Poblanas Don Adrian
14902 Victory Blvd., Van Nuys
(818) 786-0328
Recommended: Cemitas poblanas, tacos arabes

Gorditas Durango Mexican Grill
11720 Vanowen St., North Hollywood
(818) 821-3574
Recommended: Gorditas

Tortas Ahogadas Los Tripones
6102 Vineland Ave., North Hollywood
(818) 821-8077
Recommended: Tortas ahogadas, tostadas

BARES Y ANTROS

Club Vive
7230 Topanga Canyon Blvd., Canoga Park
(818) 226-9911, clubvive.net
Recommended: Banda, norteña, dancing

Cocina Condesa
11616 Ventura Blvd., Studio City
(818) 824-6177, cocinacondesa.com
Recommended: Tacos, brisket taquitos

Hacienda Corona
11700 Victory Blvd., North Hollywood
Recommended: Live music, cubetas

La Sierra Nightclub
8632 Van Nuys Blvd., Panorama City
(818) 830-1919, lasierranightclub.com
Recommended: Live music, cubetas

BEBIDAS

Wine and Liquor Depot
16,938 Saticoy St., Lake Balboa
(747) 254-0110, wineandliquordepot.com
Recommended: Tequila, mezcal

CAFEÍNA Y PAN DULCE

Café de Olla
12918 Riverside Dr., Sherman Oaks
(818) 783-4445, cafedemexico.net
Recommended: Café de olla, iced café de olla,
chilaquiles suizos

AMBULANTES

Don Cuco's Taco Truck
12898 Foothill Blvd., Pacoima
Recommended: Carnitas, morisqueta

Tacos La Fonda
N.W. corner of Vanowen and Vineland, North
Hollywood
(323) 221-0313
Recommended: Mexican American–style tacos

MERCADOS

Carniceria Don Juan
14103 Victory Blvd., Van Nuys
(818) 901-8971
Recommended: Meats, produce, sundries

Tresierras Supermarkets
13158 Van Nuys Blvd., Pacoima
(818) 896-6618

Vallarta Supermarkets
Various locations
vallartasupermarkets.com
Full-service Mexican and Latin American
supermarket

TORTILLERIAS

Carrillo's Tortilleria
1242 Pico St., San Fernando
(818) 365-1636, carrillostortilleria.com
Recommended: Corn tortillas

La Corona Tortilleria
508 S. Kalisher St., San Fernando
(818) 365-7408
Recommended: Corn tortillas

Lenchita's
13612 Van Nuys Blvd., Pacoima
(818) 899-2623
Recommended: Corn tortiilas, bistec ranchero,
caldo de pollo

WESTSIDE

It's a long-running cliché that you have to travel east of the 405 for real Mexican food, but that couldn't be farther from the truth. West L.A. is well established as one of California's more important destinations for Oaxacan cuisine, with a gaggle of Oaxacalifornia food trucks, and Santa Monica is home to one of the region's first Oaxacan restaurants, El Texate. Other westside restaurants like Frida's and Tlapazola Grill first introduced Los Angeles to fancy Mexican cuisine. Today, Santa Monica is a hot spot for tequila, mezcal, and tacos, as well as plenty of Mexican American standbys, regional Mexican spots, and a new breed of pocho restaurateurs who are changing the way westsiders eat Mexican food.

Strip-mall Oaxacan heaven

POCHO CUISINE

Casa Sanchez
4500 S. Centinela Ave., Del Rey
(310) 397-9999, casa-sanchez.com
Recommended: Chamorro de puerco,
carne tampiqueña, salmon Vallarta

El Texate
316 Pico Blvd., Santa Monica
(310) 399-1115
Recommended: El Texate's enchiladas,
mole de chichilo, tostada de tinga

Frida's Mexican Cuisine
236 S. Beverly Dr., Beverly Hills
(310) 278-7666, fridabeverlyhills.com
Recommended: Camarón rasurado,
fajitas Tlaquepaque, arrachera norteña

La Cabaña
738 Rose Ave., Venice
(310) 392-7973, lacabanavenice.com
Recommended: Tostada, el rojo burrito,
chile colorado

Maradentro
1168 S. Barrington Ave., Brentwood
(424) 273-1377, cocinasycalaveras.com
Recommended: Tacos de langosta,
chile relleno de siete mares, craiqueso

Tacomiendo
11462 Gateway Blvd., Sawtelle
(310) 481-0804, tacomiendo.net
Recommended: Taco de adobada, super plato,
chanclas

Tacos Por Favor
1408 Olympic Blvd., Santa Monica
(310) 392-5768, tacosporfavor.net
Recommended: Breakfast burrito, chicken taquito,
potato hard taco, California burrito

Tlapazola Grill
636 Venice Blvd., Venice
(310) 822-7561, tlapazolagrill.com
Recommended: Wild lobster tail chile relleno,
grilled salmon in pipián, grilled free-range chicken
in two moles

REGIONAL MEXICAN

Casa Oaxaca
9609 Venice Blvd., Palms
(310) 838-3000
Recommended: Filete en hoja de platano,
tacos de Jamaica, red mole enchiladas

El Sazon Oaxaqueño
12131 Washington Pl., Mar Vista
(310) 391-4721
Recommended: Memelas con asiento, amarillo de
pollo, enfrijoladas

Juquila Restaurant
11619 Santa Monica Blvd., Sawtelle
(310) 312-1079, juquilarestaurantlosangeles.com
Recommended: Alambre oaxaqueño, chile relleno,
tamal de rajas

Loqui
8850 Washington Blvd., Culver City
eatloqui.com
Recommended: Mushroom tacos, chicken tacos, Mexican craft beer, Mexican wine

Monte Alban Restaurant
11929 Santa Monica Blvd., Sawtelle
(310) 444-7736, montealbanrestaurante.com
Recommended: Molotes, mole negro, caldo de res

Sonorita's Prime Tacos
2004 Sawtelle Blvd., Sawtelle
(310) 444-9100, sonoritas.com
Recommended: Grilled romaine hearts, ribeye taco, carne asada taco

ALTA CALIFORNIA

Tacos Punta Cabras
2311 Santa Monica Blvd., Santa Monica
(310) 917-2244, tacospuntacabras.com
Recommended: Fish tacos, scallop tostada, shrimp coctele

BEBIDAS

Beverage Warehouse
4935 McConnell Ave., Ste. 21, Del Rey
(310) 306-2822, beveragewarehouse.com
Recommended: Tequila, mezcal

CAFEÍNA Y PAN DULCE

Churros Calientes
11521 Santa Monica Blvd., Sawtelle
(424) 248-3890, churroscalientes.com
Recommended: Churros, chocolate, coffee

La Monarca Bakery
1300 Wilshire Blvd., Santa Monica
(310) 451-1114, lamonarcabakery.com
Recommended: Iced café de olla, organic Oaxacan dark roast, pan dulce, cakes, molletes

AMBULANTES

El Paladar Oaxaqueño Truck
11654 Santa Monica Blvd., Sawtelle
(310) 691-0138
Recommended: Mulitas, taco de quesillo, tostada

El Torito Oaxaqueño Truck
Santa Monica Blvd. at Stoner, Sawtelle
(323) 282-8577
Recommended: Tlayudas, super alambre, enchiladas de mole

Juquila Truck
Santa Monica Blvd. at Stoner, Sawtelle
(424) 250-5181
Recommended: Memelas, tacos de cecina, tlayuda mixta

Oaxaca on Wheels
11975 Santa Monica Blvd., Sawtelle
(323) 805-3028, oaxacaonwheels.com
Recommended: Tacos guila, memelas, blanditas

MERCADOS

Eden L. Market
11933 Santa Monica Blvd., Sawtelle
(310) 996-7755
Recommended: Oaxacan food products, tlayudas,
pan dulce, produce, sundries

El Camaguey Meat Market
10925 Venice Blvd., Palms
(310) 839-4037
Recommended: Meats, produce, condiments,
sundries, groceries

Northgate Gonzalez Market
4700 Inglewood Blvd., Del Rey
(310) 390-9639, northgatemarkets.com
Full-service Mexican and
Latin American supermarket

SOUTH BAY

The South Bay would be a Mexican food desert if it weren't for Inglewood and Lennox, which are home to a pair of the most important Mexican seafood restaurants in the greater L.A. area, Mariscos Chente's and Coni'Seafood. In Lennox, a sleepy, dog-eared strip of mixed-use development yields a modest congregation of serious eateries and a wildly popular food truck that's got a name, Dollar Taco, more likely to cause a riot in L.A. than a marquee flashing "Free Beer." In the beach cities, fish tacos, chips, and guacamole are washed down with Coronas by aging, sunburned surfers under the shade of sombreros. If you'll excuse the thundering flow of jets coming and going from LAX, here is where you'll find the best airport food in town.

Airport dining at Don Rogelio's

POCHO CUISINE

Don Rogelio's
10618 S. Inglewood Ave., Lennox
(310) 677-1510
Recommended: Beef guisado, chile verde, taquitos

Rico's Tacos El Tio
2150 W. El Segundo Blvd., Gardena
(310) 329-9667
Recommended: Mexican American steak burritos

REGIONAL MEXICAN

Coni'Seafood
3544 W. Imperial Hwy., Inglewood
(310) 672-2339
Recommended: Pescado zarandeado, aguachile,
shrimp ceviche, camarones borrachos

La Finca Restaurante
10533 S. Inglewood Ave., Lennox
(323) 331-2431
Recommended: Mole, pipián, costillas de puerco
en adobo

Lennox Pollo
10822 S. Inglewood Ave., Inglewood
(310) 672-4850
Recommended: Rotisserie chicken

Mariscos Chente's
10020 S. Inglewood Ave., Lennox
(310) 672-0226
Recommended: Shrimp ceviche, cocteles,
campechanas

CAFEÍNA Y PAN DULCE

Jalisco Bakery
431 W. Arbor Vitae St., Inglewood
(310) 673-7876
Recommended: Pan dulce

Panaderia Mi Lupita
1640 W. Carson St., Torrance, Harbor Gateway
(310) 533-1884
Recommended: Pan dulce

AMBULANTES

Taco Dollar
Between 104th & Lennox on Inglewood Blvd., Inglewood
(310) 680-7511
Recommended: Tacos de tripa

MERCADOS

Gardena Supermarket
1012 W. Gardena Blvd., Gardena
(310) 324-7434
Recommended: Produce, hominy, chiles, meats, aguas frescas

La Sinaloense Market
10500 S. Prairie Ave., Inglewood
(310) 419-8127
Recommended: Pan dulce, tortillas, cakes, produce, chiles, sundries

La Venadita Meat Market
22035 Main St., Carson
(310) 830-7099, lavenadita.com
Recommended: Meats, tortillas, produce, sundries

Northgate Gonzalez Market
10801 Prairie Ave., Inglewood
(310) 419-4091, northgatemarkets.com
Full-service Mexican and Latin American market

HARBOR

If there's one thing that unites Mexican food lovers in this underappreciated stop lodged between the strong regional-Mexican hubs in Central L.A., East L.A., and Southeast L.A. (not to mention Orange County's formidable Central Mexican restaurants), it's hulking burritos covered in a red-orange sauce and fatty pools of melted yellow cheese. Even though most of the regional Mexican restaurants in Long Beach serve adulterated versions of traditional foods, chefs Eduardo Ruiz (Public Beer and Wine) and Tommy Ortega (Playa Amor) are a couple of bright lights—and we're down with the burritos, too.

Mural outside Playa Amor in Long Beach

POCHO CUISINE

El Pocho Grill
610 E. Carson Ave., Long Beach
(562) 290-0400, elpochogrill.com
Recommended: Quesataco, Cali burrito

Los Compadres
1144 Pine Ave., Long Beach
(562) 432-0061, loscompadreslbc.com
Recommended: Fajitas, chile verde,
pollo en crema chipotle

REGIONAL MEXICAN

Mariscos La Islitas
1585 Santa Fe Ave., Long Beach
(562) 436-2829
Recommended: Ceviche, cocteles

ALTA CALIFORNIA

Playa Amor
6527 E. Pacific Coast Hwy., Long Beach
(562) 430-2667, playaamorlb.com
Recommended: Mole tot poutine, New Mexico
green hatch spaghetti, Puerto Nuevo style lobster

BARES Y ANTROS

Public Beer and Wine Shop
121 W. 4th St., Long Beach
(562) 499-0415, publicbeerwineshop.com
Recommended: Avocado salad, taco de mi abuela,
ceviche, craft beer

CAFEÍNA Y PAN DULCE

Tierra Mia
425 E. Pacific Coast Hwy., Long Beach
(562) 912-4522, tierramiacoffee.com
Recommended: Coffee

Viento y Agua Coffeehouse and Gallery
4007 E. 4th St., Long Beach
(562) 434-1182, vientoyaguacoffeehouse.com
Recommended: Coffee

AMBULANTES

*Street vendors are illegal in Long Beach, so alas, the
vibrant scene that could exist does not.*

MERCADO

Northgate Gonzalez Markets
4700 Cherry Ave., Long Beach
(562) 423-1300, northgatemarkets.com
Recommended: Full-service Mexican and
Latino supermarket

TORTILLERIA

Julian's Tortilleria
12321 Carson St., Ste. 10, Hawaiian Gardens
(562) 865-3100, juliansmexicanrestaurant.com
Recommended: Corn tortillas

SOUTH L.A.

South L.A. is unrivaled in its Mexican street-food offerings. On weekends it teems with regional barbacoa from several states, the best Mexico City–style tortas, and a variety of regional tacos. At night, the streets are festooned with the fuzzy white lights of street stands, tire shops are transformed into taquerias, and professional taqueros plucked from Mexico City's famed al pastor destinations work the vertical spits of outlaw stands. On weekend mornings, not long after the grills fired by mesquite and propane have gone cold and the graveyard shift has packed up and gone home, vendors serving a dazzling array of Mexican dishes encircle the major thoroughfares and lie hidden in driveways and backyards astride the 110, in a barrio that never sleeps.

The Los Guichos truck on Slauson

REGIONAL MEXICAN

Carnitas Los 3 Puerquitos
981 E. Vernon Ave., Central Alameda
(323) 369-3111
Recommended: Carnitas

Chichén Itzá
3655 S. Grand Ave., University Park
(213) 741-1075, chichenitzarestaurant.com
Recommended: Cochinita pibil, papdzules,
huevos motuleños

Flautas
Baldwin Hills Crenshaw Plaza
3650 W. Martin Luther King Jr. Blvd., Baldwin Hills
Recommended: Toto-esquites, shredded beef
flautas, mercado flautas

Mexicano
Baldwin Hills Crenshaw Plaza
3650 W. Martin Luther King Jr. Blvd., Baldwin Hills
(323) 296-0798, mexicanola.com
Recommended: Enchiladas 3 moles,
chile en nogada, mole rojo

Mi Lindo Nayarit
1020 E. Florence Ave., Florence
(323) 589-5109
Recommended: Live music, vaso loco,
patas de jaiba, micheladas

Oaxacalifornia Café and Juice Bar
3655 S. Grand Ave., University Park
(213) 747-8622, oaxacali.com
Recommended: Juice, aguas frescas, tortas

Pollos Asados Al Carbón El Güero
274 E. Slauson Ave., Florence
(323) 233-2274
Recommended: Grilled chicken

AMBULANTES

Carnitas El Momo
6015 S. Avalon, Florence
(323) 627-8540
Recommended: Carnitas

Carnitas El Momo (Saturday only)
S. Alameda St. near E. 135th, Willowbrook
Recommended: Carnitas

El Rey de la Barbacoa
Hill St. between W. Adams and 27th St.,
University Park
(213) 248-3008, (213) 248-3068
Recommended: Crispy lamb tacos

Super Tortas D.F.
1098 E. 41st St., South L.A.
(323) 351-8379
Recommended: Torta cubana, Mexico City–style
tortas

Tacos Los Güichos
320 W. Slauson Ave., Florence
Recommended: Tacos al pastor, carnitas

Tamales Elena
Wilmington Ave. at 110th St., Watts
(323) 919-2509
Recommended: Tamales en hoja de platano, barbacoa de res, pozole, menudo

Tire Shop Taqueria
4069 S. Avalon Blvd., South L.A.
Recommended: Tacos de asada, mulitas

Tortas Gigantes El Chilango
1832-1834 E. Slauson Ave., Central Alameda
(323) 483-2047
Recommended: Tortas gigantes, tortas cubanas, tortas chilangas

MERCADOS

Alameda Swap Meet
4501 S. Alameda St., Central Alameda
(323) 233-2764
Recommended: Produce, chiles, herbs, spices, seeds, Mexican products, cookware, antojitos, tacos, churros, aguas frescas

El Faro Plaza
4433 S. Alameda St., Central Alameda
(323) 234-2838
Swap-meet-style mercado with produce, cookware, seafood, cheeses, meats, tacos de canasta, antojitos, fondas

El Super
1100 W. Slauson Ave., South L.A.
(323) 565-4005, elsupermarkets.com
Full service Mexican and Latin American supermarket

Northgate Gonzalez Markets
944 E. Slauson Ave., Florence
(323) 846-8804, www.northgatemarkets.com
Full-service Mexican and Latin American supermarket

SOUTHEAST

Blessed with a combination of upwardly mobile Mexican Americans who left Boyle Heights for these pocho 'burbs and a steady flow of skilled cooks and restaurateurs, L.A.'s southeast region has become the most important Mexican food hub in town. The states of Sinaloa, Jalisco, and Nayarit rule these streets with a range of seafood restaurants and loncheras, fondas and specialists. Three of L.A.'s best Mexican chefs—Rocio Camacho, Jaime Martín del Campo, and Ramiro Arvizu—have established their flagships in these parts, and street vendors representing very specific styles have solidified L.A.'s position as the US capital of provincial Mexican cooking. Like the Alameda Swap Meet and El Faro Plaza in the neighboring South L.A. region, Plaza Mexico is a replica of the markets and public squares in Mexico, which explains the draw for L.A.'s Latino community— they are homes away from home.

An old-country feel in Compton

POCHO CUISINE

El Pescador
9535 Long Beach Blvd., South Gate
(323) 564-7993, elpescadorsouthgate.com
Recommended: Costa azul, fajitas campestre,
piña el pescador

REGIONAL MEXICAN

Aqui es Texcoco
5850 S. Eastern Ave., Commerce
(323) 725-1429, aquiestexcoco.com
Recommended: Lamb barbacoa, lamb brain
quesadillas, rabbit mixiotes

Cenaduria Gumacus
8646 State St., South Gate
(323) 566-5522
Recommended: Enchiladas del suelo, asado de res,
chilorio, mochomos

El Coraloense by Leonardo's
6600 Florence Ave., Bell Gardens
(562) 776-8800, elcoraloense.com
Recommended: Tostada changoneada,
lobster nachos, taco a la diabla

El Sinaloense
7601 State St., Huntington Park
(323) 581-1532
Recommended: Chilorio, machaca, white menudo,
asado

El Sinaloense #2
15503 Paramount Blvd., Paramount
(562) 529-5120
Recommended: Taco enchilado,
albondigas de pescado, bistec ranchero

La Casita Mexicana
4030 Gage Ave., Bell
(323) 773-1898
Recommended: Mole, pipián, chamorro de res,
chile en nogada

Mariscos Los Dorados
8111 Rosecrans Ave., Paramount
(562) 531-6200, mariscoslosdorados.com
Recommended: Botana callo de hacha,
albondigas de camaron, camarones culichis

Rocio's Mexican Kitchen
7891 Garfield Ave., Bell Gardens
(562) 659-7800
Recommended: Mole negro, mole verde, chilate,
tacos de cazuela

Tortas Ahogadas Guadalajara
6042 Santa Fe Ave., Huntington Park
(323) 587-3115, tortasahogadasinla.com
Recommended: Tortas ahogadas,
tacos de barbacoa, menudo Jalisco style

ALTA CALIFORNIA

Amor y Tacos
13333 South St., Cerritos
(562) 860-2667, amorytacos.com
Recommended: Taco de queso quemado, Doritos chilaquiles, mole tots

BARES Y ANTROS

20/20 Draft House
8228 Firestone Blvd., Downey
(562) 861-7970
Recommended: Micheladas, Botana familiar, cucumber shots

Don Chente Bar and Grill
2144 E. Florence Ave., Huntington Park
(323) 585-8900, donchentebarandgrill.com
Recommended: Cazuelas, cactus pear margaritas, palomitas, mole

Lido's Restaurant
9100 Long Beach Blvd., South Gate
(323) 564-5436, lidorestaurant.com
Recommended: Live music, cubetas

CAFEÍNA Y PAN DULCE

La Monarca Bakery
6365 Pacific Blvd., Huntington Park
(323) 585-5500, lamonarcabakery.com
Recommended: Iced café de olla, organic Oaxacan dark roast, molletes, pan dulce, cakes

Tierra Mia
6706 Pacific Blvd., Huntington Park
(323) 589-2065, tierramiacoffee.com
Recommended: Mocha mexicano, horchata latte, coffee

AMBULANTES

Tacos La Carreta
413 N. Wilmington Ave., Compton
(562) 500-5581
Recommended: Chorreadas, vampiros, tacos de carne asada

Tacos La Güera
Santa Fe Ave. at Center St., Walnut Park
Recommended: Tacos de fritanga, buche, suadero, tripa

MERCADO

Plaza Mexico
3100 E. Imperial Hwy., Lynwood
(310) 631-6789, plazamexico.com
Recommended: Mexican products, produce, meats and poultry, seafood, sweets, chiles, herbs, spices, restaurants, desserts, live music

TORTILLERIAS

Amapola Market

7223 S. Compton Ave., Huntington Park
Also in Downey, Paramount & West Covina
(323) 587-7118, amapolamarket.com
Recommended: Corn tortillas, produce, meats and
poultry, fish, sundries

Amapola-Mexican Deli

6000 Atlantic Blvd., Maywood
(323) 560-4527
Recommended: Corn tortillas, produce, sundries,
Mexican products

Arevalo Tortilleria

1537 W. Mines Ave., Montebello
(323) 888-1711, arevalos.com
Recommended: Flour tortillas, corn tortillas

Tortilleria Guamuchil

River Dr., Bell
(562) 852-3868
Recommended: Flour tortillas

DICCIONARIO

Adobada: A marinade of dried chiles, citrus, and spices for roasted meats

Aguachile: A ceviche of raw shrimp in a spicy lime and chile mixture

Al pastor: Vertical spit-roasted pork in adobo, or naturally roasted kid

Alambres: A hash of various meats, vegetables, bacon, and cheese

Albondigas: Meatballs

Amarillo de pollo: Yellow mole with chicken

Ambulantes: Roving vendors

Antros: Nightclubs

Asiento: Unrefined pork lard

Barbacoa: Pit-roasted meats, usually lamb or goat, and beef in northern Mexico

Bares: Bars

Bebidas: Beverages

Birria: A stew of chiles and spices made with drippings from roasted goat and lamb (Central Mexico) or beef (northern Mexico)

Bistec: Steak, usually cooked on a flattop for tacos

Blanditas: Regional name for a large corn tortilla in Oaxaca

Botana: Snack

Buche: Pork stomach

Cachetadas: Slaps, an original taco created by Mexicali Taco Co. made with a hard-toasted corn tortilla

Cafeína: Caffeine

Caldo de pollo: Chicken soup

Caldo de res: Beef soup

Callo de hacha: Raw pen-shell clams served in aguachile (lime and fresh or dried chiles)

Camarones: Shrimp

Camote: Sweet potato

Campechana: Mixed seafood cocktail, or a combo taco (campechano)

Carne a la tampiqueña: Dish created by Don José Inés Loredo at Mexico City's Tampico Club (1939) with carne asada or cecina, green enchiladas, beans, and cheese

Carnitas: Pork slowly fried in its own fat

Cazuela: Casserole

Cecina: Salted, dried pork (Oaxacan)

Cemita: A sesame seed roll used in cemitas poblanas, a sandwich from Puebla

Ceviche: Seafood cooked in lime

Chapulines: Grasshoppers

Chavindecas: Regional name for mulitas in Michoacán; a taco sandwich

Chicharrón: Deep-fried pork rind (sometimes with a small amount of meat attached) for making stews, eating as a snack, or to add texture to a dish

Chilaquiles: Tortilla chips covered in sauce or mole, garnished with Mexican cream and crumbled cheese

Chilate: A chile and tomato stew with chicken from Huajuapan de León, Oaxaca

Chile colorado: Dried red chile from Sonora; also a beef stew cooked with chile colorado

Chile en nogada: Seasonal chile relleno from Puebla, a roasted chile poblano stuffed with a sweet and savory mix of ground meat and seasonal fruit covered in a white walnut sauce, dressed with pomegranate seeds

Chile relleno: Fried, stuffed chiles; the traditional version is from Puebla and uses a poblano chile

Chile verde: Stew of meat in a green salsa

Chilhuacle negro chile: Rare dried chile from Oaxaca used in moles

Chilorio: Spicy pork (Sinaloa)

Chipotle chile (chile chipotle): Smoked, dried jalapeño, sometimes canned in adobo

Chochoyotes: Masa dumplings

Chorizo: Sausage; varies by region

Chorreadas: A taco on a thick tortilla made with unrefined lard and melted cheese from Mazatlan

Cochinita pibil: A Yucatán dish of achiote-marinated pork roasted in banana leaves

Cocteles: Seafood cocktails or cocktails (beverages)

Costa azul: Bacon-wrapped stuffed shrimp

Cotija cheese: Regional dry cheese from Cotija de la Paz, Michoacán

Crema mexicana: Mexican sour cream

Duritos: Wheat snacks

Elotes: Grilled or boiled corn on the cob smeared with mayonnaise or another fat, salt, chile powder, lime juice, crumbled cheese, and other ingredients depending on the region

Enfrijoladas: Warm corn tortillas covered in a bean sauce, dressed with Mexican cream and crumbled cheese

Enmoladas: Rolled tortillas filled with chicken or cheese covered in mole

Entomatada: Warm corn tortillas covered in a tomato sauce

Estofado: Stew (in Oaxaca a type of mole)

Fritanga: Meats fried in a stainless steel disc

Guajillo chile (chile guajillo): A versatile dried chile widely used in Mexican cuisine

Gorditas: A masa pocket filled with regional stews

Güeritos rellenos: Stuffed blond chiles

Habanero chile (chile habanero): A fiery fresh chile from the Yucatán popular all over Mexico. It is the hottest chile used in Mexican cuisine

Horchata: Sweet rice water drink

Huaraches: Sandal-shape masa boat covered with regional stews

Huevos divorciados: Divorced eggs, a breakfast dish made with separated red and green salsas

Huevos rancheros: Eggs with ranch salsa

Jalapeño chile (chile jalapeño): Popular fresh chile that varies from medium to hot

Langosta: Lobster

Lengua: Tongue

Licuado: Mexican-style smoothies

Masa: Corn dough for tortillas, tamales, or other antojitos

Machaca: Beef jerky

Memelitas: Masa boat topped with refried beans,

salsa and crumbled cheese

Menudo: Beef tripe and stomach stew

Mercado: Market

Michelada: Spicy beer cocktail

Migas: Pork leg stew thickened with breadcrumbs and tortillas

Mixiote: Meat roasted in parchment

Mochomos: Shredded meat dish from Sinaloa and Chihuahua

Molcajete: A mix of meats, vegetables and cheese cooked in a lava rock mortar (which is called a molcajete), or raw seafood cooked in lime inside of a molcajete

Mole: A pre-Hispanic dish of chiles, thickeners, nuts, spices, and vegetables among other ingredients

Molletes: An open faced sandwich smeared with beans, cheese and other toppings

Morisqueta: A Michoacán dish of beans, rice and stewed pork

Mulato chile (chile mulato): A dried chile used in moles

Mulitas: A taco with a tortilla on top, like a taco sandwich

Pachucos: Mexican American subculture from the zoot suit era in the 1940s

Pambazos: A potato and chorizo torta with chile-dipped bread dressed with lettuce, crema mexicana, and crumbled cheese

Pan dulce oaxaqueño: Oaxacan-style sweet bread

Pasilla chile (chile pasilla): A dried chile used in sauces, and in moles in Oaxaca

Pescado zarandeado: Shaken fish; manglar wood grilled, butterflied whole fish in regional marinades from Nayarit, Sinaloa, and other Pacific Coast states

Pipián: Pumpkin-seed mole

Platano: Banana

Poblano chile (chile poblano): Large mild green chile used for chiles rellenos and other dishes

Pocho, pocha: A Mexican born in the United States

Queso fresco: Fresh cheese

Queso Oaxaca: String cheese

Rajas: Chile strips

Suadero: Brisket

Sopes: Masa boat topped with beans, lettuce, Mexican cream, crumbled cheese, and a regional stew

Sopitos: A regional sope with ground meat from Colima

Tamal: Steamed masa dough filled with regional stews and wrapped in corn husks, banana leaves, or other natural wrappers

Tasajo: Soft beef jerky (Oaxacan)

Tinga: Spicy meat

Tlayuda: Large, thin Oaxaca tortilla

Torta: Sandwich

Tripa: Tripe

Vampiros: Regional taco from Sinaloa of grilled meat on a hard-toasted corn tortilla topped with salsas; at Mexicali Taco, a quesadilla with meat and a garlic aioli

Garbanzo Entero
Garbanzo Molido
Maiz Azul Molido
MAIZ BLANCO

RECONOCIMIENTO
ACKNOWLEDGMENTS

This incredible journey in food would not have been possible without my family, whose celebrations, reunions, and tables nourished this pocho with the flavors of Mexico. To grandmas Lupe and Ruby and to my dad, thanks for making me crazy about our food—I wish you were still here so I could tell you how much you've influenced me. To my mom, thank you for your patience this past year as I hunkered down at my place in Hollywood while writing *L.A. Mexicano*. And thank you to the rest of my family and close friends for always supporting me, unconditionally.

To mi raza, the people of *L.A. Mexicano*, I thank you from the bottom of my heart for your time, your invaluable contributions to L.A.'s culture, and your friendship. Jaime, Ramiro, Wes, Ricardo C., Ricardo D., familia Acosta, Eddie, Carlos, Ricky, Susanna, Soledad, Zeferino, familia Cossio, Ray, Tommy, Hualterio, Francisco, Esdras, Elena R., Gilberto Jr. and Sr., familia Ramirez, David, Cindy, Cecilia, Elena Lorenzo and the familia Irra, Josef, Rocio, Christy, familia Burgos, Oscar, Alberto and Lauren, John, Jimmy, Josh, Paco, David and Maria R., Roberto, Ulysses, Andrew, Raul—you are all national treasures.

Special thanks to the people who've believed in me and given me opportunities to share Latin American culture with the world. Andrew Zimmern, thank you for giving me my first break and for your continuing friendship. Thanks to my manager, Eileen Stringer, for sticking with me—you are like family to me. And to my brother from another mother, Bill Chait, I'm forever grateful. Gustavo, it's you and me against the world—thanks for being an inspiration, a friend, and a comrade in arms.

I wouldn't have gotten to write this book if it wasn't for Betty Hallock, who recruited me for my first professional story at the *Los Angeles Times*, and my *Los Angeles Magazine* family, Lesley Barger Suter, Patric Kuh, Mary Melton, and Matt Segal, who've all helped me become a better writer. Thanks to Phil Rosenthal, Zero Point Zero productions, Eddie Huang, Bravo, and the Travel Channel for letting me share Latin American cuisine with your audiences.

Thanks to my Tacolandia teammates at *LA Weekly*—Erin, Tamara, and Joel—for making this event a place where dreams come true.

Finally, Colleen Dunn Bates and the Prospect Park Books team—thank you, Colleen, for the phone call that changed my life, and for giving me the opportunity, and the freedom, to tell this story. Thanks to Staci Valentine for making the food and beautiful people of *L.A. Mexicano* come to life, and to designer Amy Inouye for her tireless work and creativity in helping me document an essential L.A. story, long overdue.

INDEX

20/20 Draft House, 229

Acapulco Mexicatessen, 204
Acapulco Tortilleria, 200
Acosta, Romulo, 166
adobada, 17, 216, 231
aguachile, 18, 120-121, 159, 171, 173, 202-203, 210, 220, 231
Aguascalientes, 8-11, 17, 24, 166, 210
Al and Bea's, 202
al pastor, 17-18, 84, 119, 180, 193, 199-200, 208, 224-225, 231
alambres, 18, 84, 142, 199-200, 203, 231
Alameda Swap Meet, 171, 226
albondigas, 17-18, 228, 231
Alhambra, 210
Altadena, 205, 208
Amapola Market, 230
Amapola-Mexican Deli, 230
amarillo de pollo, 216, 231
Amor y Tacos, 145, 229
Andrés, José, 14
Antequera de Oaxaca, 197
Anthony, John, 49-50
Aqui es Texcoco, 92-94, 96, 228
Arellano, Gustavo, 6-7
Arevalo Tortilleria, 230
Arlington Heights, 197, 200
Arts District, 133, 196
Arvizu, Ramiro, 71, 80, 82, 227
asiento, 64, 216, 231
Atwater, 154, 198, 205-206
Avila, Wes, 13-14, 97, 129, 132, 134, 170, 181
avocado, how to slice, 135
Avocado Sauce, 36

B.S. Taqueria, 124, 198
Babita Mexicuisine, 109-111, 209-210
Bäco Mercat, 140-142

Baja California, 17, 23, 49, 110, 114-115, 128-129, 132, 145
bakeries, 30, 80, 190-191, 193
Baldwin Hills, 81, 225
Baldwin Park, 66, 211
Bañuelos, Alberto, 66, 68
Bar Amá, 140-142, 198
barbacoa, 92-94, 96-98
bars (bares), 198, 203, 207, 213, 223, 229, 231
Basic Beans, 24
Bayless, Rick, 16, 49, 88
Bayo beans, 22
bean recipes
    Basic, 24
    Black, 25
    Enfrijoladas, 103
    Refried, 64
    Refried Black, 65
    Tlayuda, 63
beef recipes
    Carne Asada Vampiros, 78
    Chirmole, 107
    Molcajete, 41
    Steak Fajitas, 213
    Steak Picado Ciro's, 32
    Taquitos with Avocado Sauce, 36
    Tlayuda, 63
    Torta La Rusa, 168
Bell Gardens, 70-71, 228
Bell, 71, 80-81, 129, 154, 228, 230
Berrelleza, Roberto, 16, 108, 110-111
Beverage Warehouse, 217
beverages, 153, 158, 159, 162, 163, 203, 214, 217, 231
Beverly Hills, 14, 85, 216
birria, 6-7, 68-69, 202-203, 208, 210, 213, 231
Birrieria Apatzingan, 213
Birrieria Calvillo Aguascalientes, 210
Birrieria Nochistlán, 202
bistec, 202, 214, 228, 231
Bizarra Capital, 137, 154, 210

blanditas, 22, 85, 87, 217, 231
BLVD Restaurant Group, 129
boar, 130
Botana callo de hacha, 228, 231
Boyle Heights, 13, 16, 30-31, 43-45, 47, 137, 145, 154, 167, 170-171, 188-189, 191, 193, 202-204, 227
Brentwood, 216
Broken Spanish, 122-124, 149, 189, 198
Buche, 229, 231
Burbank, 109, 213
Burritos La Palma, 66-69, 209-210
burritos, 43-44, 47, 49, 66-69, 76, 197, 205-206, 220, 222
burrito recipes
    Hollenbeck, 44-46
    Chile Relleno, 47
    Tinga (Chicken Chipotle), 68

Cacao Mexicatessen, 13, 148-150, 205-206
cachetadas, 77, 198, 231
cactus, 23, 87, 110, 129, 193, 229
Café de Leche, 207
café de olla, 190-191, 203, 207, 214, 217, 229
caldo de pollo, 214, 231
caldo de res, 217, 231
California chiles, 22, 82, 100
Camacho, Rocio, 16, 70, 72, 227
camarones, 18, 53, 197, 208, 220, 228, 231
Camote, 198, 231
Campechana, 186, 198, 231
Campeche, 17
Canoga Park, 213
Carne a la tampiqueña, 231
Carniceria Don Juan, 214

Carniceria La Oaxaqueña, 200
Carnitas El Momo, 16, 167, 203, 225
Carnitas Los 3 Puerquitos, 225
Carrillo's Tortilleria, 214
Carson, 221, 223
Casa Oaxaca, 216
Casa Sanchez, 216
Casa Vega Margarita, 158
Casa Vega, 38-39, 41, 44, 158, 213
cazuela de barro, 20
cazuela, 18, 20, 62, 84, 228, 231
cecina, 17-18, 63-64, 84, 203, 217, 231
Cemita, 18, 203, 231
Cemitas Los Poblanos Truck, 203
Cemitas Poblanas Don Adrian, 213
Cenaduria Gumacus, 228
Centeno, Josef, 13, 140-142
Central Alameda, 225-226
Cerritos, 144-145, 229
Cervantes, Ricardo, 190, 192
Cetina, Gilberto Jr., 88, 90
Cetina, Gilberto, 88, 90
ceviche, 17-18, 53-54, 115, 120, 136, 171, 203, 210, 220, 223, 231
Ceviche, Shrimp (recipe), 54
Chano's Drive-in, 210
chapulines, 18, 197, 231
chavindecas, 17, 213, 231
cheeses (quesos), 23
Chiapas, 17, 62, 156
chicharrón, 18, 22, 56, 139, 145, 198-199, 206, 231
Chichén Itzá, 16, 88-90, 149, 189, 225
chicken recipes
    Chicken Relleno Negro, 106
    Chicken Stock, 74
    Chicken with Pipián Rojo, 82
    Molcajete, 41

Mole Negro Oaxaqueño, 72
    Tamales de Pollo, 178
    Tinga Burritos, 68
Chicken Relleno Negro, 106
Chicken Stock (recipe), 74
Chicken with Pipián Rojo, 82
Chihuahua, 17, 23, 30, 47, 67, 126, 142, 233
chilaquiles, 44, 123, 129-132, 145, 198-199, 206, 214, 229, 231
Chilaquiles, Wild Boar (recipe) 130
chilate, 17, 228, 231
chile colorado, 206, 213, 216, 232
Chile de Árbol Salsa, 27
chile en nogada, 225, 228, 232
chile relleno, 149, 197, 202, 210, 216, 232
Chile Relleno Burrito, La Azteca Style, 47
Chile Rojo, 46
chile verde (in restaurants), 202, 206, 208, 220, 223, 232
chiles
    ancho, 82, 130
    California, 22, 82, 100
    chile de árbol, 21-22, 27, 46, 65, 79, 82, 98
    chilhuacle negro, 22, 72, 232
    chipotle, 22, 68, 72, 94, 147, 173, 232
    costeño, 22, 178
    guajillo, 22, 46, 72, 87, 94, 130, 178 232
    güeros, 22, 37
    habanero, 22, 90, 116, 117, 173, 232
    jalapeño, 22, 32, 48, 54, 60, 111, 130, 139, 168, 173, 176, 184, 232
    mulato, 22, 72, 233
    pasilla, 22,47, 72, 96, 130, 233
    poblano, 47, 125, 142, 233

roasting chiles, 21
Chiles Secos, 200
chilorio, 17-18, 228, 232
Chinatown, 77, 197-198
Chinois, 20
chipotle chiles, 22, 68, 72, 94, 147, 173, 232
Chipotle Cream (recipes), 100, 169
Chirmole, 106-107
chochoyotes, 18, 198, 232
chocolate, Mexican, 22
chorizo, 17, 63-64, 84, 115, 119, 191, 232-233
chorreadas, 18, 229, 232
Churros Calientes, 217
Cielito Lindo, 12, 33-34, 36, 134, 197
Cinco Puntos, 13, 36, 44, 193, 201, 204
Ciro's Restaurant, 13, 30-32, 202
Cities Restaurant, 203
Club Mayan, 198
Club Vive, 213
Coahuila, 17, 142
Cochinita Pibil Tacos, 90, 197
cochinita pibil, 18, 90-91, 105, 137, 197-198, 225, 232
Cochon 555, 123
Cocina Condesa, 213
Cocktail Sauce, 117
cocktails, 158, 159, 162, 207
cocktails, seafood (cocteles), 52, 54, 116, 134, 171, 173, 207, 210, 217, 220, 223
coffee making, 156-157
coffeehouses, 199, 203, 207, 214, 217, 221, 223, 229, 231
Colima, 17, 23, 130, 156, 233
Colonia Publica, 137, 139, 154, 159, 210
Colonia Tacos Guisados, 137, 210
comal, 20-21
Commerce, 93, 203, 228
Compton, 174, 227, 229-230
Conga Room, The 199
Coni'Seafood, 53, 219-220
Consommé, 94
Cook's Tortas, 13, 97, 136-137, 149, 210

Corazón y Miel, 129, 130
Corazón de Tierra, 14, 128
Corn & Summer Squash Tamales, 124
corn husks, 124, 126, 233
Corn-Poblano Sauce, 125-126
Cornbread, Isthmus Style, 192
Cossio, Vicente, Connie & Bianka, 52
Costa Azul, 202, 210, 228, 232
costeño chiles, 22, 178
cotija cheese, 232
Crab Huarache on Cactus Paddle, 110
crema mexicana, 22, 57, 100, 103, 110, 130, 169, 182, 232-233
Culver City, 217
Cypress Park, 122, 206

dancing, 198-199, 213
Del Rey, 216-218
Diaz, Katarine A., 90
Diaz, Ricardo, 13, 136, 139, 149, 154, 159, 209
Districto Federal (D.F.), 17, 168, 225
Don Chente Bar and Grill, 71, 229
Don Cuco's Taco Truck, 214
Don Rogelio's, 219-220
Downey, 229-230
Downtown, 44, 76-78, 84, 114, 133, 140-141, 154, 157, 167, 187, 196-200
Durango, 17, 132, 213
Duritos, 198, 232

Eagle Rock, 13, 148-150, 205-206
East L.A., 13-14, 30-31, 38, 43, 47, 49-50, 71, 98, 128, 136, 144, 170-171, 178, 188, 191, 201-204, 212, 222
Eastside Luv Wine Bar y Queso, 203
Eastside Pico de Gallo, 46-48
Echo Park, 141, 199-200
Eden L. Market, 218
El 7 Mares, 136-137
El Arco Iris, 44, 205-206
El Atacor, 206

El Camaguey Meat Market, 218
El Carmen, 199
El Chato Taco Truck, 199
El Cholo, the Original, 197
El Compadre, 197
El Coraloense by Leonardo's, 228
El Faro Plaza, 171, 226
El Huarache Azteca, 206
El Mar Azul Truck, 207
El Mercado de Los Angeles, 204
El Monte, 66-68, 210-211
El Paladar Oaxaqueño Truck, 217
El Pescador, 228
El Pocho Grill, 223
El Rey de la Barbacoa, 225
El Sazon Oaxaqueño, 216
El Sinaloense #2, 228
El Sinaloense, 228
El Super, 193, 208, 226
El Taquito Mexicano, 206
El Taquito Truck, 207
El Tepeyac Café, 30, 43, 45, 202
El Texate, 16, 62, 215-216
El Torito Oaxaqueño Truck, 217
El Valle Oaxaqueño, 200
Elotes (Corn Man), 207
Enchilada Sauce, 42
Enfrijoladas, 103
Enmoladas, 210, 232
Ensenada, 7, 114, 129, 180-182
Entomatada, 198, 232
epazote, 22, 25, 87, 106-107
estofado, 18, 197, 232
Estrada, Cindy, Gloria & Adrian, 97
Expresión Oaxaqueña, 84-86, 197

Fairfax, 55, 198
fajitas, 213, 223, 228
Fajitas, Steak, 213
Farmers Market, 55-56, 71, 198
fideos, 22, 33, 129, 137, 139-140
Fideos (recipe), 139
Fiesta Taco, 213
Fig, 123, 206
fish tacos, 182, 199, 210, 217

Fish Tacos (recipe), 182
flautas, 30-31, 67, 81, 186, 202, 225
Florence, 98, 225-226, 228-229
Frida's Mexican Cuisine, 216
fritanga, 17, 201, 229, 232

Garcia, Ray, 13, 122, 124, 170, 188
Garcia, Zeferino, 84, 86
Gardena Supermarket, 221
Gardena, 220-221
Gil, Josh, 114, 116
Gish Bac, 15, 102-103, 197
Glassell Park, 207-208
Gold, Jonathan, 16, 109, 205
Gonzalez, Oscar, 30, 32
Gorditas Durango Mexican Grill, 213
gorditas, 17-18, 213, 232
guacamole, 19, 27, 31-32, 41-43, 46, 50, 78, 84, 197, 202, 219
Guacamole (recipe), 27
guajillo chile, 232
Guanajuato, 17, 166
Guelaguetza, 16, 61-63, 161, 197
Güeritos rellenos, 210, 232
güeros chiles, 22, 37
Guerrero Produce Market, 208
Guerrero, 17, 92, 160, 174-176, 178
Guerrero, Aurora, 12, 33-34
Guerrilla Tacos, 13, 97, 132-134, 189, 198
guisados, 13, 32, 70, 85, 136-137, 180, 202, 210
Guisados (restaurant), 137, 202

habanero chile, 22, 90, 116, 117, 173, 232
Habanero Salsa, Charred, 116
Hacienda Corona, 213
Handsome Roasters, 133
Hansen, Barbara, 16, 167
Harbor, 221-222
Hawaiian Gardens, 223
Henry's Tacos, 213
Hermosillo, The 207

Hernandez, Diego, 14, 128
Hidalgo, 17, 92-93
Hollenbeck Burrito, 44-46, 202
Hollywood, 14, 56, 170, 191, 196-200, 213-214, 239
Homegirl Café, 196-197
Homestate, 197
horchata, 157, 207, 229, 232
huaraches, 17, 110, 206, 232
Huevos Ahogados, 86
Huevos Divorciados (recipe), 57
huevos divorciados, 57, 198, 206, 232
huevos rancheros, 57, 202, 232
Huntington Park, 14, 98, 114, 136, 157, 191, 228-230

Inglewood, 53, 218-221
Isthmus-Style Cornbread, 192

jalapeño chile, 22, 32, 48, 54, 60, 111, 130, 139, 168, 173, 176, 184, 232
Jalisco Bakery, 221
Jalisco, 16-17, 22, 80, 97-99, 119, 156, 201, 227-228
Julian's Tortilleria, 223
Juquila Restaurant, 216
Juquila Truck, 217

Koreatown, 16, 196, 199-200
Koslow, Jessica, 170-171

La Azteca Tortilleria, 13, 47, 202
La Blanquita Tortilleria, 211
La Cabaña, 44, 216
La Cabañita, 206
La Casita Mexicana, 16, 71, 80-82, 109, 228
La Chapalita Tortilleria, 211
La Chuperia, 155, 203
La Cita, 199
La Corona Tortilleria, 214
La Cuevita Bar, 207
La Estrella Taco Truck, 207
La Finca Restaurante, 220
La Flor de Yucatán, 16, 104-106, 198

La Gloria Foods Corporation, 204
La Golondrina Café, 197
La Huatulco, 162
La Imperial Tortilleria, 204
La Monarca Bakery, 190-192, 203, 207, 217, 229
La Niña del Mezcal, 161
La Perla Bakery, 207
La Princesita #1, 204
La Princesita #3, 204
La Serenata de Garibaldi, 16, 109, 149, 202
La Sierra Nightclub, 213
La Sinaloense Market, 221
La Venadita Meat, 221
Lake Balboa, 214
Lamb Barbacoa with Consommé, 94
Larchmont, 197
Las 7 Regiones de Oaxaca, 198
Las Molenderas, 202
Las Palomas, 203
Las Perlas, 161, 199
Lazy Ox, 141
Ledlow, 141
Lenchita's, 214
lengua, 6, 210, 232
Lennox Pollo, 220
Lennox, 52-53, 219-221
Leo's Taco Truck, 199
licuado, 232
Lido's Restaurant, 229
Lincoln Heights, 13, 34, 43, 154-155, 188, 202-203, 207
Livas, Alfredo, 190-192
lobster (langosta), 146, 216, 232
Lobster, Puerto Nuevo, 146
Long Beach, 129, 145, 157, 222-223, 228-229
Lopez, Soledad, 16, 61, 63, 163
Loqui, 189, 217
Lorenzo, Maria Elena, 174, 176, 178
Los Candiles, 207
Los Cinco Puntos, 13, 36, 44, 193, 201, 204
Los Compadres, 223
Los Feliz, 197
Lotería Grill, 55-57, 71, 149, 198-199
Lujan, Andrew, 148, 150

Lupe's No. 2, 13, 44, 49-50, 202
Lupita's, 206
Lynwood, 71, 156, 229

machaca, 17-18, 31, 36, 228, 232
MacManus, Susanna, 33, 36
mandoline, 20, 173
Manny's El Tepeyac, 44, 202
Manresa, 141
Mar Vista, 216
Maradentro, 216
Margarita, Casa Vega, 158
Mariscos 4 Vientos, 171
Mariscos Chente's, 53-54, 219-220
Mariscos Jalisco, 170-171, 173, 187, 203
Mariscos La Islitas, 223
Mariscos Los Dorados, 228
Marisela, 11
markets, 193, 201-230
Martín del Campo, Jaime, 71, 80, 82
Mas Malo, 199
masa, 15, 22, 36, 71, 110, 118, 125-126, 134, 178-179, 188-189, 193, 200, 211, 232-233
Memelitas, 198, 233
menudo, 206, 226, 228, 233
Mercado Benito Juarez, 200
Mercado Olympic, 96, 200
Merino, Hualterio, 186
Mexicali Taco Co., 189, 198, 231
Mexican Village, The 199
Mexicano, 81-82, 225, 229
mezcal, 17-18, 56, 61-62, 64, 101, 160-162, 199, 207, 214-215, 217
Mi Lindo Nayarit, 225
Michelada Verde, 159
Michoacán, 16-17, 23, 104, 191, 212, 231-233
Mid-City, 16, 196, 199
Mid-Wilshire, 199
migas, 17, 197, 233
milanesas, 22, 168-169
Mini-Mercadito @ El Mercado, 204

Mixiote, 210, 233
Mo Chica, 89
mochomos, 18, 228, 233
molcajete, 20-21, 70, 41-42, 129, 213, 233
mole, 17-18, 21-26, 61-62, 70-74, 81-82, 101-102, 119, 137, 197-198, 200, 202, 204, 206, 216-217, 220, 223, 225, 228-229, 231-233
Mole Negro Oaxaqueño, 72
mole recipes, 82, 72
molletes, 203, 207, 217, 229, 233
Monte Alban Restaurant, 217
Montebello, 230
Monterey Park, 97, 210
Montrose, 206
Mora, David, 154
Morelos, 18
morisqueta, 17, 214, 233
mulato chile, 233
mulitas, 200, 208, 217, 226, 231, 233
Murrietta, Cecilia, 160
My Taco, 206

Nayarit, 16, 18, 52-54, 120, 202, 210, 225, 227, 233
nightclubs (antros), 198, 203, 207, 213, 223, 229, 231
Nixtamal, 22, 174
nopal (cactus), 23, 110
North Hollywood, 213-214
Northeast & the Verdugos, 205
Northgate Gonzalez Markets, 193, 223, 226
Nuevo León, 18, 67, 142, 191

Oaxaca on Wheels, 217
Oaxaca, 16, 18, 23, 61-64, 70, 72, 84-85, 88, 92, 101, 103, 126, 156, 160-162, 168, 192, 196-198, 216-217, 231-233
Oaxacalifornia Café and Juice Bar, 225
Ochoa, Esdras, 76, 78
Olvera Street, 7, 12, 33-34, 36, 38-39, 43-44, 134, 180, 196, 212

Olvera, Enrique, 14, 119, 128, 161
Oregano, Mexican, 23
Orsa & Winston, 141
Ortega, Raul, 170, 173, 187
Ortega, Thomas, 13, 144, 146

pachucos, 233
Pacoima, 14, 98, 122, 128, 212-214
Palms, 11, 62, 216, 218
pambazos, 17, 206, 233
pan dulce oaxaqueño, 199, 233
Panaderia Celaya Bakery, 199
Panaderia Mi Lupita, 221
Panaderia Santo Domingo, 199
Panorama City, 213
Papaya Cream Soup, 111
Paramount, 98, 140, 228, 230
Pasadena, 104, 109, 129, 137, 191, 205-207
pasilla chile, 22,47, 72, 96, 130, 233
Perez, Francisco, 92
peruano beans, 23-24
pescado zarandeado, 18, 53, 220, 233
Pickled Onions, 91
Pico de Gallo, Eastside, 48
Pico de Gallo, Ricky's, 184
Pico Rivera, 14, 132-133, 156-157
Pico-Union, 105, 198, 200
Piloncillo, 23, 163
Piña, Ricky, 180, 182
pipián, 17-18, 26, 216, 220, 228, 233
pipián recipe, 82
platano, 18, 216, 226, 233
Playa Amor, 145-146, 222-223
Playas de Nayarit, 210
Plaza Mexico, 227, 229
poblano chile, 47, 125, 142, 233
pocho cuisine, 13, 29
Pollos Asados Al Carbón El Güero, 225
pork recipes
   Chile Rojo, 46
   Chirmole, 107
   Cochinita Pibil Tacos, 90

Hollenbeck Burrito, 46
Pozole Blanco, 176-178
Tlayuda, 64
Pozole Blanco Guerrero Style, 176
Presidente Restaurants, 213
Primera Taza Coffee House, 203
Public Beer and Wine Shop, 129, 223
Puebla, 16, 18, 92, 97, 188, 201, 231-232
Puerto Nuevo Lobster, 146
Puertos del Pacifico, 202
pumpkin seeds, 72, 82, 105, 150-151
PYT, 141

Querétaro, 18
Quesadillas Oaxaqueñas, 200
queso chihuahua, 23, 126
queso cotija, 23, 57, 130-131
queso fresco, 23-24, 41-42, 57, 81, 118, 130-131, 137, 139, 233
queso Oaxaca, 23, 64, 126, 168, 233
Quintana Roo, 18

Rajas, 216, 233
Ramirez Beverage Center, 203
Ramirez Liquor, 203
Ramirez Meat Market, 211
Ramirez, Francisco, 188
Ramirez, Martín, 171
Ramos, Maria, 15, 101, 103
Raspados Nayarit, 202
Raw Tomatillo Salsa, 134-135
recado, 90-91, 105-107
Red Aguachile Tostada, 173
regional dishes, 17-18
Rice, Mexican, 26
Rice, White, 26
Ricky's Fish Tacos (recipe), 182
Ricky's Fish Tacos (truck), 199
Ricky's Pico de Gallo, 184
Ricky's Salsa Verde, 182, 184
Rico's Tacos El Tio, 220

Roasted Tomatillo Salsa, 146-147
Rocio's Mexican Kitchen, 70-72, 228
Rojas, Elena, 43-44
Rojas, Manny, 30, 45
Romero, Ulysses, 156
Ruiz, Eduardo, 13, 128-130, 154, 188, 222

Sal de Colima, 23, 130
Sal de San Felipe, 23, 130
Saladitas crackers, 23, 116
Salazar, 77-78, 198
Salgado, Carlos, 13, 118, 120, 129, 170, 188
Salsas
    Borracha (Drunken), 96
    Chile de Árbol, 27
    Habanero, Charred, 117
    Huichol, 23, 116, 173
    Mexicana, 111
    Ranchera, 57, 59
    Ricky's Salsa Verde, 184
    Soledad's, 64-65
    Tatemada, 79
    Tomatillo, Raw, 135
    Tomatillo, Roasted, 147
    Verde, 27, 60, 184
San Fernando, 6, 38, 66, 122, 212, 214
San Gabriel, 71, 109, 111, 114, 174, 209-210
San Luis Potosi, 18
Santa Monica, 16, 115, 123, 166, 190-191, 198, 200, 215-218
Sawtelle, 55, 216-218
Scallops in Aguachile, 120
Seafood Cocktail, 116
seafood cocktails, 54, 116, 120, 134, 173, 231
seafood recipes
    Crab Huarache, 110
    Fish Tacos, 182
    Puerto Nuevo Lobster, 146
    Red Aguachile Tostada, 173
    Scallops in Aguachile, 120
    Seafood Cocktail, 116
    Shrimp Ceviche, 54
    Shrimp Tortas, 99-100
    Tuna Tostada, 134

Shaw, Jimmy, 55-57, 71
Sherman Oaks, 38-39, 213-214
Shrimp Tortas Ahogadas Gemma Style, 99-100
Silver Lake, 154, 157, 180-181
Sinaloa, 16, 18, 33, 53, 108, 120, 145, 159, 186-187, 227, 232-233
Sofrito, 112
Soledad's Salsa, 65
Soledad's Tepache, 163
Sonora, 17-18, 33, 67, 232
Sonorita's Prime Tacos, 217
sopes, 18, 56, 118, 233
sopitos, 17, 233
South Bay, 219
South Gate, 128, 156, 228-229
South L.A., 174-175, 224-226
South Pasadena, 191
Spanglish Kitchen, 210
Steak Fajitas, 213
Steak Picado Ciro's, 32
Studio City, 213
Suadero, 229, 233
Super Tortas D.F., 168, 225
Superior, 208

Taco Dollar, 221
Taco Maria, 14, 119-120, 149
taco recipes
    Carne Asada Vampiros, 78
    Cochinita Pibil, 90
    Fish, 182
    Squash with Pumpkin Seeds, 150
Taco Zone Truck, 200
Tacolandia, 7, 11, 189, 239-240
Tacomiendo, 216
Tacos Baja, 210
Tacos Cuernavaca, 203
Tacos El Pelon, 208
Tacos El Pique, 208
Tacos La Carreta, 229
Tacos La Fonda, 214
Tacos La Güera, 229
Tacos Los Güichos, 225
Tacos Por Favor, 216
Tacos Punta Cabras, 115-116, 217
Tacos Quetzalcoatl, 204

Tacos Tamix, 200
Tacos Villa Corona, 206
tacos, cochinita pibil, 90, 197
tacos, fish, 182, 199, 210, 217
tacos, squash, 150
tamale recipes
    Chicken, 178
    Corn & Summer Squash, 124
Tamales de Pollo, 178
Tamales Elena, 175-176, 178, 226
tamales, 20, 22, 122-126, 174-176, 178-179, 193, 197-198, 201, 204, 226, 232
Tamaulipas, 18
Taquitos with Avocado Sauce, 36, 197
tasajo, 63-64, 84, 233
Tepache, Soledad's, 163
telera rolls, 23, 168
Tierra Mia Coffee, 207
tinga, 56, 68, 216, 233
Tinga (Chicken Chipotle) Burritos, 68
Tire Shop Taqueria, 226
Tlacolula Panaderia y Carniceria, 199
Tlapazola Grill, 16, 62, 160, 215-216
Tlayuda L.A., 198
Tlayuda (recipe), 63
tlayudas, 61, 63-65, 197-198, 217, 233
tomatillo salsas, 27, 60, 79, 135, 147, 151, 184
tomatillos, 23, 27, 37, 45, 60, 79, 135, 146-147, 150-151, 184
Torrance, 174, 221
torta recipes
    Shrimp Tortas Ahogadas, 100
    Torta La Rusa, 168
Torta La Rusa, 168
Tortas Ahogadas Guadalajara, 98-99, 228
Tortas Ahogadas Los Tripones, 213
Tortas Gigantes El Chilango, 226
tortas, 99-100, 168-169, 203, 210, 213, 225-226, 228

Tortilla Chips, Homemade, 131
tortilla press, 20
tortilla warmer, 20-21
Tortilleria Guamuchil, 230
Tortilleria La California, 208
Tortilleria San Marcos, 204
tortillerias, 188-189, 204, 208, 211, 214, 230
Tostada, Tuna (recipe), 134
Tresierras Supermarkets, 214
tripa, 221, 229, 233
Tuna Tostada, 134

University Park, 225
Urbano Mexican Kitchen, 207

Vallarta Supermarkets, 204, 214
Vampiro Sauce, 78-79
Vampiros, Carne Asada, 78
Van Nuys, 85, 186, 213-214
vaporera, 20, 94-96, 126, 178-179
Vega Fowler, Christy, 38-39, 41, 158
vegetarian recipes
    Avocado Sauce, 37
    Avocado-Tomatillo Salsa, 151
    Basic Beans, 24
    Black Beans, 25
    Charred Habanero Salsa, 117
    Chile de Árbol Salsa, 27
    Chile Relleno Burrito, 47
    Cocktail Sauce, 117
    Corn & Summer Squash Tamales, 124
    Eastside Pico de Gallo, 48
    Enfrijoladas (if made with oil), 103
    Guacamole, 27
    Homemade Tortilla Chips, 131
    Huevos Ahogados, 86
    Huevos Divorciados, 57

Isthmus-Style Cornbread, 192
Pickled Onions, 91
Raw Tomatillo Salsa, 135
Recado Rojo, 91
Refried Black Beans, 65
Ricky's Pico de Gallo, 184
Ricky's Salsa Verde, 184
Roasted Tomatillo Salsa, 147
Salsa Borracha, 96
Salsa Mexicana, 111
Salsa Ranchera, 59
Salsa Tatemada, 79
Salsa Verde, 27 & 60
Sofrito, 112
Soledad's Salsa, 65
Squash Tacos with Pumpkin Seeds & Avocado-Tomatillo Salsa, 150
Vampiro Sauce, 79
White Rice, 26
Venice, 114, 199, 216, 218
Veracruz, 18, 88, 156-157
Viento y Agua Coffeehouse, 223
Villalobos Meat Market, 200

Walnut Park, 229
Watts, 174-175, 226
Whittier, 14, 109, 136-137, 139, 154-155, 191, 201-204, 209-210
Wild Boar Chilaquiles, 130
Willowbrook, 225
Wine and Liquor Depot, 214

Yuca's Hut, 197
Yuca's on Hollywood, 197
Yucatán, 16, 18, 22, 80, 88-91, 104-106, 137, 198, 232

Zacatecas, 6, 18, 33-34, 66, 68, 136, 201

The winner of a James Beard award for his coverage of the L.A. taco scene in *Los Angeles Magazine*, **Bill Esparza** is one of the country's leading experts on Mexican food. The California native curates the annual Tacolandia festival in Los Angeles; writes about Mexican food for *Los Angeles Magazine* and others; and appears regularly on CNN, KCRW's radio show *Good Food*, and such television shows as *I'll Have What Phil's Having*, *Bizarre Foods*, and *Top Chef*. A noted saxophone player, Esparza has traveled and eaten extensively throughout Mexico, Latin America, and, of course, Southern California.

Gustavo Arellano (foreword) is the author of *Taco USA: How Mexican Food Conquered America* and *¡Ask a Mexican!* He is also the publisher and editor of *OC Weekly* in Southern California.

Staci Valentine (photographer) is a Los Angeles–based photographer whose work has appeared in *Sweet Paul*, Goop, and many cookbooks, including *Little Flower Baking*, *The Seasonal Jewish Kitchen*, *Das Cookbook*, and *The Perfect Peach*.

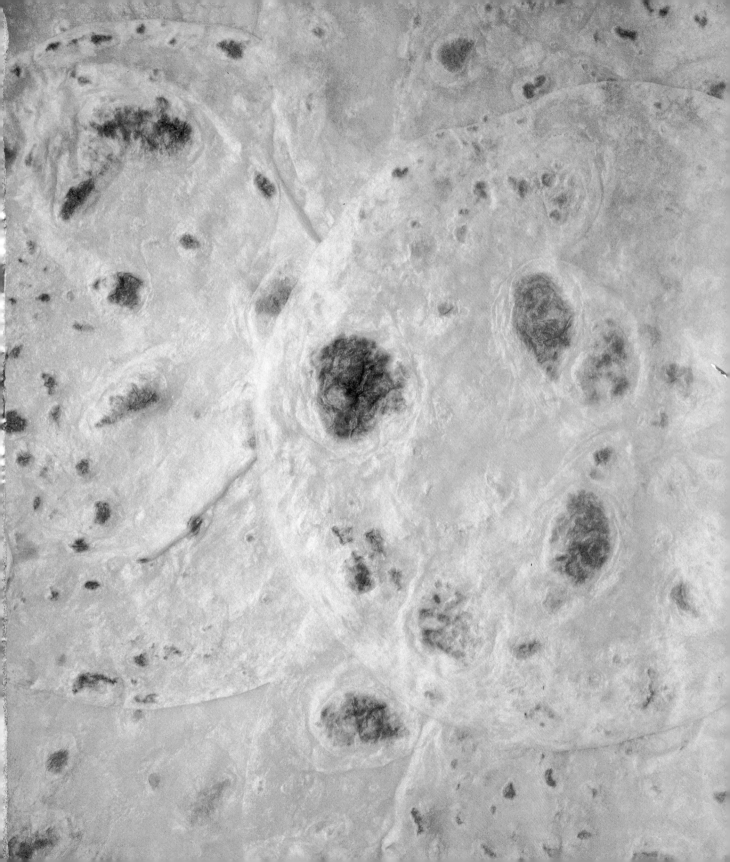